THE BEST OF THE FICTION MAGAZINE

New stories, poems, essays: an exciting
collection of today's best writing

In 1982 *The Fiction Magazine* was widely welcomed
as a much needed outlet for writers, the untried as
well as the famous. It was heralded as 'a spirited
assault on precious elitism' (*The Guardian*),
'wonderful entertainment' (Molly Keane) and as
Nadine Gordimer said 'the emphasis on writers
and writing justifies its existence among so many
journals that are given over to endless comment.'
While taking fiction seriously, the magazine has
also succeeded in being lively and visually
inviting, with top-quality illustrations,
cartoons and photographs.
Paul Cox's exuberant drawings complement this
exciting introduction to some of today's best
writing: a varied and entertaining selection of
stories, poems and essays. None of the stories is
available elsewhere in book form, and work by
Brian Aldiss, Desmond Hogan, John McGahern
and Richard Rayner has been written especially for
this anthology.

The Crown Tavern
The Strand Magazine

The Best of the

Fiction

Magazine

Edited by JUDY COOKE & ELIZABETH BUNSTER

J.M. DENT & SONS LTD
in association with
THE FICTION MAGAZINE
LONDON · MELBOURNE

This anthology first published in Great Britain by J.M. Dent &
Sons Ltd in association with *The Fiction Magazine* 1986
Selection ©*The Fiction Magazine* 1986
Foreword ©Judy Cooke 1986
Illustrations ©Paul Cox
The copyright information constitutes an extension to
this copyright notice

Designed by Paul Watkins

This book is set in 10/12pt Plantin Medium by The Chesham
Press Ltd, 16 Germain Street, Chesham, Buckinghamshire.
Printed in Great Britain by Hunt Barnard for J.M.Dent & Sons
Ltd, Aldine House, 33 Welbeck Street, London W1M 8LX,
in association with *The Fiction Magazine*, 12/13 Clerkenwell
Green, London EC1.

British Library Cataloguing in Publication Data
    The Best of Fiction magazine — (Everyman fiction)
    1. English literature — 20th century
    I. Cooke, Judy II. Fiction magazine

820′.8′00912   PR1148
ISBN 0-460-02464-7

Copyright

Contents

ROBERT COOVER

GERALD'S PARTY

'WHAT A NOVEL! ...

'A crazed comic strip, a zany metaphysical murder mystery, outrageous satire and humour at its blackest. Robert Coover's furious new novel takes on all the queasy affluence of Reagan's America and hits it right below the belt. He is unfair, rude, cruel and murderously funny. A master'

Angela Carter

'Robert Coover is one of the greatest innovative writers of the United States, and this novel, a wonderful pastiche of the murder mystery, manages, like THE PUBLIC BURNING, to convey the pains and corruptions of modern American life while remaining a totally exact and cunning work of fictional experiment'.

Malcolm Bradbury

Publication 14 April   £9.95   352 pages ISBN 0 434 14290 5

WILLIAM HEINEMANN

Foreword/Judy Cooke

In April 1982 the first issue of *The Fiction Magazine* was published, its aim being to 'encourage the innovatory without excluding the traditional; to promote new and young writers; to print work which is lively, communicative, inventive, reflective — writers' writing, in fact, which cannot be defined in advance other than by the term "professional".' I would hope that this anthology remains true to that aim and dedicate it to the writers who contributed to our first issue.

'It's a risky business,' the distributor used to say as we tried to make sense of his computer print-outs and our print bills. He proved to be right, so much so that the enterprise was near to foundering on a number of occasions. Thanks to three generous individuals, the magazine has not only survived but prospered. Philippa Toomey helped us out in 1983, Robert Macleod in 1984 and Keith Young, who took over the magazine in 1985, has set it on the firm basis of monthly publication.

There are many people whose hard work and advice have been crucial. We are indebted to David Profumo, Thomas Blaikie and Simon Gooch on the editorial and production side, and to many friends in writing and publishing, especially to John Brushfield, Antonia Byatt, Liz Calder, Mel Calman, Richard Cohen, Frank Delaney, Martyn Goff, James Hale, Robert McCrum, John Murray, Deborah Owen, Ruth Rendell, Tom Rosenthal, Sarah Peel, Steven Williams and Robyn Sisman, fiction editor at Dent, with whom we have collaborated on this book.

My special thanks to Paul Watkins, the designer; to Paul Cox and Ken Sharp, whose drawings and photographs, respectively, introduced a whole new dimension to the magazine; to Charlotte Everest-Phillips, of The Dragonfly Press; to Dominic le Poer Power, of Mind's Eye Theatre; to Elizabeth Bunster, the assistant editor; to my sons Daniel and Oliver, who shared our cottage with an industry for three crowded years and to Paul Barker, Eric Paice and Alison Rimmer, whose friendship and expertise supported the venture from the start.

THE BOLT HOTEL

Simon Burt

'This isn't your home', my father said, running a soup plate under the hot tap and shaking off the excess water. 'It hasn't been for how many years? Four? Five? You only use it as a bolt hole.'

He handed me the plate. I dried it and stacked it on the draining board. Every now and then things get too much and I have to run to cover. I'd spent most of the meal we were now washing up trying to convince my father of my profound conviction that this time was different. My father wasn't convinced.

'A bolt hotel,' I said, 'You make me pay. I have to listen to your crap, just as you have to listen to mine.'

My father held up a half empty wine glass.

'Yours or mine?' he said.

'Mine I think,' I said. 'You finish it.'

My father drank off the wine and washed the glass.

'Are we going to get drunk?' he said. 'I mean I am, and I expect you are. But are we? I hope you've brought a bottle or two with you. I wasn't expecting you. There isn't much in.'

'A couple of bottles,' I said.

'Rent,' I said.

'Good,' my father said. 'Your aunt Elizabeth may drop by.'

'I hope not,' I said.

'You never were any good at sharing,' my father said. 'Would you deny an old man his fleshly pleasures, just because yours have got on top of you?'

I picked up the pile of plates.

'Where do these live?' I said.

'I leave them,' my father said. 'We'll use them for breakfast. Why waste effort?'

I put the pile of plates down again.

'It isn't working, is it?' my father said. 'It isn't working yet. The balm of paternal consolation.'

'I keep on telling you,' I said. 'I don't need consolation. Not this time. I got it on the train.'

'I wonder if they knew,' my father said. 'The makers of your chic and expensive pinefragrant aftershave.'

'You're changing the subject again,' I said. 'That must be part of the rent this time. Silence on certain subjects.'

'The lavatorial connotations of that particular smell in this country. Very poor market research, I call it.'

My father swilled out the washing up bowl and turned it upsidedown in the sink.

'Right,' he said. 'Let's get those bottles then.'

I looked at my father's hands as he poured our fourth whisky. They were mottled, and thatched with greying hair. Otherwise they were the same as mine: longfingered, bony, spatulate, with fleshy palms. The likeness saddened me. He was old. I drank.

'I can see your point,' my father said. 'Your difficulty rather. There is no past here. No bathing in the pool of your recollections. Not like there was in the old house.'

My father drank. I noticed that we drank in the same way, swallowing, and pressing our lips into a firm line.

'There are correspondences,' I said. 'You are as trapped as I. The furniture is arranged in the same way. The layout of the rooms is similar.'

'You see only so far, as usual,' my father said. 'There is such a thing as solidity. And there is such a thing as slavery. I keep things the same because I like them that way. I have discovered what I like, and keep it.'

'And I?' I said. 'What does your crackerbarrel tell you about me?'

'You'll be off again,' my father said. 'Just like last time. And the time before. You can't stay away. And you can't stay away from here. That's slavery. You live here, and you live there. Which means you really live in neither place.'

'Very clever,' I said.

'And,' he said, 'I don't know if you've thought of it, not very nice for me. Who wants to be anybody's anchor? You think I like being your solid base? The point from which you stray? What are you running away from, every time you come down here, if not from that? If not because you have become someone's, or some people's, solid base, and you can't live with it. And you run home to daddy.'

'To daddy's house,' I said. 'To daddy's hotel. For a bit of peace. To escape the feeling that I voluntarily make the same mistake every time I meet someone. The feeling that I turn them into you. Give me another drink.'

My father passed the bottle. I filled my glass. He held out his glass and I filled that too.

'Glass for glass,' he said. 'Fair's fair.'

'The feeling,' I said, 'that I need you so much that I have to reinvent you in everyone I meet. I come home to dispel that. Don't tell me I can't recognise slavery.'

'But this time is different,' my father said. 'No slavery this time.'

'This time is different,' I said. 'Plenty of slavery, just as usual. But this time it doesn't matter. I've found something else.'

'Something else,' my father said. 'Something else to lean on. You think it makes any difference what you lean on when you still need to lean?'

'No,' I said. 'No. So you can stop playing the sage. The fount of ancient wisdom. No. I've got beyond that.'

'On the train,' my father said. 'Oh God, he found enlightenment on the train.'

'I tried to tell you,' I said. 'All evening I've tried to tell you. I've had an experience.'

'I don't want to hear,' my father said.

He put down his glass and covered his ears.

'I don't want to hear.'

I sat still. When it became obvious I wasn't going to speak, my father took his hands from his ears.

'It's only a gesture,' he said. 'Any fool knows you can't shut out noise that easily.'

'It's all right,' I said. 'You're quite safe. I don't think it's the sort of thing that can be put into words anyway.'

'Oh, how handy,' my father said. 'How very convenient. I pray to God that when I achieve enlightenment I won't be able to put it into words either. Think of the trouble it will save. Think of the time it will save. Drink up.'

We drank. We filled our glasses again. We sat and looked at our glasses. From time to time we drank.

'I have a life too,' my father said. 'I have my difficulties too. I want to run away too. Often.'

I couldn't think of anything to say. My father looked at me. I was still trying to think of something to say when the doorbell rang and saved me the trouble.

'That will be your aunt Elizabeth,' my father said.

It was eleven o'clock. My father and my aunt Elizabeth sat side

5

by side. Sometimes they held hands. Sometimes she put her hand on his leg. Sometimes, maybe less often but I wasn't counting, he on hers. My aunt moved her hands a lot, and shifted about on the sofa, sitting forward, lying back. She reached for cigarettes. She stubbed them out. I won't say she couldn't sit still, but she didn't. We were well into the second bottle. My aunt seemed pleased to see me. Presumably she was good at sharing.

'You should come home more often,' she said. 'We have good times.'

'Home,' I said. 'Where's that?'

'Your father needs you,' my aunt said.

'My father needs no one,' I said.

'That's right,' my father said. 'You talk amongst yourselves.'

'He needs you,' my aunt said.

'I decide what I need,' my father said. 'That is my secret.'

'Family,' my aunt said. 'You should come more often.'

'I come when I need to,' I said.

'I need a pee,' my father said.

He stood up and walked unsteadily to the door.

'Just talk amongst yourselves,' he said.

When he had gone my aunt sat still. She lit a cigarette from the butt of the previous one.

'It's not just the drink,' she said.

I looked interrogatively. I wasn't giving her anything. I don't like sharing.

'You must have noticed,' my aunt said. 'He can't walk straight. It's not just the drink.'

I took a deep, deep breath. I hadn't noticed.

'He's getting thin,' my aunt said.

'Thin nothing,' I said. 'He's twice my size.'

'Yes,' my aunt said.

She paused to make sure I got the point. I pantomimed patience. 'He lives more and more . . .'

My aunt groped for the word. She achieved it.

'Vicariously,' she said. 'He leans on people. On me specifically. He likes watching. He likes listening at doors.'

I glanced towards the door. My aunt shrugged. She smiled. I went to the door and opened it.

'Still at it,' my father said.

'You're a ghoul,' I said. 'A ghoul, you know that? A bloody

ghoul.'

'Your aunt would say,' my father said, as he walked past me, not that unsteadily I noticed, 'a vampire.'

He leaned over my aunt and made as if to bite her neck. He lost his balance and fell on her heavily. My aunt squealed. My father rolled from her lap onto the floor, upsetting table, drinks, ashtrays. My aunt leaped to her feet. I rushed from the door. My father lay on the floor in a cloud of cigarette ash, gasping; struggling, it appeared, for air. My aunt knelt at his side. I hovered.

My father hissed and whistled through his teeth. He said something I didn't hear. My aunt sat back on her heels.

'What?' I said.

My aunt laughed.

'What did he say?' I said.

'Hogarth!' my father said.

My aunt quaked with laughter.

'Hogarth!' she said.

My father was purple in the face.

'Hogarth!' he said.

'Stop it!' I said. 'Stop it!'

My father and my aunt shook and moaned and hiccoughed into silence.

'Christ!' I said. 'You fools! A couple of old, old, bloody fools.'

'Sit down,' my aunt said. 'Sit down, and concentrate on your manners.'

I sat down. My father, giggling, picked himself up. He helped my aunt to her feet. My aunt made to straighten up the mess.

'Leave it,' my father said.

They sat on the sofa. My father looked at me. I looked back. Then I got up and picked up the table, collected debris, poured more drink. I emptied the bottle.

'My son, you must understand,' my father said, 'has this little problem. He cannot handle love. Most of his time is spent looking for it. He hangs around bars looking for it. He invests great deserts of time indulging in what I believe is known as casual trade. He goes to clubs where he meets the sort of people who like going to clubs. He goes to saunas where he meets the sort of people who like going to saunas. He complains of loneliness, with an address book full of phone numbers he can't recognise, or daren't use. He is very active. He bounces around on top of total strangers. He achieves complicated positions and engulfing orgasms with total strangers. But then, oh then, he meets someone who doesn't want to stay a stranger. Maybe even he doesn't want them to stay a stranger. That's when I get the letter. Love, love, love, I've found love. Oh God, those letters. But, you see, he has this problem. It's all very well, you see, to bounce around on a total stranger. But a time comes when they're not a stranger any more, and what does he do then? Then, when all the magical ingredients are there, and love itself stands beckoning? He can't do it any more, that's what happens. He lies on his back with his eyes closed, and the ex-stranger bounces around on top of him, and my son the Casanova can't take it. He lies there, brushing aside kisses and pudenda, concentrating like crazy on his own erection, lest it vanish. And he writes another letter, saying Love, love, where has it gone? Why must I hunger? Whither joy? Only this letter he doesn't send. He comes in person, to tap the inspiration at source. He sits and he gets drunk. Then he goes back, takes the unposted letter from the hall table, and tears it up. He washes, and showers, and drenches himself in lavatorial scent, and off again to the bars. I haven't left anything out, have I? That's it, isn't it?'

'Put baldly,' I said. 'Put baldly I guess that's it.'

'Only this time,' my father said, 'it's different. He's going to tell us. Oh God, is he going to tell us? He's had an experience. On the train. And he's going to tell us. How can we wait?'

I went to bed.

I woke drenched in sweat. The sheets clung to my body. Moisture collected in my navel, and the pit of my groin. I pushed back the covers and sat on the edge of the bed. There was drumming on the ceiling. My father is a meticulous house keeper. His only slovenliness is nylon sheets. I always sleep badly in nylon sheets.

I stood up and dragged the covers off the bed to air it. I opened the window and let the night air dry me. There was a further drumming on the ceiling. My father's bedroom is directly above mine. I went upstairs.

My father sat, wrapped in a towel, in an armchair facing the foot of his bed. The bedclothes were heaped and tangled.

'I couldn't sleep,' my father said.

'I was awake,' I said.

I pointed at the bed.

'We ought to make it again,' I said.

'She went home,' my father said. 'There's no need to worry.'

As we were making the bed my father said, 'Funny. Any time during the day I can sleep. I sit down to read and I'm asleep. Night time though. I hate it. You have no idea.'

I plumped up the pillows.

'Get in,' I said.

He got in, and settled the pillows behind his head.

'You don't see yourself clearly if you don't sleep,' he said. 'After a while you panic. It's a false emotion. But strong while it lasts.'

I sat on the edge of the bed.

'The experience,' I said.

'Yes,' he said.

'It's already fading,' I said. 'At least the vision is. If you can call it that. But not the aftermath. The taste it left in the mouth. Not that.'

'No,' my father said.

'We were just leaving Reading,' I said. 'You know the place. Acres of industry, and slums, and floating newspapers. Old tyres and trash. I was looking out of the window. Not really seeing it. Suddenly it was as if everything was attached to me. To *me*, you understand. With tiny threads. And as the train moved, these threads meshed and crossed and remeshed. Each had its separate note, like a harp. Everything was separate, and everything was me. And we sounded. Like the music of the spheres. Only we were the music. Just outside Reading.'

'You are very like me,' my father said. 'You know that? We stand in the same way. We drink in the same way. Our voices are the same. Your aunt noticed it.'

'I noticed it,' I said. 'She doesn't have the monopoly of observation.'

'It's tactless,' my father said, 'to show how much you dislike her. She is, as they say, a good woman.'

'My aunt,' I said. 'She's fat. And silly. She twitches. The whole affair seems rather squalid to me.'

'And yours aren't?' my father said.

'We've been through that,' I said. 'Thank you very much.'

'Rent,' my father said. 'Surely not too much to ask. To deflect your merciless eye from me to you. She's good for me.'

'She makes a mess of the bed,' I said. 'And I have to make it.'

'Has it occurred to you,' my father said, 'that I deserve some love in my old age? Some comfort.'

'Not for a moment,' I said.

My father chuckled.

'My son,' he said.

'I learned something,' I said. 'I learned not to be afraid of patterns. Even patterns of failure.'

'It's all part of the tapestry,' I said.

'That's nothing,' my father said. 'Experiences like that. We all have them. They don't mean anything.'

'Even not being able to sleep,' he said, 'is more important. You don't understand anything. You come home with a story like that. Some sordid twopenny halfpenny ecstasy. What's the use of it, if you don't like your aunt?'

I bent forward and kissed him on the cheek.

'Goodnight daddy,' I said.

My father closed his eyes.

'All your life,' he said. 'All your life. You've been asleep.'

Mad
About
The
Boy

Georgina
Hammick

He got her through school which she hated. On Saturdays, and on weekday evenings after prep, they were allowed to play the gramophone. She would take hers, a German machine in a blue-black leather case her father had found in Berlin at the end of the war, into a corner of the gym and set herself up. The inside of the gramophone had an intoxicating smell. Each time she lifted the lid she sniffed hard. Years later, searching a junk shop for something to stand plants on, she came across an old gramophone and opened it up and sniffed and was immediately taken back; she could see that German machine: the catches on the case that released the lid, the heavy head tucked safely to the side, the winder secured by two brackets inside the lid, the sliding compartment for needles, the needles themselves in their shiny tin boxes.

She was nine or ten when the passion started and her collection of his records amounted to less than a dozen. She had stolen them from her mother and her aunts. All, with the exception of *Don't Let's be Beastly to the Germans*, were pre-war and recorded before she was born. Three were twelve-inch and scenes from plays (*Private Lives; Cavalcade; Tonight at 8.30*). The rest were ten-inch and songs, sung solo by Noel with a piano accompaniment. Sometimes she listened in silence, kneeling close against the gramophone with her head inside the lid so as not to miss a syllable; more often she sang along with him in a clipped light tenor as near his own as she could manage: *Let Our Affair be a Gay Thing* — there was no joke to be got out of that in 1950 — *All these Sweet Moments We've Known* . . . Soon she was spending all her pocket money on records: *Don't Make Fun of the Festival; There are Bad Times Just Around the Corner; Matelot*. His voice in these seemed rounder – or was it thicker? – which fitted in with his being almost bald now and not as thin as he'd been in the photographs she owned of *Private Lives*.

Noel's popularity was at a low ebb in the early nineteen fifties, a fact she discovered from the gossip columns of the daily newspapers. He seemed to be in trouble with the press for living most of the time in Bermuda or Jamaica and thereby avoiding income tax, and he was having a rough time with the critics for writing plays which, they were all agreed, showed none of his pre-war brilliance. He was not popular at her school, Belmont, but that was because most people had never heard of him, the few that

13

had knowing him only as a vague figure – like Fred Astaire or Jack Buchanan – from their parents' youth. The decline in his fortunes suited her very well and made her feel protective. She alone really appreciated him. She alone understood him and his problems. She alone knew, and sympathized with, the weaknesses of his literary style. These included an over-fondness for adjectives and an inability to resist, in his plays, the witty line even when it was at odds with the character who had to speak it.

By the time she was twelve she knew, she was sure, everything there was to know about him; not just about the plays – date, theatre, cast, length of run were all at her fingertips – but his private life and his character. He was kind and sentimental and generous and tremendously hardworking, someone who never put off till the afternoon what he could do in the morning. He did not suffer fools. He was of course clever, but perhaps not in an intellectual way. He was witty and funny. He had no false modesty about his talents. He was not a believer, except in himself, and this was bothering because God might strike him down. She was keen on God and often spent as much as an hour on her knees on the splintery boards of Burne-Jones (the dormitories were named after painters) before getting into bed. She had once heard Colonel Symes, a friend of her father's, refer to Noel as 'that old pansy'. This, so far as she could gather, meant that he preferred men to women in some respects. If he did, it didn't bother her. It was so obvious that he liked women and that he loved them too. He was always loyal about the women he loved. She knew who they were: his mother and G. E. Calthrop (Gladys) and Lorn Loraine and Joyce Carey. And Gertrude Lawrence. She loved Gertie almost as much as she loved Noel and kept a scrap book for each of them into which she pasted newspaper cuttings, theatre programmes and notices.

In the school holidays she haunted the second-hand bookshop in the market town where her mother did most of her shopping. The shop, Burkes, had high ceilings and the bookshelves went right up to them. There were books everywhere, not just on the shelves but in untidy stacks on the floor and in parked trolleys that blocked the aisles. A rickety staircase led to more books upstairs, but she seldom climbed them because the theatre section was on the ground floor. The shop, poorly lit and with alleyways that turned corners and resembled streets, made her think of a town at dusk.

Among her finds at Burkes was a brown book with a battered spine entitled *The Amazing Mr. Noel Coward* by Patrick Braybrooke. The book, in itself disappointing, had been made special by its previous owner who'd stuck photographs and press cuttings on all the available space of the end papers. There was a caricature of Noel and Gertie taken from *The New Yorker*, a newspaper clip of Noel and Beatrice Lillie dining 'intimately' at a restaurant, and another cutting, so large it had had to be folded over, the caption of which read: 'At Goldenhurst Farm: Gertrude Lawrence, Noel Coward and Jack Wilson his Business Partner'. The photograph showed a tea party on a lawn. Gertie, sitting up very straight, poured out from a silver tea pot while a huge dog, a setter possibly, leaned across the table and licked her nose. Noel lay in a wicker chair, which was old-fashioned and had a wheel at the back. One of his knees was bent up. He held a saucer in his left hand and a cup in his right which partly obscured his face, and he eyed Gertie over the rim. The business partner who sat astride another wicker chair which did not have a wheel, was reading a magazine. Behind him a bag of golf clubs posed against a brick pillar. The domesticity of the scene was thrilling, although Goldenhurst – from the photograph all diamond panes and beams – was not to her taste.

Reading Noel was not easy to do at Belmont, where books brought back by the girls had to be passed as suitable by the headmistress, Miss Church. You put your books on an oak chest outside her drawing-room door and at some time, probably in the middle of the night for no one ever saw them go, they were taken inside. If they passed, they reappeared two days later in the same miraculous fashion, and you were then free to remove them and read them. She'd put *Fallen Angels* and *The Vortex* out once but had not seen them again until the end of term, when they were handed to her with a wan smile. After that she smuggled his plays in and kept them under a packet of sanitary towels in her underclothes drawer. She learned them, in bed and with a torch, after lights out.

Before falling asleep she invented a 'dream' about him. The dream was always the same. On a foggy afternoon she would escape down the drive (pitted tarmac and enclosed by species rhododendrons and ponticums, now glistening unpleasantly in the fog) and walk the two miles to the station and the London train. At

15

Waterloo she'd take a taxi to 17 Gerald Road, the studio flat he lived in when he wasn't in Jamaica or wherever. He came to the door himself, peered down, saw at a glance how fascinating she was under her cloak of shyness, and invited her in for tea. Tea was crumpets in a silver dish, accompanied by light and witty conversation. She made him laugh a lot. After tea he showed her his treasures and his books and pictures (these included two landscapes he'd painted himself) until they were interrupted by actor friends dropping in for cocktails. He was proprietorial about her and introduced her to them with pride, as though he himself had invented her. Occasionally he'd pat her head, which made her blush with pleasure. When his visitors were invited to stay on for supper she stayed too and helped Cole (she knew about Cole from reading *Present Indicative*) serve it. They had cold roast mutton and baked potatoes and onion sauce and salad, followed by apple pie and cheese and biscuits. There was red wine to drink.

Coffee was served in the drawing-room. Noel ('Do stop calling me Mr. Coward, there's a darling') sat down at the grand piano and played a few bars. 'Antonia!' – he beckoned her with a finger – 'Come and sing a duet with me.' They sang *You Were There* from *Shadow Play*. She owned the record of this, and had sung Gertie's part so often, copying every idiosyncratic note, that she sounded just like her, she thought. Noel seemed to think so too. Eventually the visitors began to drift away, fetching sable wraps – the women – and capes and white silk scarves – the men – from Noel's bedroom. Then she said 'I must go now.' He said 'Not in this fog dear, and in any case you've missed the last train.' So she stayed. Dressed in a pair of his pyjamas – they were slub silk and striped in pink and grey – she slept, curled up beside him in his huge double bed under a black satin quilt with scarlet roses on it.

At home she was teased about her passion, but not unkindly. Her mother – 'I was a Coward fan long before you were born' – quite liked him, and her sister Fran, who was eighteen, liked him very much. Fran's teasing often took the form of trying to trip her up on dialogue from the plays. They might be sitting at lunch when Fran would suddenly stare out of the window and point and say: 'That hedge over there is called Cupressus Macrocapa', to which the only possible reply (there were no hedges of the sort in their garden) was: 'Do you swear it?' Or again, she might be minding her own business in an arm chair with a book, when Fran would

materialize at her side and ask: 'Are you engaged for this dance?'
The correct answer, which of course she always gave, being: 'I was,
but I'll cut it if you promise to love me always and never let anyone
or anything come between us, ever'. Her father addressed her,
with gentle irony and often in the third person, as Lady Coward,
even though Noel at the time was plain Mr. 'Some more roast beef
for Lady C?' – he would turn from the sideboard with his carving
knife and his eyebrows raised. Or 'Lady Coward is in a pretty
bloody mood today, it seems'. His icy staccato was an impressive
imitation of the master in a rage. Asked for something for her
autograph book, he wrote unkindly on one page: Nobody loves a
fat girl/Nobody gives me a date/The only game I play with the
boys/Is sitting and guessing my weight, and on the facing one, right
in the middle: I am a Nole and I live in a hole. He drew a picture of
the hole, and beside it a signpost on which he printed: Montego
Bay 3 miles.

One day, feeling fat and bored and sad, she looked Noel up in
the A-D volume of the London Telephone Directory, not
expecting to find him there. Yet there he was, his name in ordinary
print like everyone else's, and there was his telephone number:
SLOane 2965. For three days she did nothing except chant the
number. Say she got through and managed to speak to him? A
furious: 'Who are you? What do you want? Go away, please.' Click
– the likely outcome – would put paid to her fantasy for ever. So she
compromised. The compromise consisted of asking the operator
for SLOane 2965 and then sweating with fear while the number
was obtained. When it was engaged, which was often, the
anti-climax was balanced by a dull relief. Whenever the operator
said: 'It's ringing now, caller,' she felt sick with terror and replaced
her receiver as soon as his was lifted. Sitting in her father's worn
green velvet chair in the empty drawing-room (the only extension
was in her parents' bedroom) she would shake and speculate: Who
had lifted the receiver? Was it him? Or Cole? A maid? A friend? A
lover? The thrill lay in the knowledge that she had caused a bell to
ring in his house and that if he were in he must surely hear it. If only
in the minutest way she had affected his life. Because of something
she had done he had perhaps called out: 'Answer that, Coley,
would you?' or 'Who the hell's that? Tell them I'm not in'. Or, if
Coley and maids and cooks and friends and lovers were absent, he
himself might have padded – in his dressing-gown? – to the

telephone and picked up the receiver with his own hands. The possibilities were endless.

As with a drug, the telephone episodes satisfied for a time and produced highs and lows. Soon a stronger dose was needed. So that when her best friend from school with whom she sometimes stayed in the holidays, dared her to speak to him, she decided to take on the dare. They did it from a telephone box outside the Post Office and Stores in the Suffolk village where Christina lived. There was a good deal of preliminary giggling and pinching – Christina carried on like that much of the time in any case – and scrabbling on the filthy floor of the call box for the pennies they kept dropping. Eventually the operator said: 'You're through now, caller', and after a pause and some clicks, a male voice that was not his said: 'SLOane 2965.' 'Hello', she said. 'Could I speak to Mr. Coward please?' 'He's at the theatre at the moment, I'm afraid'. The voice sounded wary (but it could have been true, she decided afterwards. He was playing King Magnus in *The Apple Cart* that summer). 'Can I take a message?' My name is Amanda Prynne,' she spoke very fast, turning her back on Christina who was bent up with laughter and clutching her stomach. 'Isn't that a coincidence?' 'It certainly is,' the voice said politely, disbelievingly. 'I can't wait. I can't, I can't,' Christina had started to wail. 'I'm going to do it NOW.' She wasn't sure what to say next to the voice on the telephone. Instead, it spoke to her: 'Mr Coward will be most interested to hear about you. Thank you for calling. Goodbye.' 'Wait!' she shouted, but the line had gone dead. Christina uncrossed her skinny legs and unleased a stream of pee that struck the floor of the box as a waterfall strikes rocks, splashing their bare legs and soaking their sandals. They quarrelled all the way home to the cold Regency rectory where Christina lived, but by the time they reached the bathroom and were unpeeling their smelly clothes they were giggling again. 'What did he say? What did he say?' Christina aimed a loaded sponge at her and missed. 'Who's this Amanda person, anyway?'

The following day she shut herself in the lavatory, which had a noisy cistern, and took up her pen: 'Dear Mr. Coward, As you may have heard, I telephoned you yesterday . . .' She covered two whole sides. She told him how much she admired him and how she knew everything he'd ever written. She said she hoped he didn't mind her writing to him. She signed herself Amanda

Prynne. The letter was written on Christina's mother's headed paper: Bumpstead Hall, nr Haverhill, Suffolk, which she hoped would impress him. Leaning out of the carriage window as her train pulled out of Audley End station, she asked Christina, as casually as she could, to forward any letters that came for Amanda Prynne.

Silence is ambiguous stuff, she discovered. Almost anything could be read into it. Sometimes he opened her letter, scanned its contents briefly, crumpled it and dropped it in a wastepaper basket. Sometimes (he did this more often) he read her letter carefully and with increasing interest, then sat down at his desk, unscrewed his Parker 51, filled it with Quink and wrote a reply. It was a kind note, quite short, and it ended with an invitation (to tea, but she knew where *that* would lead). When the weeks that went by became months and she could no longer believe in his letter, she allowed herself to think that he didn't want to spoil things by writing, but that he kept hers on his bedside table, tucked inside a favourite book – *Barchester Towers*, perhaps. She knew everything about him. She knew of his addiction to Trollope.

It was about this time that something happened to bring the real world and the fantasy world briefly if thrillingly, closer. Copies of *The Times*, the only newspaper considered suitable reading for the girls at Belmont, were kept in a Jacobean oak cradle in the hall, disproportionately large and imposing for the house which had been built at the turn of the century in baronial style for, rumour had it, a Spanish ambassador who for some reason had never arrived. The floor of the hall was on two levels, the lower level, nearest the front door, being paved with large black and white stone squares and empty except for an enormous J. Arthur Rank gong struck at mealtimes by Brooks the butler whom everybody hated; the higher level oak-boarded and part-covered by an ancient (that was easy to believe: it was almost threadbare) and, so they were always being told, priceless, Persian carpet no one was allowed to tread on. No one, that is, except for Miss Church. The cradle was on the higher level, and beside it was an oak chest you sat on if you wanted to read the paper (it was forbidden to remove *The Times* from the hall). She was seated there one morning at break, kicking her heels against the chest and giving the personal columns on the front page her usual close attention, when a small paragraph winked at her like a neon sign: 'Mr. Noel Coward will be at the Times Bookshop at noon tomorrow (Tuesday) to sign copies of *The Noel Coward Song Book*.'

There was no chance of escaping in fog (it was in any case July) on the London train. She'd spent her pocket money for the term and had nothing for the fare. She did not know where the Times Bookshop was. She tore a page from her rough note book (it was forbidden to tear pages from your rough note book) and wrote to Fran who was doing a secretarial course in Bayswater and who lived with three friends in a basement flat off Royal Avenue:

> Darling Fran, Noel Coward is signing copies of the N.C. Song Book TOMORROW (Tues.) at the Times Bookshop. Please get one for me in yr lunch hour. I swear I will repay. I'm sorry to be such a nuisance. Please please PLEASE!
> T.O.L.
> Ant.

She gave her letter to the under-matron, Miss Tankland, who stopped in the town on Monday afternoons. Miss Tankland did not like her any more than she, or any other of the girls, liked Miss Tankland, who was spiteful, two-faced, a snob and stupid (she had once said to Camilla Arbuthnot: 'I believe you're quite well connected' and had not perceived the irony in Camilla's reply: 'Yes. The ninth earl died last week'). It was quite on the cards that Tank would lose her letter on purpose.

The next day was a day of suffering. Would Fran get her letter – always supposing Tank had posted it – before she left for Bayswater? If she did get it, would she act on it? She had a feeling she hadn't told Fran what time Noel was supposed to be at the shop.

After tea, which as usual had been buns and compo strawberry jam out of a tin with woodshavings added for pips, she was searching her desk for Geography Today Bk 3 – there was a prep on watersheds that evening – when Alice Hodges from Remove skated over the glassy boards into Vb form room. 'Antonia *Pen*rose – you're wanted in the study'. She sang this with relish and then skated away again.

The study, which was also Miss Church's drawing-room, was furnished with highly-polished Edwardian Sheraton pieces and Persian rugs. There was an ornate break-fronted bookcase full of unappetising books on one side of the fireplace, and the wall opposite to where she now stood, her back to the double doors, was taken up by a mullioned bay window, from which she could see the top of the latticed stone terrace wall and beyond it yellowing lawns sloping down to the tennis courts, on the left, and The Military Building, a leftover from the Army's occupation of the house during the war, on the right. In this dark and draughty shed (its north side was entirely open to the elements) which had a tarmacadam floor that minced your knees if you fell over, they played team games with bean bags when the weather was considered too bad for tennis or lacrosse.

Miss Church faced her from a chintz-covered arm chair by the fire. She had a smallish, square head, a beaky nose and highly-coloured cheeks. Her hair, cut like a man's at the back, was thick and wiry and not yet entirely grey, and it stuck out in tufts above her ears. The head sat oddly on a huge unfit body that tended to wobble in an unpleasant way when she walked and was always draped in loose navy or maroon garments, uninfluenced by fashion of any period and peculiar to Miss Church.

She had once seen a photograph of Miss Church as a young woman during the first world war. It was difficult to think of the thin and flat-chested person who held a boat-shaped tennis raquet with what looked like purpose, and who smiled at the camera from under an amusing hat, as having anything to do with the headmistress she knew. Miss Church taught English literature and scripture. She had a habit, when seated before the class, of holding her fountain pen vertically and letting her thumb and index finger slip down it to the nib. She would then about-turn the pen very slowly, tapping on the table as she did so. The action was usually accompanied by some ominously quiet instructions, apparently directed to the book in front of her: 'Jessica. I believe you learned the Gospel according to St Mark, Chapter 4, for preparation. Would you,' a pause, and she would look up at this point with a little smile that was not a smile at all, 'recite verses 10–23 for me please, darling.'

Miss Church did her pen trick now, tapping it on the notebook in her lap. She did this for some moments and then put the pen down on a little table which, when visiting parents were present, sometimes supported minute glasses of dry sherry. She opened the notebook. There was a small yellow envelope between its pages which she handed to Antonia. It was a telegram. 'What does this mean, darling?' Miss Church asked her.

She unfolded the telegram – it had already been opened – and read: 'All is performed stop arent I a good sister Fran'.

'Yippee,' she said, and did a little jump. Miss Church looked at her unsmilingly. 'Children are not permitted to receive telegrams here,' she said, 'except on matters of the utmost gravity. I should like some explanation, please.'

She did not fancy telling Miss Church about Noel and his Song Book and what she'd asked Fran to do. It was not Miss Church's business. 'It's a private matter. Nothing to do with school,' she said brightly. 'I see,' said Miss Church, turning a nasty shade of purple. 'I'm afraid you are a rather silly and superficial person, Antonia. I think you like to imagine yourself as different from other people, superior in some way. I have to say I have not found your work to be superior. You tend to run away from anything at all difficult.' There was a pause, during which she felt uncomfortable for a moment, knowing that Miss Church referred to the music exam she'd been supposed to take last term but had refused, at the last minute, to sit because she knew she'd fail.

'It is perhaps your parents' fault that you are spineless and spoonfed', Miss Church went on, 'but if you can't cure this you will never achieve anything very much.'

Out of the window she could see a group of figures straggling up from the tennis courts. Caroline Timpson, or it might have been Rosemary Bailey – it was hard to tell from this distance – was bouncing a tennis ball on her raquet. Every so often the ball bounced out of the raquet's reach and rolled away over the tussocky lawn, and Caroline – or Rosemary – chased after it. Meanwhile, Miss Church was winding up: 'You will be late for your preparation, Antonia, and must do an extra half hour. Before you return to your classroom, run up to Matron, will you, and tell her I'm sorry to have to bother her – I know how busy she is – but that I had to send you for a clean tunic because your own is so,' she looked briefly at the lentil soup and ink stains on the brown serge bosom, and then turned away, 'soiled'.

She had to wait until December 25th for the Song Book, which Fran said was her Christmas present. She made Fran go endlessly through her experience in the Times Bookshop. There had been a long queue. Noel had sat at a large table, piled with books, signing away. He'd worn a grey pinstripe suit, a pink shirt, a navy blue and white spotted bow-tie. When her turn had come, she'd said:

'Would you sign my book please?' and he'd said: 'It will be a pleasure.' When he'd signed his name, which he did rather fast in blue biro, she said 'Thank you very much' and he'd said: 'Not at all.'

The book when it came was large and important-looking, the paper cover designed, not very well she thought, by G. E. Calthrop. The signature was eccentric and bold and ran diagonally across the title page, fitting neatly between '*The Noel Coward Song Book*' in large lettering at the top, and '*London, Michael Joseph*' in much smaller print at the bottom. The flourish of the 'd' in Coward sliced through '*with an introduction and annotations by Noel Coward*'. On the facing page was a portrait by Clemence Dane of Noel in a yellow jumper. His hair was unflatteringly short. His forehead and ears looked pink and cross, and his pursed mouth was a bright lipstick red.

She ran her fingers over the signature as though it had been in braille. His ballpoint pen had nearly pierced the paper on some strokes; how nearly was obvious when she turned the page over. He had written this with his pen. She copied the signature over and over in her rough note book and was soon able to execute a perfect forgery and at speed.

It dawned on her gradually that Noel was never going to be interested in the real Antonia Penrose, who at fourteen was not just fat but spotty and greasy-haired and uncomfortable like Mrs. Worthington's daughter. He could only be drawn to the Antonia Penrose she had invented for him, who was thin, attractive (not beautiful: she hadn't thought that necessary) and talented in the same sort of ways that he was. The only chance she had of winning, if not his love, then at least his respect, was by *doing* something. She removed a new exercise book from the form room cupboard and started work on a play. It was to be a musical play, she decided. She called it *Court Circular* and it centred on the social round and marital difficulties, two subjects she knew next to nothing about, of a couple in their thirties whose names were Paul and Theresa Felton.

Getting the dialogue to sound convincing wasn't as easy as she'd anticipated. But she enjoyed writing the songs, or lyrics as she always thought of them (as in 'book and lyrics by so-and-so'), and she composed the tunes and fitted the words to them while walking round and round the lacrosse pitch while supposedly 'off games'. 'Off games' was the expression employed by the school to denote

23

the first three days of your 'period'. 'Period' was the word Matron used for what your mother called 'the curse'.

Of the songs *Queen of Sheba*:

I think you're the Queen of Sheba,
You know I do
And somehow I sort of feel a
Passion for you.
I don't care if the Atlantic's between us
So long as it's still romantic between us
I think you're a bit of my heaven come true –

had perhaps the best tune, but the smartest lyric was undoubtedly

When the Moon is Blue:
When the moon is blue, darling,
I'll be true, darling, to you.
There are quite a few, honey,
Apart from you, honey,
I'm fond of too.
But I'll be faithful sometime,
You may be sure
When I've had my fun time,
Then I'll be your
Baby
When the moon is blue, darling
I'll be true, darling,
To you.

The cover of her notebook said: *Court Circular*, A Musical Play in Three Acts, but she ran out of steam after the first Act and wrote nothing more. Noel was not to know this, however. She copied the First Act into a new notebook and wrote him a letter:

Dear Mr. Coward,

I thought you might be interested to see the first Act of my new musical play, *Court Circular* . . .

He would be obliged to reply now, if only to return her manuscript, and for weeks she believed this, sometimes racing to the Junior Room – the mail was given out there – at break, sometimes staying edgily in her form room in the hope that the prefect in charge of the mail would seek her out: 'Huge envelope for you, Antonia'. 'Oh, thanks,' was her bored reply as she took the packet without even glancing at it. It was years before she realized that he probably received hundreds of unsolicited manuscripts a week, and that the only ones that had even a hope of being returned, possibly accompanied by a brief and discouraging note from a member of his staff, were those which had self-addressed and stamped envelopes attached to them.

The silence that greeted *Court Circular* marked the end of her obsession as it had been. She still loved him, and she still wrote to him sometimes, but she never posted the letters. What she did post to him, every year, was a birthday card, drawn and painted by herself. The wording never varied: 'To the Master, With best wishes for a Happy Birthday, from Antonia Penrose.' She always wrote her address on the bottom left hand corner, just in case, but she no longer expected a reply. What was permitted was to picture him at breakfast, slitting the heaped envelopes with a silver paperknife. He hurried through them until he came to hers, exclaimed with pleasure, called everyone round to look, and then stood the card up in a place of honour on the piano.

One December when she was nineteen and teaching English and Art at a girls' preparatory school – a post she had no qualification for and had managed to get because her parents knew one of the governors – she read in the paper that he was ill in bed at the Dorchester Hotel. She read this on the 13th. There were three days to go before the birthday. She took great pains with the card, an ink and wash drawing, rather Cecil Beatonish, of an Edwardian couple walking in a park. The woman held a parasoll and a little dog on a lead. Behind the couple, who walked arm in arm, was a suggestion of railings and a park bench. She pasted the picture onto a stiff blue card and wrote inside: 'To the Master. Happy Birthday. I hope you're feeling better'. She was about to sign her name as usual when she hesitated, and wrote *Anthony* Penrose instead.

Two days later she was just setting off for the school when the post arrived. Among a pile of stuff for her parents, there were two other items: a communication for her from Lloyds Bank which she did not open, and a white, square envelope addressed in blue type to Anthony Penrose, esq., The Glebe House, Monkerswell, nr Salisbury. She opened it quickly and took out a greetings card. Its entire front was taken up by a black and white photograph of Noel.

He was sitting cross-legged in a white tubular chair on top of a rock in the middle of the sea. He wore a dark jacket and white trousers and espadrilles and he had a book on his knee. It was impossible to tell what book. He was seated sideways to the camera, his face half turned towards it with an amused expression that was not quite a smile. She opened the card. At the top, a blue seal, the sort some people stick on Christmas parcels, said: "Merry Xmas" in fancy silver lettering above two silver holly leaves and berries. Underneath this was a signature: Noel, in red biro. There was nothing else at all.

This card, and how she came by it, became in time her 'Noel Coward story', and she told it through the years at what she judged to be the right time to the right company. It was not a story that improved with embellishment. It depended for its effect – gratifyingly hilarious, nine times out of ten – on a fast Coward delivery:

Cue (approximate): 'As Noel Coward might say . . .'
A: I can't remember if I ever told you my Noel Coward story?
Cue: No, Do tell.
A: I was madly in love with him from about the age of eight and used to write to him from school, and ring him up – SLOane 2965 – and always for his birthday I drew him a card and he never replied. And then one year when I was about nineteen I did him a rather Cecil Beatonish card – he was in bed at the Dorchester with 'flu – and I wrote 'To the Master' at the top as usual, and was just about to sign my name 'Antonia Penrose' when I stopped and wrote Anthony Penrose instead. And I got a reply by return of post.

She felt no disloyalty at telling this story, being certain that, if he could hear it, he'd laugh louder and longer than anyone else.

She had been married to James for six years and had had three of her five children when the Great Coward Revival began in the mid-nineteen sixties. She went twice to see him – his last stage appearance – in *Suite In Three Keys*. Separated from him by only the orchestra pit she was shocked to discover how like her own father, who had died the year before, he was, not just in obvious physical ways of height and shape (their ears were almost identical) but in facial expression, in speech – particularly delivery and timing – and in gesture. The way Noel sat in an arm chair, for instance, one leg crossed over at the knee, his arms stretched along the chair arms, fingers lightly drumming the ends, was instantly familiar, as was the way he held a cigarette, the way he inhaled smoke and released it, the way he nodded his head in emphasis. None of these similarities had been discernible from photographs. He seemed, curiously, to be more like her father – who she had loved but had never bothered to get to know until it was too late, than her father had been himself.

Sometimes she and the children had Noel Nostalgia Evenings, when she played them all her old scratched 78s. Flora, in particular, was attentive and appreciative. 'I really love Noel,' she said once, but Flora loved lots of things, and most people. James always absented himself from Noel Nostalgia Evenings, either going to bed earlier than usual, or shutting himself in the study with his dictaphone and his in-tray.

She thought about Noel whenever his name was mentioned in the press or on the wireless which was increasingly often. They were not real thoughts, more a feeling of tenderness. It was comforting to know that he was alive somewhere, getting up in the morning, cleaning his teeth, eating, making jokes. Nothing too terrible could happen to a world that contained him. But he was old and, according to reports, often ill. The day could not be far off that she dreaded when she'd turn on the wireless unsuspectingly and hear a newsreader announce: Sir Noel Coward died today at his home in Jamaica (or Switzerland; or wherever he happened to be), and then, after a brief biography, go on to give the cricket scores, as though the world were still the same place.

She was glad that he was being fêted in his old age, though a part of her felt resentful that he was everybody's darling now. There was nothing special or peculiar or different about loving Noel Coward. Even his critics had stopped being critical and seemed to think that everything he'd ever written was bloody marvellous. This was surely insulting, and a mistake she'd never made, even at ten years old.

When Christina, whom she had not seen for years, telephoned and suggested they go together to see *Cowardy Custard* at the Mermaid, she was tempted to refuse. Only Noel Coward could sing a Noel Coward song. She did not want to see a camp chorus perform dance routines with top hats and canes or hear them wreck his songs by sticking too closely to the melody in places where he would sing seconds or merely speak the lines. But she went because it would be nice to get away from James and the children for once, and she enjoyed herself because it was fun seeing Christina (fat now, hooray, whereas she had remained eight stone five – except during her pregnancies – for the past twenty years). *Cowardy Custard* itself was exactly as she'd thought it would be.

Three weeks later she got back from the afternoon school run to find a note stuck in one of the children's gumboots outside the front door:

Your telephone's out of order. We've got one spare ticket for *Cowardy Custard* on the 17th, and knowing your passion for N.C. thought of you. Please come if James can spare you. Supper in the Garrick afterwards.

After a little thought – it was very kind of the Evanses to ask her and she didn't want to seem ungrateful – she refused the invitation, explaining that James had already spared her once to see it, and suggesting the ticket should go to someone who hadn't because it was a wonderful . . . (she paused here, because the word 'show' was so disagreeable, but how else could she describe it?). She also said, which was true, that there was a parent-teacher meeting at Flora's school that evening, and that she ought to be there, Flora's maths being what they were.

On the morning of the eighteenth she had washed up the breakfast things, wiped some surfaces, made the beds (Jack's had to be stripped because he'd wet his sheets without telling), collected socks and knickers from the floor of every bedroom and put them in the dirty linen basket, stared out of Flora's bedroom window unseeingly for half an hour, wished she were dead, and was just about to start on the mountain of ironing she'd been avoiding for days because it was all tangled up with laddered tights and matted and odd socks, when the telephone rang. She recognized Jane Evans's voice:

'Antonia – It's Jane here. I can hardly bear to tell you this, but we were sitting in our seats at the Mermaid yesterday just before the curtain went up, when NOEL COWARD walked into our row and sat down in the seat next to yours – I mean the one you'd have been in. He got a standing ovation. The whole theatre clapped and roared for at least ten minutes. He was on his own and seemed very frail and old and his hands shook and he wept throughout the entire performance. It was rather upsetting, really, but wonderful too, of course. You never did meet him, did you? And if you'd been there you'd have sat NEXT TO HIM,' (she shouted this). 'I really can't bear it!'

After Jane had rung off, she sat on her bed and stared at the floor. Tears, for sad Noel and for herself, spilled over and ran, slowly at first and then faster and faster, down her cheeks. They fell onto a join in the carpet that had come unstuck. Its edges had curled back to reveal dusty brown underlay. The carpet, once a quite pleasing and subtle shade of blue, was shabby now, and needed not just hoovering but a good going over on hands and knees with a sponge and a bucket of *1001*, something she'd been putting off for months.

Buying a Dress

James Lasdun

Thirty a day, sufficient gin to float
A goldfish, Guinness sluicing down her throat,
The barman's spaniel, one damp eye a-cock,
Wiggling his nose like a toe in a sock
As he watched her mechanic's hands tip back
And twist the beaker till the rim's last black
Oil-heavy droplet splashed her scarlet lipstick
(Even a tampon was like a dipstick
In those hands). She had myths for everything;
I was the last of the line, the inbred king,
Witless, chinless, myopic, coughing up gold,
Herself the gene-rich gutter-urchin, bold
As ersatz brass and hungrier than a till,
Her mouth wide open, sieving the world for its krill
Of creature comforts – 'would you like that?' 'Yes.'
I'm thinking of the day we bought a dress,
She tried on most of London's stock for size –
From Columbine to Pantaloon my eyes
Were washed in primal splashes, polka dots,
In patterned mascots of the male world – yachts
Hot-air balloons and motorbikes that traced
A knee-high Capricorn, Equator waist;
My little Earth, each louvered stall a night
She'd break from, like a planet into light,
Massed colours, samite, lace, merino wool,
And where she stood, each mirror's pool seemed full
To bursting, like a swollen waterdrop's
Bulging convexity . . .
                        Outside the shops,
Where summer riots were simmering in the heat
And shoals of gauzy dresses swam the street,
Fate, in a painter's shape, began to dip
His brush in wet vermillion, letting drip
Only the most occasional beady gout
Onto the street below . . .
                        Meanwhile a shout
Of triumph signalled that the job was done –
Each wished-for detail gathered into one
Wrapped-round expanse of yellow silk, held tight
About her waist – a fluted fall of light,

Half-light and shadow, billowing at the sleeves –
Picture a ship's bell melting, harvest sheaves,
Their brilliance hatching with the crack of dawn,
Gold cobbled light on streams – I could go on,
But what I most remember is the way
She wore it; buckled turbulence, the spray
Of water on zinc, a beehive's boiling throng,
The way a budded peony breasts the strong
Rotunda of its sheath; improbable
Compression, not of flesh, but of the soul,
As if she'd torn through every veil, but found
Matter itself in Purdah, nature bound
And yashmak'd in some chemical Sharia
She'd never overthrow. Her heart's desire
Rippled in the mirror, and she turned
Quickly; the knowledge framed inside it burned
Too violently . . .
                              She wore it from the shop
And step by step we zeroed on the drop –
Slick globule that prefigured my one spurt
Of infidelity (I blabbed, the hurt
Exploded in her body like a gun)
Oh Exegetes, behold her now, the sun
Falling upon her in gambades and curls
Of gold, the whipped-cream, thixotropic swirls
Of virgin silk notating on the air
The way a body registers despair;
I see it in slow motion: the surprise,
The torso's whiplash twist, neck arced, the eyes
Widening as the tugged silk slides around,
And with it, like a perfect bullet wound,
One molten ruby. Silence. *No harm done.*
Nothing we can't put right (much later on
The same words met the same astonished look);
Endings are swift — we taxied home, she took
The dress off, checked the damage, nodded, gripped
A bunch of fabric in each fist, and ripped.

Natacha Ledwidge

BOX OF DREAMS

Maggie Brooks

Dib woke after a restless night feeling, for no reason, disturbed. As she came round, she became aware of a shadow blocking the light. It took a moment before she realised that it was Audley looming intently over her, scrutinising her drowsy face as though he might learn something. She heard him speak fondly and softly, 'Darling, you've got two little spots by your chin. I thought they were moles but they're spots.' This information took a moment to seep through her dulled brain, and when it did, she felt an overwhelming surge of irritation and, putting the flats of her hands on his chest, she pushed him away with quite unnecessary force. He heard a shoe hit the door as he closed it behind him. Puzzled at her vehemence, he retreated to the kitchen.

Some twenty minutes later, with harmony restored, Audley was sat on a high stool at the breakfast dining surface next to the sink. There had once been two stools but the leg had fallen off the other. He sat wearing his pyjama bottoms and a pair of steel-rimmed glasses. He was poised over a piece of paper. Every now and then he paused to give attention to the act of peeling and segmenting a clementine, and then he would return to his writings. Dib was beside him boiling eggs and she had begun to hum as she watched the bubbles welling in the saucepan. Her humming had the peculiar insistence, the perspectival variations of an aimless fly that needed swatting and it prevented him from following his train of thought. She put his egg down in front of him. It sat neatly in a little chicken egg cup.

'They're nice big brown eggs,' she said, 'Yours has got a feather on it. That's sort of reassuring, don't you think? Makes you think it came out of a chicken.'

'Please,' he said, frowning.

She bit her lip and stood next to him, silent, eating her hot egg with some difficulty from a serviette. The white broke and a dribble of yolk moved down her hand. He was aware of the yellow drool and stirred uneasily on his perch. It really was impossible to concentrate. She caught his glance and began to mop the yolk up nervously.

'It's very hard to eat an egg standing up,' she grumbled, scrubbing at a bead of yellow on her dressing gown.

'Well, why don't you do it in the other room, then?' he asked in a perfectly reasonable voice, 'Then you could sit down.'

Dib could feel herself becoming sulky. 'People eat breakfast

35

together, don't they?'

'Yes, I believe they do. But if we could just have quiet for five minutes . . . would that be possible? Just while I record my dreams . . .'

She was silent for five minutes, but, on the one hand he could hear her jaw clicking as it revolved on a particularly crunchy batch of toast, and on the other hand, he had a strong sense of someone hovering in resentful silence against all their inner promptings.

Finally, he put his pencil down.

'If you *really* cared about me,' he said with emphasis but without rancour, 'You'd want me to get my dreams down . . .'

Her jaw stopped. After a moment she spoke with obvious effort, 'If you *really* cared about me, you'd make sure there were two stools.'

He pushed his work away, looked at the neon for patience. 'Oh, yes, always the martyr. The stool broke if you recall.'

'That was six weeks ago,' she mumbled.

'Look.' A note of desperation came into his voice, 'I'm *trying* to do this. It's important.' and then, more gently, appealing to her better instincts, 'Don't you want me to get better?'

She cocked her head on one side and thought about it. The concept of getting better seemed to be an abstract one when they only had the analyst's word that there was anything wrong with him in the first place. So far, the treatment had resulted in a box of dreams so heavy that it needed two hands to lift it, and he spent most of his waking hours pouring out still more messages from his active unconscious, waiting for expert code-cracking by the mysterious and venerated Mervyn Baldock. Dib was beginning to dislike Mervyn Baldock intensely. For one thing, she suspected he shared an intimacy with Audley which, by its nature, she could never equal, and for another, she had a dim foreboding that Mervyn's view of total health was total self-obsession.

'Well, would you like *me* to buy a stool?' she asked, knowing full well he wouldn't.

'That would be one idea,' he conceded. He was aware he had a curious resistance to this idea. She had been living with him for six months but, somehow, confirming it with furniture was a little too emphatic, 'But in the meantime . . . it's not a lot to ask . . .' he said nodding to the toast, 'Just for ten minutes . . .'

'And then what?'

'And then I'm going to see Mervyn. It's Thursday.'

She poured herself a bowl of Grape Nuts. He watched coldly as the nuts scooted noisily into the bowl. He looked up at her pointedly.

'Now, are you really able to eat all those Grape Nuts?'

She was in the action of pouring the milk on, but suddenly something seemed to halt her arm in mid-action, and it shot up as though someone had tapped her funny bone with a gavel, and she threw the cereal bowl in the air instead. At the same time, to his astonishment, she bent in half, shrieking at him, reminding him of nothing more forcibly than the small, savage terrier down the road who snapped at heels and bit the postman's fingers as he sneaked the letters through the slit.

'Well, ask *Mervyn*,' she shrieked, giving the name its full contemptuous weight, 'Ask Mervyn why you *say* you love me, why you *ask* me to live here, but there's only one egg cup and there's only one stool. Ask him that will you? Ask him if it means anything . . .'

'All right,' he nodded tersely, 'I will,' and he carried on forming spiders with elaborate care.

As he drove along, his mind was ticking over in tune with the elderly engine. The incident with the Grape Nuts was hard to explain away. He re-ran it in his mind's eye – saw the movement of her hand. It had tremored slightly. Then the cereal bowl revolving in the air – the milk cascading, fanning out and upwards balletically, then falling in a wet slop, heavy with sodden pellets. The Grape Nuts had lodged in the narrow spaces between the tiles and would be a devil to pick out. It would either take a needle or a toothbrush. Why had she suddenly, out of the blue, from a perfectly calm conversation, sent the hooped bowl spinning through the air like a frisbee? Perhaps she was on the verge of a nervous breakdown. He thought hard. Her hand *had* trembled before she tossed it, he remembered that. Dammit. What if she ⸰ *were* on the verge of a nervous breakdown. Could he cope? Would it be fair to ask him to cope? He saw her, now, in a long Victorian nightgown, wandering the flat in fevered agitation, a circlet of wild flowers in her hair, red rims under her eyes, listlessly emptying a box of Grape Nuts as though scattering seeds on the brown loam of the foam-back carpet, singing a weird little song in a cracked voice.

Rochester's words came into his head:

> 'Your mind is my treasure
> If it were broken it would be my treasure
> still . . .'

Audley wasn't entirely convinced. One committed oneself to a person. If their mind subsequently wobbled off-centre, they weren't necessarily the same person one had committed oneself to. Certainly Rochester had sung a different tune with poor old Bertha Mason. And, there again, Rochester had the room to accommodate a mad person. Audley had not. He saw here now, in the diaphanous gown, drifting dippily towards the window, candle in hand, the flame dancing and snatching, perilously close to the drapes. Would it be fair to ask him to cope?

His jowls wobbled as he shook his head.

Wasn't there something women got when they became obsessed with the gas taps? They had to keep going back time after time to check. And cleaning. They had to keep vacuuming long after every speck of dust was gone. No danger of that with Dib, more like a pathological ability to create crumbs even when she wasn't eating. An obsessive desire to clean should she manifest it, whilst being a distressing neurosis, would not be unacceptable, but it was too much to hope the malaise would take that course. This thing was more like an obsession with trivial detail.

He thought about the stool and the egg cup. For God's sake, if it mattered that much they could take turns. In fact he would offer her a turn on the stool tomorrow. If they took alternate days they would more or less even up. He scowled. Of course, it would be hard to get his dreams down, standing on one leg like a stork. And after all, it was *his* flat. She didn't have to write her dreams down for an exacting medical practitioner. All she wanted to do in the morning was witter. He had started her on a programme to record her own dreams so that he could get an hour of peace, but her dreams struck him as rather uninteresting. His own were jammed solid with rich, archetypal imagery obligingly packaged and sent up from the unconscious as though on a rather efficient conveyor belt system through the dark grottoes and canyons of his sleeping brain. Fairground horses, unicorns, keys and medieval boxes, mazes and parfait gentil knights, even trains coming out of tunnels. They all popped out obligingly like images on a zoetrope.

Dib, by contrast, seemed to be plumbed in to some vast

department store packed with consumer durables. In the last dream she'd recounted, for instance, Audley had bought a monstrous King-size bed with a hideous Dralon Cintique headboard and matching side tables attached. He had made her carry it home on her head. He was cycling beside her as she bobbed along and he was announcing gleefully, 'Why it's big enough for *three!*' She'd kept asking him about this dream.

'I take it to mean you're rather manipulative,' she'd said cautiously, 'Well, either that or there's another woman . . .'

'A dream tells you about *you,* not about someone else,' he'd informed her. Privately, he thought it related to her refusal to explore her unconscious, 'We all carry a mattress,' he said enigmatically.

'It was *your* mattress I was carrying,' Audley shrugged but she persisted, 'And it felt very unwieldy and extremely heavy.'

As he lay now in the rather anonymous office looking at the stained Regency wallpaper, the stool issue came again into his mind. Mervyn Baldock sat listening with a placid non-commital look of professional blankness on his face.

'Dib threw a plate full of cereal today, quite out of the blue. Do you think she might be unstable? She wanted a stool of her own. She seemed to think it was significant that I hadn't glued the leg back on.'

Mervyn stirred.

'We are concerned with you not with Dib.'

Audley settled back. He found the words quite reassuring.

Dib wandered through the run-down market in a black, desperate gloom, buying nothing but stopping now and then to stare bleakly at inexplicable West Indian vegetables laid out like old brown socks; at the hair pieces in the garish wig shop, marked *horse* and *Yak* and *Javanese human.* She felt a pang for the small Javanese human who had sold her switch of long black hair for a pittance so it could set on a wig block here in Shepherd's Bush where no-one could afford to buy it. It drizzled fitfully and the water splattered off the striped awnings down her collar. The puddles seeped moisture through the gum seams of her inadequate shoes and the cold seemed to penetrate right through to her bones. She kept going over and over it – like probing a tooth cavity trying to work out where it hurt most. Maybe he did love her in his way, but it was indisputable that love went further than stretching one's mouth around the phrase 'I love you'. It involved small caring attentions like, well, egg cups and stools.

The greasy smoke from the hamburger stall hung in the air, folding gently towards the small table and chair where the harrassed Irish women queued, gazing dolefully at the placard which announced Madame Chirene to be at her tea break. Dib thought of joining the women with their fretful, criss-cross foreheads and their knobbly bags of shopping. But there were some things it didn't take a clairvoyant to reveal. Lately, she'd begun to feel that she was fading, not like the Invisible Man, all in one go, but in portions that came and went. She'd even toyed with the idea that it was the box of dreams that was doing it. The relentless stockpile of phantoms was beginning to outweigh reality by its sheer volume and she found that depressing. What's more, she herself was markedly absent from the dreams. In a pile of paper, thick as two stacked volumes of the Longer Oxford Dictionary, she'd found only four references to 'D', none of them particularly flattering. Other letters from the alphabet occurred in more exotic, alluring locations or in different centuries, mostly in states of undress, and whilst she could hardly be jealous of the uninvited guest stars of his sleeping brain, she had begun to have a sense of herself as an insubstantial ghost in his waking life, just as she seemed to be in his sleep. The position now was that the initials were beginning to appear in her own dreams, without the benefit of her knowing who they were – giant dancing letters, Ls and Rs and Gs, soft and spongey like the noodles in alphabet soup. The awful certainty was that *she* loved him, how else to explain this hollow, haunting ache just like a hunger.

Noon found her outside the wet-fish shop, staring into a cardboard box of severed mullet heads. They were all gaping with blind tiddley-wink eyes and their expressions were uniformly aghast. A tray of eels pulsated on the slab. One of them lifted its grey-green head to peer myopically over the rim as though planning its escape route. It opened its mouth to gasp and she could see the pink membrane of its lower lip. She felt a sudden urge to save the thing. It would only need some water. A moment's thought dispelled the scheme. She could see it now, a big black wriggle, doing lengths in Audley's avocado bath. Audley, all squeaky indignation, demanding it be gone before his bath night. She stopped herself short in this flight of fancy and forced herself to face the facts in hand. No more Audley, no more bath nights, no more confidences shared and, in the arbitrary way of things, what stood at risk had never seemed more precious or more real. She still nursed a forlorn hope that the situation could be saved. The stool had taken on immense significance. Objects didn't matter but, just right now, they did. If he would only give her some sign that she had substance in his thoughts, that she existed for him at all. The crabs under the plastic palm pot rattled their claws feebly as she walked away. The eel knew he wasn't sitting beside a sprig of parsley for nothing, and she knew with the same bitter satisfaction that there wouldn't be a sign, and there certainly wouldn't be a stool.

There was a brief thunderstorm as Audley drove back from Hampstead, thinking hard. He was still feeling vaguely tetchy because one of the dreams had got away. It was essential to pin them down on waking because they tended to evaporate during the day like candy floss. Grasping for the elusive memory in the afternoon was as exasperating as running round a hedgerow trying to catch a butterfly. Who was the woman standing in shadow holding the jewel-studded scabard? Was it E? He could remember a few small details and the general texture but every time he tried to close his fist around it, it scampered off like a wily daddy long legs. He worried away at it until he noticed with a start that he had taken entirely the wrong turning and was proceeding down Ladbroke Grove, where he had no conceivable reason to be. He also became aware that he was humming under his breath, and when he analysed it, it was from My Fair Lady.

'I have often walked
Down this street before . . .'

On some impulse he couldn't have explained, he took a further wrong turning into Oxford Gardens, which, even in the weather, looked like a gay wedding bower. The blossom-heavy trees bowed under the weight of water and, here and there down the long festive avenue, boughs hung down limp like festoons of sodden ribbons.

Half way down he parked. He stood in the rain, in a puddle that was full of petals, gazing up speculatively at the house where Estelle lived. He didn't know her well but he seemed to recall a stack of discarded furniture in her hallway, he seemed to recall a stool amongst the pile and he supposed that was why he was here. He also had an inkling, just the merest suspicion as yet, one that he had not previously had the pretext to explore, that he might be in love with her. Before he could think better of it, he rang the buzzer of her entryphone and stood with his ear to the metal box, hoping she was out. Her cool voice came through the speaker, tinny. He noted, just out of scientific interest, that his heart was thumping as he sprang lightly up the stairs two at a time.

The rain ouside had stopped, leaving the sky a luminous dark grey. Audley knew that, if he just craned out, there would be a rainbow. The sun streamed in and made the china cups transluscent. It lit up the amber stream of tea that she was pouring. His eyes strayed back continually to the way the heavy bronze earring, sandwiched with its threads of turquoise, nestled in the hollow space formed by the softened angle of her jaw. She tossed the dark snake of hair with artless indifference, as though unaware of his earnest, anxious gaze. The bracelets shimmied up and down her sparrow wrist as she handed him his cup. He was not entirely sure whether she fascinated or repelled him, and the distinction was as fine and precarious and finally inconsequential as the flip of a coin.

'Funnily enough,' she was saying lightly, 'I dreamt of you only the other day.' She dipped her eyes, 'I can't imagine why . . .' She stirred the tea in the pot as she spoke and the silver tinkling against the fragile china together with the bangles made a sound like the jangling of wind chimes. She began to recount the dream but he didn't hear it. He continued to gaze at her in a disconcerting, wistful fashion as though the act of staring would uncover something new. If she'd been crystals in a test tube, he might have waved her over a bunsen burner, if she'd been liquid he might have shaken her up and tested her with litmus but, since she was none of these things but unpredictable flesh and blood, he could only stare cautiously at her as though in close proximity to some exotic spider.

'You're such a good listener,' she was saying, 'I have this sense, you're very still and wise . . .'

Through the door he could just glimpse his ear-marked stool as it balanced on the cartons of packed books. The things belonged to a departed lover but wouldn't be collected for two weeks. In the meantime he was perfectly welcome to borrow the stool just so long as it returned in the fortnight. As for an egg-cup, she was sure she could sort him something out. He nestled down more snugly in the comfy armchair. His eyes drifted from the luxuriant plants to the small mahogany piano, and he monitored calm readings from the meter in his chest. All was harmonious – it was only when his eyes came to rest and met *her* eyes, that the needle flickered and threatened to fly off the scale.

Dib stood in the kitchen staring at the stool and the cracked rabbit egg-cup. She had an inscrutable, perplexed expression like St. Bernadette beholding the Holy Spring. She didn't speak but moved towards him and he noticed she was rather pink and pleased. She pulled him to her clumsily, then burrowed urgently into his arm-pit with her head, emitting faint squeaks of pleasure like a contented hamster. They clung together sharing a mysterious sense of relief as though some dreadful crisis had been passed particularly mysterious to Audley because he had no idea of what it was. There was a faint waft of hamburger and soap coming from her sandy hair. Now was not the time to tell her of the drastic changes impending in his life. Across her head, his eyes came level with the calendar. Two weeks. That was plenty of time. He felt unaccountably excited like a bottle of soda that had been shaken up.

He gave a heave and swung her boisterously around, squeezing the air out of her until she gasped for breath. Dib laughed protestingly and he felt a great benevolent surge of tenderness towards her as one might feel for some long-loved family dog. She seemed in *such* high good humour, he was almost tempted to tell her of the pleasures of the day. And Audley held onto her that fraction longer than the hug demanded as though he were reluctant to let her go.

That night she slept as though a great weight had been lifted from her. She dreamt she wandered over to the bureau and then to the window that overlooked the square. She was carrying the box-file. It was heavy. She balanced it half on the sill, half on her knee while she threw up the sash. Then, taking reams of paper in great handfuls, she tossed them out into the midnight air. The sheets seemed to hover suspended, twittering and spinning in the atmosphere until suddenly with a great whoosh, they took off as one great mass, swooping upwards like a flock of birds. Audley clapped his hands to see the paper doing aerobatics in the sky. Not all of the sheets made it. Some of his dreams were wrapped round the branches of the tree, others were impaled in clusters on the railings, but the main body of the flight of dreams kept climbing until it was only a distant flutter like the tail of a kite.

She felt a deep sense of satisfaction, as though it were something noble that she'd done – liberating restless spirits who were never meant to be kept confined in a cardboard box.

As she sat rather self-importantly beside him on the brand-new stool, eating her egg from the small cracked rabbit, she began to tell him the dream. Audley listened politely for a moment, his pen hovering discreetly – Estelle had featured in the chaotic travails of the night as a bejewelled snake charmer and it was important that he shouldn't lose the thread. He broke in at a tactful moment and suggested that, just for practice, she might like to write it down. Dib tailed off into silence, unresentful. He continued to fill the page with fevered, unintelligible scribble and, perched upon the stool that felt so stable, she was perfectly content to simply sit and watch his hand.

LOST
IN A
NIGHTMARE

Richard Rayner

She was sick with fear but she thought: '*I'm not going to let him do this.*'

It was nearly three in the afternoon and the thin, cold rain which had been drizzling for so long was turning into a downpour. Through the bus window she saw the crowds begin to move more urgently, heading for shelter. A man with a moustache and a red golf umbrella slipped and fell on the suddenly treacherous pavement. She scanned the street. There was no sign of him.

More and more passengers filed on board. Lurching forward through the City, the bus stopped with unbearable frequency. Progress was negligible.

Jane picked at a mark on the patterned seat cover with her finger nail. She rubbed her eyes and wanted to howl with frustration, asking herself whether she should have bothered to pack the small suitcase which now rested at her feet or whether she should have rushed out of the house, the house which had become so cold and chill these days, as soon as she heard his voice on the phone, laughing and teasing, as calm as ever, saying they would be seeing each other again, soon. Her eyes strained against the light.

She should have taken a taxi to the station, it would have been quicker, then again it might have been stuck in the same jam and the bus *had* come along first. Perhaps she'd done the right thing. It was impossible to say.

She could no longer think straight. He was paralysing her capacity for logical thinking, she realised.

Her plan was vague: to get out of London by train, head North. She could have taken the car but the train seemed safer — more people. Except the train involved taking the bus and the bus seemed to be going nowhere. She had no clear idea of her final destination. It didn't matter much, she had to get away from the house, it was as simple and as difficult as that; she had to *try*. The house seemed filled with an unnatural silence. Now even the sound of the phone ringing made her flinch, so she kept the answering machine on all the time. Anywhere would do, anywhere at all. She'd decide at King's Cross; she'd decide, that is, *if* he allowed her to leave.

Something touched her shoulder. Her heart knocked at her ribs and her shoulders jumped in an uncontrollable reflex as if subjected to an electric shock. Slowly, with a feeling of dread, she twisted her head to look at the seat behind.

It was only a small, frail-looking woman with glasses and a green hat who was saying, 'Are you all right?'

'Fine,' Jane said, 'I'm fine, Thank you.'

The English habit, she thought, not saying what you feel.

'Bit nervy, aren't you?' The woman screwed up her face. She had piercing eyes and her voice was surprisingly deep.

'I'm sorry.'

'No need to apologise, dearie. Not to me. I don't like to see it, that's all. Nice girl like you, in such a state. You was chattering away to yourself like a little monkey. I thought you were talking to the man in front. But he got off at the last stop.'

'The first sign of madness,' Jane said, managing a smile before she turned away.

The bus edged along a canyon formed by vast buildings of glass and concrete on either side. Driving rain bounced off the pavements.

She was talking to herself more and more. When she was alone in the house it didn't seem so bad, just a little crazy. In public it was more of a humiliation.

She'd noticed it first ten days before. She was wearing a grey silk suit and carrying her briefcase, walking up Holborn to get a cab, on her way across the West End to Curzon St where she had an important meeting with her lawyer. She was preoccupied. She didn't want to be late. A cab was trundling up the hill from the *Daily Mirror* building and she was about to hail it when suddenly Michael was beside her, suggesting in rather earnest fashion they should go to the country at the weekend, maybe to Devon to find that quiet hotel they'd stayed in before and she'd replied yes, why not, they could take the MG and drive with the top down if it was fine.

Then she realised what she was doing and she found herself on the corner of Furnival Street, shouting. 'NO. I CAN'T BE TALKING TO YOU. I CAN'T.' The crowd on the pavement parted like an Old Testament miracle and flowed round her. Faces stared at her and at each other, exchanging glances of shock, pity and embarrassment.

That same night she'd had the dream. She woke with a start, sweating, and lifted her head. From next door she heard Buddy Holly: *Love is love and not fade away, love is love and not fade away.* She reached out and turned on the bedside lamp. In the dream she was with Michael. They were in a bathroom, decorated in vivid blue. She approached Michael who lay in the bath with water up to his neck. She approached him slowly and then pushed his shoulders down, hard, until his body was below the surface. Her nails scratched against the enamel. Moving gently, his hair made sweeping patterns through the bath and bubbles of expelled air burst upwards as his lungs inhaled water. And all the while his green eyes, magnified by the water, remained open, staring, watching her with curiosity as she killed him. After several minutes, when she was sure he must be dead, she took her hands from his shoulders. There was no movement in the water, just the slow motion of swirling of his hair. It wasn't until she was drying her hands on a thick blue towel that Michael stood up in the bath and with water dripping from his body asked: 'Would you like to try that again?'

That was when she woke. She felt cold and drew the bedclothes close round her body. Then she saw it, a spot of red on the ceiling. She knew instinctively that it was blood, his blood. The mark grew in size and slowly assumed the shape of five fingers and a palm as though his bleeding hand were pressing down from above, leaving a stain which became more and more clearly defined with each passing second. The plaster on the ceiling began to bulge and the hand came down to meet her.

Someone was banging on the wall and she was screaming, 'WHAT MORE CAN I GIVE YOU?' Her breath came in panicky shudders. When at last she realised that she really was awake she got up and tried to compose herself, repeating over and over that it was only a dream, that he couldn't hurt her anymore. She went to the bathroom and turned on the light. Her body was still shaking as she glanced at the mirror and saw the message there, sprayed in red paint. It was just a single word, typical of Michael's fondness for the terse and the dramatic and the sick: HI!!! It was one of his jokes, of course, but she couldn't find it within herself to laugh. A part of her sensed the horror was just beginning.

At last the bus reached King's Cross. She stood to get off and rang the bell. As she walked down the aisle the woman with the green hat caught her sleeve. She was looking at Jane with desperate conviction, her eyes glazed. She pulled a leaflet from a Sainsbury's bag and thrust it into Jane's hand. 'Remember,' the old woman said, 'JESUS SAVES.' Jane glanced at the copy of 'Watchtower'

49

and smiled. Praying certainly hadn't helped so far. And she'd tried, even after all these years, she *had* tried.

The station was busy. A train was leaving for the North — Leeds, York, Edinburgh — in twenty minutes. That would do as well as any. She was in the queue at the ticket counter when a young man barged in front of her. He wore jeans and a T-shirt. He had dark hair. Terror rose in her throat but he turned to her almost immediately and she saw his face — skin smooth as a child's and a hint of a scar on the left side of his mouth. It wasn't him. Relief exploded in her chest.

'This isn't how it's supposed to go at all,' he said. 'You're supposed to be annoyed with me because I've been rude. You should have said something. That's according to Procedure A for meeting attractive women in railway stations. But as you can see, being a man with an infinite capacity for making the best of things, I've already launched on Procedure B, the one I follow when Procedure A goes off the rails. Which, if truth be told, it does with sickening regularity.'

He smiled, a friendly, unassuming smile and Jane studied his face. He could be useful. She'd feel easier if she were with someone, at least for a while. In normal circumstances she would have deflected such an advance. Now she said, 'That's probably because Procedure A is in considerable need of improvement.'

'You're right, I know. Meeting cute is always so easy in the movies. I never seem to be able to bring it off.' He smiled again. 'Where are you going?'

'Edinburgh.'

'*Great*. Edinburgh. 'I'm going there too. For a holiday. Well, to see my parents. Not quite the same thing I suppose. What about you?'

'Business.'

'Business. I thought you were a tourist. You are from the States aren't you.'

'Half and half. I was brought up there. Near San Francisco. But I live here now.'

'Where?'

'In the East End.'

'I'm up North. Camden Town.' He pulled a face. 'Very trendy.' He made a stiff little bow and asked: 'Might I take it that we'll be travelling together?'

She shrugged. 'Why not?'

'Terrific.'

She felt some of her anxiety begin to lift. It seemed as though she'd been alone for weeks, with no-one to talk to. No wonder she thought she was going mad. 'We haven't introduced ourselves. My name is Jane Morrissey.'

'Paul Thompson.' He extended his hand. She shook it briefly.

They were at the front of the queue now and a voice on the PA was announcing the departure of their train in fifteen minutes. 'Excuse me,' Paul said. He swivelled away from her to buy his ticket at the counter.

She was opening her purse and deciding whether to pay by cash or credit card. She asked, 'What do you do? I mean, what's your line of work.'

'I'm an actor.'

He was still facing the counter and she was thinking a credit card would be better, after all she might need the cash and —

she knew that voice

— she didn't know when she'd next get to the bank.

Christ, she knew that voice. An actor. Sweet Jesus.

She knew he was facing her again. She could feel his eyes as though they were launching a physical assault. But she didn't look at him. That was the last thing she wanted to do. What she wanted to do was run, run like the wind as she used to do on the track when she was a kid, but she couldn't. A nightmare feeling of dullness weighed down her body. Against her will, she felt her eyes raised towards his and the face she saw was no longer the face of Paul Thompson but a more familiar one with startling green eyes and fair eyebrows that were almost invisible on his forehead.

Michael.

He smiled.

And then she was running, across the rubber tiled station concourse, head down, running blindly towards the Euston Road, out into the street, until she crashed into something hard, bounced away and hit the wet concrete flagstones. She bit the inside of her cheek as she fell and tasted blood in her mouth. A newspaper vendor was shouting at her, words she couldn't understand. She'd knocked his stand over. She got up slowly, dizzily.

'You're a menace,' the newspaper vendor said. 'Someone should put you away.'

But now she was running again, fast and with a more controlled motion, pumping her arms and legs rhythmically, heading down the steps into the King's Cross Underground. She didn't buy a ticket. She vaulted over the automatic steel barrier. As she ran towards the escalator she heard a man shouting, 'Come back. You can't do that.' It almost forced a smile from her lips. She swallowed the blood which was filling her mouth and took a few deep breaths. Her composure was beginning to return.

She rode the escalator down to the Northbound Piccadilly platform, thinking all the time, *'I'm not going to let you do this, you bastard.'* She wondered whether she was imagining all this, whether something really had come loose in her mind. That was wishful thinking. She knew it was happening. It was impossible but he was here. She thought about where he'd come from next. Was there any way of fighting him off? She looked round on the escalator to see if he was following her. Nothing. She'd read somewhere how it was easy to trap someone in the Underground. Well, it was too late to worry about that now.

The platform was crowded. A train pulled out, disappearing into the tunnel with a clatter and a shower of sparks and people were hurrying past her to the exits, brandishing cases and umbrellas. A drunk lay on the platform, swilling sherry from a bottle. She almost fell over his legs.

She hated the Tube, it was dirty, fizzing, weird, a chaos of noise and bodies and smells where anything could happen. This time it was worse than ever for this time she kept seeing faces, half-expecting each one to turn to her with his eyes and begin to speak to her in that soft, persuasive manner she knew so well. *'Janey, would you like to . . .'*

She shivered. A beggar stood in front of her, an old woman with greying, matted hair stuck to the side of her face and plastic bags rolled round her feet. Jane pushed a few coins into her hand and the old woman smiled primly before shuffling away. She looked up and down the platform. No train came.

She felt unbearably tired. Her head ached and she had that peculiar feeling of being in a dream — unable to focus her mind. There were so many memories of Michael, she knew, but it all seemed so long ago, so distant and confused. She could hear the beat of her heart and she realised this was the moment, he was coming for her. Sensing him close, feeling her stomach sink, she closed her eyes. And waited.

She remembered something her father told her when she was young and having nightmares which concerned a man in an iron mask who would wait until she was asleep before opening the cupboard at the bottom of her bed, walking out, and coming to take her away. 'Fear doesn't exist,' her father said. 'No such thing. There's nothing in that cupboard. Just your own imagination. You can make it go away.' Like many of her father's pronouncements this had proved misleading; she had known terror, it was real, and it was here and now.

She opened her eyes and was looking straight into Michael's face. 'Hello,' he began and then instinctively she rammed her palms against his chest and pushed as hard as she could, surprising herself with her own strength. His scream knifed briefly through her mind but the sound was soon drowned by the roar of the next train as it sped on to the platform, crushing his body beneath it.

It was twenty minutes later when she heard them coming for her, their footsteps echoing down the long, empty corridor. They were in a group and as they grew closer she heard voices calling out. A man was saying that someone had been pushed under a southbound train on the Piccadilly line, murdered.

She was kneeling on the ground, head pressed against the coldness of the wall, neck outstretched, as if waiting for her own execution. 'There she is,' someone shouted, 'she's the one.'

She looked up. Above her she saw the letters S-M-I-L-E spelled out in brightly coloured tile, curving along the top of the corridor. They had surrounded her now and were examining her with suspicion. He eyes moved across each bulging face, examining them carefully.

'Where's Michael?,' she asked.

No one answered.

'Where is he?,' she asked again.

Then it was all right because she did see him, there he was, moving forward, pushing towards her. And she did smile.

London Pubs

Paul Cox's Sketchbook

Chas with accordian Cheshire Cheese

Cheshire Cheese

Cheshire Cheese

Beryl
with ten Glasses

Cheshire Cheese

Curlis 'n' Johnny's

Brokers at the
Tottenham

Black Friars

Trevor, Brian, Norman, Tom.

Dirty Dicks

Full Fathom Five

Marina Warner

Father – for so I'm told I must call him – gave us the bunk in the middle of the boat, the 'bridal suite', though it was hardly as wide as a single bed, and really a part of the corridor. That's not the right word – is 'companionway'? I don't remember now. There was a curtain we could pull across if we wanted privacy, Father said with a half-wink that I wasn't meant to catch. I can't bear to be overheard in bed, and I can't enjoy myself much if I'm always thinking I must keep quiet. Besides, I didn't feel like it anyway then. James likewise, to give him his due.

That first night, we couldn't sleep. The boat had looked so huge when it stood in Fathers garden, hulking in its leggy cradle like a monster lobster. It embarrassed me, it looked so expensive. But when the water swept us away we felt carried on the brittle back of a leaf, no sturdier than the twigs I used to break off to play poohsticks in the waterfall.

It was the waterfall, that beautiful torrent, brought the flood.

We used to watch while the stems bounced on the brown water, then went under the head of foam by the first reefs, then sometimes spun up again and shot over the falls into the forth by the pool where the sheep came down to drink. Even in full spate, the stream below the waterfall was friendly, a laughing brook as they say, no broader than a jump anywhere, full of turns and spills. We used to dam it and divert it with the great grey loaves of slate it brought down from the mountain.

You used to take me up there – to the moraine, as you called it – in the old days.

The first night on board, our bunk was soaked through, and it never dried out again. The waves touched hands over us, like giants saying hello, and we'd skid around their skirts and just as they crashed together and fell in one huge breaker we'd somehow each time shoot down and away and escape, Father or one of the boys in a safety harness leaning on the wheel so they wouldn't be dashed overboard. I felt sick as a dog below, so I'd come up and tie myself to the rails until I couldn't take the sting of the wet to my cheeks any more and my nose could have been snapped off like an icicle. I couldn't ever get dry. We women gave up trying to dry ourselves, or anything else. James' mother hated it most of all, she wasn't used to wearing yesterday's shirts.

Perpetual greyness, perpetual rain. The men had two sets of oilskins between them, from Father's old yachting gear, and they took turns in them on deck. (A lovely boat, you used to say. Lovely lines. Then, rolling your eyes to heaven. But for 'weekend leisure sports', I asked you? You envied Father.) 'The seams are bursting,' said James, when he came back from his watch, that first night. His eyes were scared. We lay there, and water spouted in our faces. It was rancid and full of grit. The boat tossed and shrieked, and though I wanted comfort from him I couldn't move or ask or speak.

We used to go up there to the moraine, as you called it, in the old days. You knew an awful lot about everything, it always seemed to me, even about stones and rocks and strata. The scenery up there was beautiful, in a kind of harsh, grand way, and you liked its bleakness. You were so good at that, at seeing what there was to something. So good at telling stories about how things came about, about how things were to be.

The last time, before I was married, it was dry and dusty, the wind lifted the black silt and filled our ears and nostrils with light powder. I laughed at you, with your miner's face and white clown's eyes behind your glasses, and you looked bewildered, short-sighted as you always did when you provoked laughter and had not told a joke. I stopped laughing and I listened. You showed me the stain of the glacier's slow heavy journey, higher up, and gathered pieces of rock and loose pebbles and called them by their names – mostly the slate from which we built our dams in the stream below, but some of it feldspar, scintillating, with purple flecks. You were worried, that last time, that the glacier seemed to be on the move, so fast, suddenly. Then you said you were an old man, and your memory was playing tricks on you. You laughed, and said it was impossible, the glacier couldn't flow that fast, not unless some freak conditions were at work. 'Wouldn't old Crane be pleased if his catastrophic predictions are proved right?' And you imitated the old anti-nuclear nuclear physicist, screwing up your dusty lips and spitting out the words through the tiny hole you made. 'Even if it means Armageddon will carry him off as well as everyone else.'

I laughed, though I'd heard stories about this old sparring partner of yours all my life, and most of them over and over. I didn't give the glacier another thought. But then the spring came, and with it the best weather anyone alive had ever known. You suggested a real dam be built, to contain the coming watershed. You spoke of hydro-electric power and new jobs in the region. I was impatient, all through May and June, whenever I was with you. I wanted to be with James, and you and James didn't get on, so I always went to see you alone. But it was never enough.

If I had our time again together I'd be different, I swear. You said that I never came to see you, and that when I did I wanted to get away again as fast as possible, that you were a foolish, fond old man, you knew, but since Violet – my mother – died you liked to see us now and then. And I writhed and suddenly my tights would feel itchy and my T-shirt too hot – or too cold – and I'd try and tell you what I was up to, but as that revolved round James, he'd soon come into our conversation, and a malignant gleam would begin to cover your face, and you'd give a dry cough of a laugh and scorn the project, the enterprise, whatever James was up to. I suppose he's wearing a badge of that charlatan now, is he? (I'd mentioned James' new interest in China.) You could never forget the one time you visited the flat we'd taken together, when you gave vent to your spleen about our living together at all. Whatever, it was, you attacked the poster of Che Guevara James had put up in our kitchenette.

Now I want to go back to that time again more than anything in the world. You would certainly have said to me now, Too much of water hast thou poor Ophelia. Whenever it rained and Mummy went out shopping and came in wet, that's what you'd say.

I can't remember ever feeling as sad as I did then. It was a sadness that was constantly interrupted by other feelings, by fear of the water whirling us God knows where, by the struggles to get the simplest task done, yet it never let me go even in the hell of the continual night, with the sky dark and close and cold as a wringing wet towel. Before the Flood, I used to luxuriate in grief, concentrating on it, growing it carefully, feeling it stretch my soul, making me deep and important. (When something floated by and so much floated by I saw you, I was scared it was you I was seeing, Daddy). I snapped at everyone, especially at James, and I knew it was because I couldn't fight with Father. He had me pinned down, like everyone else. Even the few animals we'd saved were meek with him, unruly with us. 'Pa is an autocrat,' James says proudly. I have to admit I was impressed by that too, when I first met James. That his father was who he was, the legendary magistrate, who could sit in judgement on two men in the same day for the same offence and sentence one to three years and let the other one clean

61

off with a chuckle. 'If he likes the cut of your gib, that's the phrase,'
James explained, 'he'll shout out from the bench, "I'm letting you
off with a caution, this time," and then he'll bring down the gavel
and bellow "Next", while the lad in the dock's ready to go out of
his head with disbelief. The boys in blue having given him to know
he'd be lucky to get away with his life.' I couldn't find it in me to
admire him exactly, but I was impressed. (I know you really looked
down on him as a show-off, a loud mouth. Though you would have
found better words, dictionary words.)

When something floated by and so much floated by I saw you, I
was scared it was you I was seeing, Daddy. The bodies of men float
by face upwards, staring at the sky, they look like rag dolls with
lidless eyes. Sometimes their faces had lost their eyes, then they
were like old toys. The women's bodies float face down, as if
weeping. I don't know if I could have told it was you, the water
swells everything up. I remember when I was going to school I used
to come into the bathroom to brush my teeth and often you'd be in
the bath, white and warm and lazy. I never saw you bask except
those times, when you'd lie in the tub, turning the hot tap with
your toes to top it up. In the garden, you'd never lie on the lawn
with us, but weed and move the hose, even this last sweltering
summer.

I wanted us to take you. I didn't want to leave you. There wasn't
room in the boat, Father said. You said I should go – with my
husband, my new family, you said. 'Instead of some animals', I
pleaded, as Father tossed a hutch onto the deck, 'Can't we take
him?'

It's your family now, you said. I shall be dead soon, anyway, you
said. Sooner or later, what's the difference?

The sun unlocked the glacier and it swept down over the
moraine. Your talk of dams was useless now. We waited in the
boat, on its spindly cradle, in Father's garden, as the level began to
rise. I had no idea then, listening to the strained voice of the radio
reporter, how much I was going to mind leaving you behind. 'It's
your duty, little woman,' you wote to me just before, using the
words of childhood, 'to stay with your husband. The race must go
on; the old be replaced by the new.' I could hear you sigh over your
usual tag, 'Eheu fugaces, Postume, Postume.' You said you would
wait, in the garden, that whatever measures the government might
try to provide should not be used by the old. 'P.S.' you wrote. 'No

mourning.' And underlined it three times. Then, in brackets: '(Should only be for the young).'

I was safe on the boat, or as safe as anyone could be, with my husband and the father law has provided for me. All I could think of was sadness, how I let you down by joining them. I do mourn. I wouldn't have left you, then, when I was still separate from them, before my marriage. And I stuck to James in the first place partly to defy you, because you were so set against him and his family, just as I took up smoking when you ordered me not to and blew out smoke in your face.

You'd been a teacher in a none-too-brilliant country school while Father had held sway over the imaginations of your charges. They called him 'No-No' because he always shouted from the bench, challenging the evidence. They knew how he dealt with turbulent elements, how he could turn a youth who fancied himself a leader to a pale, yammering jellyfish of self-pity and cowardice in the dock. Ten years in the quarries for him, he'd hand down, while the fuzz beamed. There were graffiti in your boys' toilets, you told me, warning, 'Judge No-No'll get your balls,' and 'Watch out, No-No's watching you.' You despised all this, but you envied him all the same. One evening soon after James and I got married, we all arranged to meet for dinner in a restaurant, so the in-laws could get to know one another. Mummy was alive then and, I remember, she registered the strain long before it began telling on James and me. Her brown eyes, usually so pensive and slow in their rhythm, were darting over the menu, then scanning our faces as if something inside her had accelerated all her workings. There were no mishaps, no open conflicts. But when the time came to pay, Father took out his credit card and slapped it down on the bill. 'It's on me,' he said. 'But *we* invited you,' said James. 'Yes,' I said, 'It was our idea. We want to take you out.' 'Nonsense,' said Father, 'Since when has that rag you write for earned you an honest penny?' Then he wheeled his frame round square to you, and raised his strong red hand from the card and jerked his jaw at it and said, 'Don't suppose you've got one of these, eh?'

You'd probably never seen a credit card, or hardly, certainly never had one. Father's was a fancy one, stamped in gold, to show how rich and important he was to anyone who wanted to notice. It was preposterous how he was pulling rank over you. It was absurd, it was cheap and yet it was agony. I wanted to laugh. And yet it worked. We were all turned into his creatures; he believed in the authority of his worldly success with such conviction that it leaked around him like gas. Mummy wilted at her end of the table. But her voice was harsh with scorn when she said they must be going.

I wish she had not died when she did, so that at least you could have sat together under the black sky waiting for the flood to come. Even though you fought, it would have been better to submit side by side.

I had to do the cooking on board, or at least take turns with the others. Miriam was having a baby and the smells from the galley made her feel sick; when she squatted over the side she looked sometimes as if she wanted to fall in and disappear. She'd lost her family too, we've talked about it often together since. So I took her shift. The boat pitched and heaved the stove about, even on the gimbals, and I banged into everything and it all seemed to be made of corners. We used to try and sit down, though the salon – as Father made clear we must call it – was cramped for all of us. Leisure sports boats – even big family ones – aren't made for the apocalypse; and the animals' stampede and yowling below as well as the ever-increasing reek made companionable eating ridiculous. But Father said we had 'to keep up our standards.' 'What were we made of if civilisation could be forgotten overnight?' So I had to lay knives and forks and spoons and they clattered and banged and jumped off the table. One night – it was always night and there were no stars or moon to tell where we were or what time it was – I folded the omelette I'd made onto my portion of bread. Father exploded, 'And where were you brought up, young woman? In a sty?'

'You know where I was brought up,' I said. I thought, I wish I was there now.

'We're not in a sty here and don't you forget it.'

I clutched my sandwich with both hands and got up. 'I don't care,' I shouted. 'I don't give a fuck.'

'Take control of yourself,' he said, with his eyes hard and cheeks red.

I staggered up and swayed and made for the ladder and heaved myself up into the storming world, scattering bits of omelette and crumbs everywhere. For once I welcomed the sharp lash of the wet and the wind.

James came, and looked helpless, and was sweet to me, though I knew it was because he wanted a peaceful life. Who could blame him? Also I was making his mother's position even more intolerable, with a tyrant on one hand and rebels on the other. I went down the ladder again, and swallowed all the witty things I'd thought of, and apologised. He told me we were all under strain, and I was to keep making myself useful, and I wouldn't buckle. I had real reserves, he knew, 'Underneath'.

So I went to fling out the muck from the animal's bedlam below, and even in the stench and roar of their terror, the cow's gently furred, blue-veined udders, her warmth and her silkiness was the greatest comfort I could have imagined. Her eye spun in a frenzied disc of blood-shot white as she tried to keep herself steady in the heaving and the pandemonium of the hold. I had no idea how to milk; none of us had. But I'd learned, and that night? that day? I felt the emptiness of the silky bag.

Father didn't like herbs in the food; I'd brought along my pots from our kitchen shelf, and though they turned yellowish in the constant darkness they were still scented and I liked to think they flavoured the tins of ham and pilchards we'd brought from the supermarket before the scare really cleaned out the shops. But when he saw the stray bits of leaf, he pushed his plate away. 'Fancy ideas about cooking, foreigners' fancies,' he said. 'Kind of thing your father liked.' And he waved at the black through the porthole as if the herbs and the tempest were one evil consequent on another. 'She's a very good cook, dear,' interposed the peace-maker, his wife. And I bit my protest back.

You had loved 'abroad' and he knew it.

It seemed for ever before the rainbow came. I was so wasted by then that I could hardly even smile at it, and when the sun burst from behind the tall chimneys of filthy grey cloud and exploded in ash-laden spokes, I blinked at the sudden light, like a nocturnal animal. James held me and squeezed me, with a kind of sensual pressure that we had never communicated for the whole stretch of eternity the boat had held us. He was quivering when he bent down and turned my face to his to kiss me.

'We'll be alone again,' he said. 'It'll be all right again.'

I felt the trembling seize me too, and I clutched tight, tight on his arm and kissed him back, babyishly dry sealed kisses like printing and felt my throat hot with the sobbing that doesn't make a sound, and thought, not yet. I can't be happy yet, not until you have been . . . and then I did not know quite what I wanted for you.

It was this: freedom to speak of you without constraint, to be proud of you. I needed to end the way you and I were kept apart, the way James' family inspired embarrassment and confusion in me on account of you and your difference from them.

Besides I needed revenge too, I suppose, though I didn't know how to get it.

James and I were doing up an old house that had stood the force of the flood. The roof had gone, but the walls were still solid and the site was beautiful, overlooking the new shore, towards the sunset, with the ruins of some town we did not know on the hill between. Father had moved into another house, further up the valley. The first summer after the flood was exceptionally fine, and everything was growing easily in the alluvial silt, a rich red-black, that the water had deposited in a layer one metre deep over everything. The fruit was sun-ripened to huge, glossy size; the vines' crabbed fingers held out grapes as big as plums. Just the smell of them when you squeezed one could give you a light head.

James and I were going over to Father's, as we often had to do – tools were in such short supply. We were walking through the new cornfield, when James heard something. A snuffle, a sigh, then a kind of groan as a weight shifted. All our survivors' talk was always of sightings – a footprint here, distant, moving shadow there – but so far we had not met a single other human being.

James crept towards the snuffling. I followed him. In front of me, he went stiff, and seemed to fall back and want to turn and run, so I held him firm and looked round his shoulder. Under a tree, sprawled like the old winos we used to see under the bridge by the river before the flood, with one arm flung out and his head thrown back, showing the mottled red gizzard above the white tidemark where his collars covered his neck when they were buttoned up, Father was spreadeagled; he grunted and huffed through his open mouth, a little smirk playing in the corner of his strained lips. The other arm lay across him, and with his hand he had taken his cock out of his flies and was grasping it, like a pet rat in a pet-lover's hand peeping through the window of a finger and thumb. James clapped his hand over my eyes, I tore his hand away, and I looked. Father pulled at himself blissfully. Then I began to laugh really loudly, and James tried to haul me away with him, and when I wouldn't come, he ran away. But for Father, it was too late; he opened one eye and swivelled it round till it landed on me and my laughter. At first a smile played lasciviously on his face, in answer. The response was fleeting, because then his other eye flew open, his hands came up and covered his face. He said, 'My God!', scrambling, but still fuddled. I said, 'Oh, it's only you. We thought it might be someone new.'

I was glad for you, after. Perhaps only for my idea of you. He swore at James, but James didn't take it so badly. He cursed us, then said our children were not blood to him. But he couldn't pull rank on you or me any more. He had been singled out all his life, privileged and beyond the reach of ordinary justice. But even death is not such a leveller as shame.

And I was glad, because I could then think of my child, who was born soon after, as belonging to our side only. I did what you told me, because you said I must. Stay with your husband, little woman, you have a new family now.

Neighbours

V. S. Pritchett

After taking a two mile walk across fields half way up the headland, to break himself in, as he put it, on the first day of his holiday, Frazier got back to the hotel. He had a bath to get the last of London off his skin, then, avoiding the bar already crowded with golf players, he went out on to the Terrace to be alone. He had been coming to this hotel for three or four years in the spring, a man who liked to stay in a place full of middle-aged people, many of them so well-known to one another that it was simple for him to avoid them and to be alone. Off he went to walk all day; off they went to the golf course or to drive about in their cars. If he was slightly known it was by his surname: Frazier – 'with an "i" ' he would say with a piercing pedantic stare and giving a roll to his stone blue eyes as he said it, like a tall schoolmaster mocking a boy. He was, in fact, a hairdresser who came to this lonely part of the Atlantic coast to slough off the name of Lionel as he was called at the rather expensive Salon de Coiffure in London where he was eagerly sought after. ('You know,' ladies said, 'how difficult it is to get an appointment with Lionel.') He was a tallish, slender man, not one of your sunken-chested barbers, gesticulating with comb and scissors as he skated about you, grown cynical with the flatteries of the trade. On the contrary, despite his doll's head of grey hair and the mesh of nervous lines on his long face, he was as still and as dispassionate as a soldier.

At this moment, on the Terrace, he was examining the distant clouds over the sea half a mile beyond the garden and the few villas, below the hotel, watching the purple, the black, the dyed-pink and the golden, as they re-styled themselves in one of those spectacular sunsets common on this coast. He broke off to stretch out a hand and to glance at the palm and the widely stretched fingers as if looking at a mirror. And then, after the lapse into this habit of his trade, he looked at the sky again, until the sound of the door opening on to the Terrace made him turn. He saw a middle-aged woman and a young man standing there. He saw her snatch the young man's arm to reprimand him in a threatening way and then push the arm away. They moved to a table at the end of the Terrace. Frazier who preferred to be alone thought this was the moment to go back inside, but the woman looked up as he got to the door.

'Lionel,' she called. Then she rushed at him. 'What on earth are you doing here? How extraordinary to find *you* at this hotel.'

'Mrs . . .' Frazier stood still and his eyes went wide with horror. 'Mrs Morris! I don't believe it. How did *you* find this place? When did you arrive?' He pulled himself together and all those fine lines on his face switched to politeness.

'What an unexpected pleasure.'

With excitemnet she said: 'This is my son. He's come over from Canada.'

And to her son she said: 'Tom, I wrote to you about Lionel. I've told you how he saved my life when Alec was taken ill.'

The son was a tall, bulky young man who gave Frazier the worldly look of a son not surprised by his mother's habit of staring at men anywhere and, the next moment, going straight up to them and saying 'We have met before.'

'I don't believe it, Lionel,' she said. And, almost archly, 'What a thrill!'

It would have been bad enough, Lionel thought, if Mrs Morris had been one of his customers. It was worse that she was a neighbour from the flat below his own in London who (one thought) one had at last shaken off! Staying here! A woman who talked and talked, never finished her sentences. A floundering over-flowing, helpless widow, her face so dramatic as it shot out of her thick hair that was like an old black curtain over her cheeks.

Frazier did what he could to hide the shock of seeing her. And then he was certain she knew how he felt, for the dramatic look went. She now gazed at him humbly, guiltily, as one given to excesses of friendship and who saw the talent unwanted.

'As a matter of fact,' she said proudly, 'Tom and I are not staying at the hotel. It's too expensive. We have taken a flat in one of the villas down the road. We just dine here. I used to live in these parts years and years ago. When you were a boy, Tom. We have a lot of old friends here.'

And then she laughed away the shock she had seen on Lionel's face and said to her son:

'I know what Lionel is going to do! Walk and walk. I don't know how you do it, Lionel. I can't face hills any more. Do you know, Tom, he walks across the park and back twice a day to work – when he's working on his feet all day! I see you going out every morning from my window, Lionel.'

'Oh,' said Frazier ashamed now, for he liked her laugh. 'I'm sure we'll meet.'

'We're just going in to dinner. Early start tomorrow,' she said to her son, 'we're driving to Land's End.'

To escape, Lionel said he was going down the road to see what the tide was doing.

'I always like to check on the tide,' he said to get away from them as he opened the door for them and then left as they went into the dining room.

Disaster! Friends here? I doubt it. She's on the war path, her non-stop tongue chasing him! Not staying, but dining *every night*. Oh God! His walk down to the sea was ruined. Had he let the name of the hotel slip out in those chats with her in London? At the Salon he often chatted in a gossipy way of trips, hotels, countries, prices, as he stood behind his customers, feeling the heat of their scalps and seeing their torpid or fretful faces in the mirror. Women came to him to be changed, to be perfected. They arrived tousled and complaining and they left transfigured, equipped for the hunt again. They were simply topknots to him. When they got up he was always surprised to see they had legs and arms and could walk. He sometimes, though not often, admired the opposite end of them: their shoes.

But Mrs Morris was not a customer. She was a close neighbour, a fellow leaseholder. For him she was virtually headless, a body, a part of the building and of ordinary life. He still thought of her after the death of her husband not as a person but simply as 'the couple downstairs' who had lived for at least ten years in the flat below and who had only one head between them – her husband's – her's being disposable from a professional point of view. To Frazier her elderly husband looked brutally placid and she as squashed as a cushion when he went up in the lift with them. What did one know about one's neighbours in a city? Nothing, until that Saturday afternoon when his door bell rang and rang and a woman was calling 'Mr Frazier. Mr Frazier'. (The porter and others called him Frazer – she had at any rate had the merit, he remembered, of giving him the 'i'.) He was marinating some breast of chicken in his perfect kitchen when he heard the bell, wearing an apron of dark blue and white stripes. He dried his hands, took the apron off and went to the door. There she was, with her winter coat open and her keys jingling in her hand.

'Mr Frazier! Please can you help me? I can't get a sound out of the Porter. My husband's fallen out of bed; he's on the floor. He's had a stroke or a fit – I can't get him up from the floor. I've rung the doctor. Would you *please* help me? I am sorry . . .'

Nothing cushiony about her now. She had a tearing grip as hard as a child's on his coat and her nails pinched through to his arm; her black hair that usually swung over her cheeks was now pushed back from a high naked forehead which startled him by revealing the curl of a white scar on it.

'Of course, Mrs Summers,' he said. She dragged him to the lift but he pulled her away saying the stairs would be quicker. He skipped down fast. She followed, more slowly, because her eyesight was not as good as his, calling out, 'He's been ill for a fortnight. He's such a weight. I found him when I came back. I went out to buy some fish because of his stomach. There was nothing in the fridge.' The door of the flat was open. He went into a thick smell, partly of spice and upholstery that seemed vegetable and hot, and the peculiar smell of a marriage. He saw the open door of the bedroom – what curtains! – and there was Mr Summers lying on his back on the floor with half the bed clothes dragged with him, blood on the sheet, a dribble of wet in one nostril and a pale belly with white hairs curling on it, half out of his pyjamas. The face was dark violet with a green streak in it and had a look of disdain about the mouth. Mrs Summers was on her sharp knees beside him at once, holding her husband by the feet.

'Not his ankles!' said Lionel. He was taking the man's pulse.

'Put a pillow under his head. Pull those sheets away,' Frazier said calmly. He got his hands under the man's shoulders from behind and heaved him to a near sitting position.

'Sit up, soldier,' said Lionel. 'Hup. Hup.'

The man opened his eyes feebly.

'I'll hold him here', Lionel said, 'you get him under the knees. Now, slowly.'

They raised the body and then let it flop to the floor again.

Mrs Summers stooped to pull up her husband's pyjamas.

'It's the weight,' she said again.

'Change round,' said Lionel. 'We'll get him nearer the bed.'

In the end, somehow or other, they man-handled the hot body and rolled it on to the bed, Frazier falling on top of him.

'We've got him the wrong way up. Now gently, your end.'

The man was awake now and grunted:

'Bloody Red Cross,' closed his eyes and his breathing roared.

'He was in the Army,' gasped Mrs Summers apologising. 'Were you in the Army?'

'Ambulance driver,' Frazier said.

She said: 'He's been climbing the wall, all the weeks. It is those pills. I found him when I got back.'

They sat, getting their breath back. Frazier looked around the room. The Summers were a heavy couple, with heavy furniture. The head of the wide bed was padded and crossed by two awful loops of pink satin. The padded part was greased by the marks left by two heads. Frazier had thought of her as a cushiony woman but in the struggle when hands and arms touched, he was shocked to feel the bones through the soft flesh at once. Those bones must be made of iron. He saw her roughly pull her hair back over her forehead and now he knew why he had paid so little attention to her. The hair was dull black, slow growing stuff, hanging in loose ridges – perhaps she had had loose curls when she was young but now the hair seemed to have been set in some out-of-date perm in a style she must have settled once and for all years ago. The strong nose and forehead stuck out boldly as if they had been, until now, staging another wilful life behind the curtain. The face reminded him of an actor who used to tell his troubles to Lionel's father whom he used to see in his father's underground barber's shop when he was a boy. Her eyes were large and brown.

'You would have done better to have put a blanket over him and to have left him on the floor,' the doctor said and called an ambulance.

Down by the sea, because the heavy weeds were hanging from the rocks, scraps of this scene came to Frazier's mind as he stood for the moment by the sea that came in quietly, making a sound of sentences without words.

Poor Mr Summers died in hospital. A crowd of friends came to console her after the funeral. She came up to thank and thank and thank him and admired his flat and the plants on the balcony. There was a look of hunger on her face as she looked back on it when she left.

Then, after a few weeks, she was at his door, asking him with apologies, to witness her signature on some document. She was wearing a red suit as bright as a geranium – an improvement. He picked up the document and saw she had signed Pamela Morris. It turned out she was two persons, indeed three, and perhaps four –

when he thought of his father's actor – for she was dramatically open-mouthed, eager to explain. The woman he had known as Mrs Summers had divorced a man called Morris who had once hit her over the head with a bottle. Mr Summers had been her solicitor and had rescued her. She had met him in an hotel in Vichy when she had gone to stay with her father who lived there as a tax exile. Her tale began to ramble about Europe. At every pause, her mouth remained half open to change to the next chapter, going back to Mr Morris, a man often on a yacht or in a race while she looked after baby Tom in a house near the Lizard – 'you know the Lizard?' Which race and where was not clear to Frazier – she was calling him Lionel now. The bright red suit turned out to have been given to her by one of her rich women friends. The shoes, too. There was a moment in this talk when she became almost a customer in his eyes. No grief, no reality, she shuffled, dealt and re-shuffled her life, a woman playing cards. The enormous distinction of Mr Summers and indeed of herself was that they had seen no point in marrying.

She paused as he got her a second glass of whisky and she said, 'What a lovely piece of cut glass. You have such lovely things.' And at this she was back to that awful night when he had been so kind, kind, kind, as if all the women in her were talking in turn. She became secretive. She repeated that she had left Mr Summers for a quarter of an hour, as she had told the doctor. But now 'not to get fish!' He had been asleep and had suddenly woken up and asked her to fetch his wallet from his jacket hanging over a chair. He pulled out a slip of paper. It was a betting slip. He had backed the winner in the afternoon's race at Newbury: he told her, ordered her, to go down to the betting ship to collect his winnings. Pamela Morris knew nothing about horse racing: the only quarrels she and Summers had – well, not the only ones – were about his betting. She knew he had not been out of the flat for ten days but he boiled up in a temper and started getting out of bed. She was so frightened by his illness that she lost her head. Perhaps he *had* got out, somehow. Men did get out.

'I didn't look at the slip. I put on my coat – *you* saw me in my coat when I came up to your flat? – and went to the shop and when I gave the slip in, the man pushed it back to me. It was two years old!'

There was awe in her face as she stopped for breath: it turned into a sudden laugh hissing along her delighted teeth.

'The wrong slip?' said Lionel who was a literal rather than a laughing man and looked at the stretched fingers of his hand. Then he understood: her laugh showed a pride in the irresistible folly of Mr Summers. Lionel saw the first tear in her great still eyes. And, even more proudly, she said:

'I didn't want to make a fool of him in front of the doctor. Alec, you know, was a solicitor.'

As he listened Lionel became even more aware that Mrs Morris was a body. His clientele were no more than heads that he gardened as he gardened the plants on his balcony.

He understood that their physical struggle with Summers had created an unwanted bond. Headless she might be, from his professional point of view, but she was alive because she was deep in the belief in the plural quality of her person.

Since she admired his flat – and goodness knows he admired it himself, never thought of anything else once he got home in the evenings – he showed her round it. It was not a stew of upholstery, a goulash of furniture, as her's was: every object had been picked up, collected with great care, and had had to show itself worthy: and, by the way, nothing, absolutely nothing, had come out of a boutique, nothing poudree, jokey or licentiously odd. He showed her the perfect kitchen, installed by *himself*, and every glittering utensil.

'Alec would have loved this,' she said, conveying that it terrified her. 'He always did the cooking, never let me near the stove – never cleaned it, either. If he had a fault, he had a cook's temper.'

And she went on, in her way of begging for an answer to a question:

'I suppose that was why he was so jealous of my husband and hated poor Tom? Wouldn't have the poor boy in the flat?'

That, no doubt, was the measure of her love for the unreasonable man.

They went into the two other rooms, one of which he said he was going to re-decorate.

'Lionel,' she said as she looked in and went out, 'I wish you'd decorate my flat. Tell me what to do.'

(He ignored that at the time, but afterwards her words came back to him.)

He bent down and picked up a piece of cotton from the carpet in the hall and then simply gazed politely at her without replying. He was vain of living alone. He shopped, cooked, cleaned and polished. His cupboards were models of order. His glass was polished. His china gleamed. The jars and packets in his refrigerator were labelled. If anything broke or went wrong, he himself repaired it. He took her out to his balcony where his plants thrived. He showed here the glazed cabinet fixed to his wall, electrically heated, where he grew his seedlings. Re-decorate? Advise? Certainly not. She was clearly incompetent. After the death of Summers the smells of saucepans burned out on the stove in her flat came up to his kitchen. Out of kindness he gave a small plant in a pot for *her* balcony.

That was a mistake. In a couple of weeks, she came up with the dying plant. Over-watered. She sat with him for an hour. After this she started telephoning to him, about things that had gone wrong in her flat and then, when he evaded her, she started slipping notes under his door when there was no reply. Once a week he did not mind seeing her, hearing about Summers's will, or her son Tom, but twice a week was too much. She sat on his sofa, often in that red coat and skirt which did not go at all with his room, talking away about every day life.

'I love sitting here looking at everything,' she said sighing naively. 'You are so cosy.'

Cosy was not a word he liked. He was a busy, practical man, not given to idle speculations.

'You ought to have been a decorator.' (Back on her theme.)

He said as drily as possible, struck, however, by the thought, 'I suppose I am.'

He was thinking of his work at the Salon.

'Of course! That is what you are!' And she laughed.

'I was never taught to do anything,' she said, but as usual the words suggested that her life was a string of accidents for which she had been avid and when these were disastrous they left an aftermath of glee. The only subject which did not end in a laugh was her son, by Mr Morris. She had 'put' him firmly into a New Zealand bank and he had left that for a job in Canada. She was proud he had done that because her ex-husband, Mr Morris, had tried to stop him. Lionel said that boys change their minds and said he himself had wanted to go on the stage.

Lionel was a listener and was unprepared when this admission made her stop talking about herself.

'Why didn't you?'

'There was a boy at school called Archie. His father was a barber like mine. He used to act in the school play. He would put girls' heads on pictures of Vikings in the History books – the girls in the class.'

'And did he go on the stage?'

'He was older than me. Killed in the war,' said Lionel.

'Oh!' said Mrs Morris, eager to mourn. 'So you became a hairdresser.'

Surprised by the intimacy of this Lionel said – not wishing to talk about Archie who had come to live in his mind – 'No, nothing to do with Archie. I suppose I used to watch my mother doing her hair when I was a boy. Brushing it, with all those hair pins in her mouth, putting up a piece of hair on top of her head and holding it there. It used to fall down and I had to hold it for her, because it often fell down when she picked up another long piece from the other side, then she would start winding it round – it always came out all right in the end like a conjuring trick. She wouldn't let father touch it with his scissors when short hair came in. She kept her's long until she died.'

'I know,' said Mrs Morris. 'I used to see her when Alec and I moved into the flats and she was living with you.'

'That was when father died,' he said.

'You used to take her to the theatre,' said Mrs Morris fondly. 'You go to the theatre a lot, don't you?'

Lionel was alarmed when she said this. He wished he had not revealed anything about himself. The next thing she would be getting round him to take her to a theatre. That evening she did something very tiresome as he stooped slightly to open the door to let her out of the flat.

'Poor Archie,' she said. 'You were so good to your mother, not every son is,' she said. And suddenly she kissed him on top of the head, rather greedily, and having ruffled his hair started to put it right.

That was too much. She was ordinary life and ordinary life always went too far. After this he made a point of putting her off when she telephoned or slipped another note under his door. He was going out, he said. Or he was washing paint, getting the spare room ready for his sister. Also, after Mrs Morris left, he had to get a cloth and wipe a stain of whisky from the seat of the velvet sofa she had been sitting on and – as he said to one of his customers at the Salon – he had to hunt for days all over London for something that really got stain off velvet and in the end he had to get the sofa re-upholstered. The expense! The visits stopped. If by chance he travelled up with her in the lift he felt that too much life was going up with him, to judge by her plaintive expression. Life abashed. But so, so . . . what? Longing to frequent.

He got back to the hotel. She and her son were dining at a distant corner of the crowded room. A long time passed before he saw them leave and they showed no sign of seeing him. He went up to his room. 'It will be intolerable. Why didn't I ask them how long they were staying? I must get out.'

He lay on his bed looking at a guide for new places.

The danger on the next morning was that he might meet them near the villas on the road. Any one of them might be the one where their flat was. Once he was on the beach below and had climbed to the cliff he knew he was safe for the day and once his feet were on the close turf his mind scattered her as his restless eyes collected all the details of the long stretch of sea and the sky like another country hanging over it. No human voices, only the screams of gulls and the hum of the wind. Below him, the sea came pouring black as whales in the deep gullies between the rocks and was sucked out like suds and then hurled in again. These walks were personal victories for Lionel and not simply for his feet – piddle-paddling (as he said) round all those ladies in the Salon. If occasionally he saw other walking men or women on some higher or lower ground keeping their distance as he kept his, or if they chanced to walk close by, they stuck as he did to passing like solitary clouds, egotists without a muddling word. They were like clouds in the sky, born out of the horizon, and as the hour went by slowly joining the rising grey populations and processions built up high and drifting away across the blue sky and the changing sunlight. Every year he felt re-born here. The sky was always young and ageless, the rocky land nevertheless got older every day. Clip, clip, clipping in the Salon Lionel also aged with every day; but here, every hour made him younger as he aged.

When he got back to the hotel at the end of the morning or the afternoon and went into the dining room he was surprised to notice that Mrs Morris and her son were not there. He was rather sorry.

What a fuss about nothing!

And so it went on, wet or fine, he was out, on top of this promontory or that, going further every day as if daring the Morrises. Four days passed. Not a sign of them. Had he been rude? What were they doing? Was she, in her slapdash way, being almost absurdly discreet? He didn't want to chat but he would have liked to tell her and her son about some of his discoveries. For example, terror. His life had been without it; her's must have had its precipitous moments, poor silly soul. The paths he followed from one cliff edge to the next would suddenly zigzag and turn inland and then seaward again round appalling ravines whose black or lichened walls dropped from great heights to inaccessible spits of sand below. Gulls and crows were so often at their savage wars there. There were sometimes the bloody feathers of dead bodies on the grass. There was one particular place, close to an estuary, where the land was in a state of debacle: huge blocks of rocks the size of houses or fallen castles had been torn off the cliffs and were stranded there in a chaos of spouting water, and closer to the shore here was a brutal coagulation of stranded rock which had struck him when he first saw it on his first holiday here – a year when he had had a row with one of the hairdressers at the Salon – like the body of a truncated man, arms chopped short, huge chest and head tipped back so that one saw only the underside of a chin: a giant in a barber's chair, tipped back and ready for a shave, like some man he might have seen in his father's shop when he was a boy. He would have liked to have shown off to Mrs Morris about rocks. She would roll her eyes and give one of her laughs as she did at grotesque things made half true: that tale of her husband hitting her on the head with a bottle and leaving that scar, for instance. Had her chin tipped back like that?

There was one more terror for the secret collector of terrors which he called 'the black wall', a ravine with a plain black wall. He studied it from one side and then the other. It dropped sheer to a spit of sand left by the tide where there was a long narrow isolated rectangle of flat rock, like the hull of a lost ship or simply a table where fifty people could sit down and eat. He had often noticed that there were boulders just below the top of the wall and from below the boulders there was a thin irregular scratched line going steeply down, vanishing behind lower boulders and then beginning again. The scratch must once have been a path used by fishermen.

He stepped down a yard or two, daring himself to go down, then frightened, crawled back.

'Better not,' Frazier said, looking at his hands. They were his living. He could not afford to break his fingers or his wrists on a giddy climb like that. Anyway, he had his eye on a black cloud coming dragging rain across the sea and he had no sooner turned back towards home than a squall did blow up and whipped him and soaked him before he was half way back to the hotel six miles away. He broke his rule and went for a large whisky in the bar.

This was on the sixth evening.

'Hullo,' said Mrs Morris's son. He was sitting on a stool at the bar with a young girl wearing jeans, his hand on her knee. She was simply pretty, with her fair hair knotted up in a careless way.

'This is Sal,' said the son. 'Mr Frazier.'

'You live in Falmouth?' said the girl.

'Get clued up,' said the worldly young man. 'Mr Frazier is a friend of Ma's in London. That's someone else. I told you.'

'Sorry,' said the girl. 'Oh, I know! We *saw* you this afternoon, out on the cliff.'

'Coming from the Coffin,' the young man said. 'How far did you get? Ma dropped us on the road and we came across the fields, it's only a mile. She's gone to have her hair done and we had to bloody walk back. We got soaked. Did you? Did you get to the bottom? It's called the Coffin,' the boy said. 'I took Sal to look at it.'

'I didn't see you,' said Lionel. Watched!

'Mas used to take us on picnics down the path there when I was a kid, very sheltered down there. We used to have a house back on the road.' – owning the place! And to the girl he said:

'In Dad's time. I told you. Before they split up.' A young know-all, thought Lionel. Carriés on as if he owned the sea cliffs and all that sea.

'Your mother took you down that wall!' said Lionel. 'It's impossible.'

'A bit dizzy but it used to be all right. I know what you mean – you can't get down now, the rock's fallen,' the boy said.

'Will you have a drink?' Lionel said.

'I think I'd better not. Sal's soaked through and I've got to drop her. Ma will be back. But thanks.'

Lionel watched them go.

"London Friend. Someone else?"

What did the knowing boy mean? And where on earth could she get her hair done in this part of the world, not that that would bother her!

'Well,' thought Lionel, 'that lets me off the hook. I suppose I've been rather stand-offish with the old bird.'

He found himself wishing to see the fat woman who had got down the 'black wall' when she was young.

He went into dinner. There were two or three large laughing parties of old friends in the middle of the crowded dining room and murmuring grey-haired couples at other tables – corks popping. Between courses, slow in being served because he was alone, Lionel tried to see if she and her son and the girl had slipped in and were at the table at the other end of the room. They were not.

In the morning, the wind was steadier, the rain quieter, but the sky was dirty and the sea looked like unwashed linen. The seagulls perched on aerials and chimneys, their indignant heads into the wind.

That was the trouble on this coast: fogs or rain would set in for days. The guests in the hotel turned their backs to the windows and sat hiding themselves behind newspapers: the heartier ones went boisterously out to their cars. One or two little groups sat about talking about their relations in the towns they came from in the tones of people sitting out a funeral. Every now and then a golfer would come back from the main door dispirited. Lionel sat in the coffee room which was usually empty in the morning. An expert in choosing chairs, he had marked one down on his first day. It was now unoccupied. He kept an eye on the puddles on the Terrace and saw at last that the rain was stopping.

Then he heard a voice saying to one of the waiters:

'I wonder if I could have some coffee?'

Mrs Morris was standing there carrying a raincoat and wearing a white scarf round her head. She came at once to sit with him. She had walked up, she said, because something had gone wrong with the power at her flat.

'Would you like me to drop down and look at it?' he said at once – to make amends. He had once or twice put something right in the stove she maltreated at her London flat.

·'No, it's the landlord's job to see to it,' she said. And then, 'No walkies today?' flirtatiously wagging a finger at him.

She did not take her scarf off and although her face looked bare, it looked shapely with thoughts of her own.

'We went to Falmouth yesterday,' she said. 'The trees in the harbour are much better than here. Taller, more sheltered.'

Then relaxing, 'Tom said he saw you yesterday at the Coffin. Mr Morris, my husband and I, had a house a couple of miles away once,' she said.

She laughed.

'He wanted to show his girl the place where he was brought up. Especially,' she said, 'the Coffin.'

That word excited her and then she said:

'I dropped them there. It's a mistake to go back to the past. I meant at my age. Our age,' she said. 'Don't you think?' Yet she said this with the pride of one who had always chosen the mistake when she was young and even now she had the warm wide open eyes of a woman hoping for another.

'Tom has got a very pretty girl,' Lionel said.

'Oh I'm so relieved he's got a girl at last – I can't tell you! I begun to think . . .' she stopped. 'He just wasn't interested. I mean he's 29. Not afraid of them, always about with them – but, indifferent. I was afraid it was my fault.'

'They seemed full of themselves,' Lional said.

'He's very good at his job,' she said.

'I was afraid,' she said, 'that the divorce had upset him. Alec hated him. I told you. It was so difficult. The funny thing is' – and it was clear she thought that this, being funny, was a revelation – 'Tom was fond of Alec! Liked him better than his own father. Tom was really sad when Alec died.'

'He was sad for you,' Lionel said, who suddenly remembered he himself had disliked Mr Summers. The man had looked so much like the soap-white bust of someone who had never existed. Perhaps there was something sexy in the blind, bland conceit of busts?

Lionel waited. She would break off sentences as if beguiling herself with the dramas hidden beyond – in the open-ended.

'You see, Lionel,' she suddenly said, 'my mother died when I was a girl, a child. Not died exactly but "put away". I mean I didn't know her. I'll never forget what you told me about your mother, doing her hair. When I grew up my father used to take me abroad with him on business. Norway, Sweden, France. He had a lot of business friends. He was in timber.'

'Lonely for a girl,' he said.

'Most people thought I was having a wonderful time, but you are right, Lionel. I *was* alone half the time, sitting in hotel rooms, reading novels. The novels I read! Eating. Talking to waiters. I used to think of my mother. Mr Morris was much older than me, in timber too, a friend of father's. After him, I mean after the divorce, I was afraid of Tom's *feeling* for me.'

She looked at him greedily and intently. Lionel saw she was working up to asking him why *he* hadn't married.

'Do you think a mother can be too frank?' she said.

Lionel was lost. He wondered if she could mean she had been chased all round Europe by her father's friends. He could see that she might have been a pretty girl, dangerous in her naiveté, either piling up day dreams or perhaps not innocent at all.

'Was it really because of your mother you took up doing women's hair?' she said, leaning forward, avid for a secret.

'No,' he said. 'Men's hairdressing was going downhill. More money in the women's trade.'

He was about to tell her about the rock that looked like a man tipped back waiting for a shave. Her habit of rambling from the point was infectious. But she was too quick.

'Ah,' she said, with all her breath. 'Money! That's it isn't it? You had to look after your mother. I mean you had her to live with you. I remember when Alec and I moved into the flats. We used to see you both going out together.' Then, looking around the room to see if anyone had come in and could hear, she said in a low voice:

'Alec *did* something fishy in the Law, I never understood it – one of those things solicitors are not allowed to do. I mean, when he died, he hardly left me anything. Well, thank goodness, the flat belongs to me. I'm so grateful to Tom. He came over to sort things out. He thinks I should sell it. What d'you think, Lionel?'

What an extraordinary thing – Mrs Morris no longer there! New people. Builders, painters, hammering. How awful!

She glowed at the surprise she had given him.

'How much of your lease have you got left?' he said.

'I must ask Tom,' she said.

'I wouldn't do it if I were you, unless you know you've got a place to go to. Prices are still going up,' he warned her. In fact, not liking change himself, he wanted to stop her.

'I don't want to be a burden on Tom. He wants me to go to

Canada with him. I suppose I could but he's very serious about this girl,' she said. 'He's fallen flat for her these last weeks. Down here! He met her with an old friend of ours we've been seeing down here. I wish I had talked to you about this before, Lionel. I'm afraid I've been very stand-offish. You must have thought I was avoiding you, but it wasn't that. We were out all the time. I've known this friend most of my life, when his wife was alive. I told him about you and Alec. But I don't know whether I'd like to go back and live in the country again. Plants die when they see me!' Her eyes were brilliant when she laughed now.

'He'd miss his garden in London,' she added, looking around the room again. 'It's stuffy in here, isn't it? And she began fidgeting with the knot on her scarf.

'He wants to marry me, but I don't know,' she said, whether offended with her scarf or the man Lionel could not tell. 'He's coming over to dinner tomorrow night. I would love you to meet. You always know *what to do!*'

And then she tugged off her scarf. He had been looking only at a face: but now, as she shook back her hair he saw that half of what he had called the old rope had gone. Her hair was chopped into short curl-like lengths, her forehead was clear, her eyebrows had come to life.

'You've changed your hair,' he said. He nearly said: 'You have come out into the open.' But the stylist said: 'But it's marvellous, so young.' Immediately he stopped saying 'I' and called himself professional 'One'.

'One can see the ears and the neck, the forehead is rounded,' he said and moved both his hands as if modelling the roundness himself.

'Not severe?' she said. 'Or gollywoggy? As though I'd fallen through a hedge?'

'It brings out the eyes,' he said. 'It's perfect. Slimming too.'

'You are a darling,' she said. 'I am frightened. It shows the grey.'

It was perhaps a touch gollywoggy: he was silent about that. But he said a slight salting of grey gave dignity to the head.

'Now you have a head,' he said. 'I am jealous.'

'Ah?' she said curiously.

'I'm jealous of the man who did it. Where did you get it done?' he asked.

'Tom's girl friend found him for me,' she said, disappointed. 'Do you really think the forehead's all right?'

He knew she was thinking of the scar.

'Perfect,' he said. And in fact the scar did not show.

'It was rather an awful place really,' she said. 'Do you know a dog got in from the street and started eating the hair that had fallen on the floor? The poor thing might have choked to death.' She gazed. An omen? she seemed to ask.

'The time!' she said, getting up. 'I must get back. Look out of this window – there's a pair of wagtails jumping at the flies. They never fly straight. Thank you, thank you, Lionel. Between ourselves?' she said with a prudish glance round the room. 'Don't say anything here, will you?'

He walked through the foyer of the hotel to the door where she refused to put her scarf on.

'I miss you,' she said and after a step or two she looked back at him with a pout of mock despair that seemed to implicate him in her continuing fate.

Another garrulous fragment of ordinary life was leaving him, going about its business. He was afloat in space and below him he began to feel the cold air of an empty London flat.

Feeding the Old Man

Tim Aspinall

The old man was a famous writer. He sat in an armchair by the bookcase like the photograph on the back of his novels.

'You are a TV director between contracts, you say?'

'Yes, Sir.'

'Do you mind if I ask you how much an ITV director makes?' I told him.

'Twenty two thousand a year,' he said crossly, 'that's more than I make.'

'I've a lot of commitments,' I said.

'Well,' he said, 'that's your business. The point is, I can't possibly come up with anything like that. I pay my housekeeper thirty pounds a week and she does everything.'

Mister B wanted a cook while his housekeeper was on holiday. Usually her sister stood in, but, this year, he told me, he wanted some decent food for a change. That was why he had advertised in *The Lady*.

'What can you cook?'

'Soups.'

'I love soup.'

'I can cook you haricot bean soup, cream of cauliflower soup, potage bonne femme. Say, potage bonne femme, followed by raie au beurre noir, a green salad with a light French dressing of lemon juice and olive oil, a little Camembert.'

He thought about it, then leaned forward and tapped me on the knee. 'Look,' he said, his blue eyes very bright, his lips purple. He was a handsome man in a thrashed-out sort of way; wrinkled and jowly but his face was very animated, 'can you handle a roast duck?'

I was commissioned to cook a trial dinner for two, to include roast duck. He gave me a cheque for twenty pounds to cover all expenses including my fee. The wine was down to him. He said he kept a modest cellar.

I decided to start with a fresh tomato soup from the Elizabeth David recipe (leaving out the ground rice). To follow: a plate of saucisson sec and a bowl of black olives (to give me time to finish the duck). Salad, goat's cheese and two Cox's Orange Pippins.

My girlfriend, Elsie, a TV PA in Light Entertainment, sat watching me prepare the duck. I rubbed the breast with rock salt and huile vierge de Provence (brought back from Aix this summer). The giblet and vegetable stock simmered away on the stove.

Elsie said: 'I suppose it's going to be nothing but food for the next two weeks.'

'I haven't got the job yet.'

'You will,' Elsie said despondently.

The duck was already in the oven when the housekeeper's sister came in to do the general housework and the washing up. She was a jolly woman.

'Don't go to too much trouble, dear,' she said. 'Just throw the burnt bits in the dustbin like I do.'

At the end of the meal Mister B called me to the dining-room and gave me a glass of port.

His crony declared: 'If you direct the ITV as well as you cook a duck it could be worth watching.'

Next night there were four for dinner. Mister B's solicitor, a Jesuit priest and his American agent.

A relatively light meal: Smoked salmon soufflé, calves' liver (my modification of the Venetian style with green peppers, a whiff of shallot, a sprinkle of parsley). Mousseline of potatoes, a chicory and orange salad. Brie. A bowl of white Vaucluse grapes.

High praise from the guests. Mister B gave me an opened but untouched bottle of Gigondas.

I told Elsie: 'You can forget your pretty cars and your pretty clothes, I don't want a new contract. Let me work with civilised food and civilised wine.' I was a bit drunk.

Elsie said: 'You feel fulfilled because you are cooking what you want to cook but a professional cook can't always cook what he wants.'

'I will always cook for civilised people,' I said.

'Sometimes you like your tele's,' Elsie said.

Elsie isn't beautiful. She's a white goose. She's got eyes tinted lettuce green by contact lenses. Her chin recedes into her neck and her neck goes into her big breasts. She has natural blonde hair like a baby's and a prodigious muff.

'Elsie,' I said, 'there's an ad here, look at this: "The Cotsworlds. Wanted couple. Cooking weekends. General housework. Chauffeur duties. Daily help in kitchen garden. Staff cottage. KB. LR. 2B. OF. Colour TV". Probably some Lord or financier. You could go riding all the time.'

'Don't be soppy,' she said.

Tomato salad (peeled), Cassoulet, baked plums, Stilton and biscuits.

I was the dinner guest.

'Let's have a little wine,' Mister B said.

He brought out three bottles of Bordeaux. A white Sauvignon called Château Reynon, a young Belair, and an eminent Petrus.

'D'you think this kind of thing does one any good?' he asked, taking two cigars from his humidor. 'I've been at it for so many years. D'you know my heart has beat more than two-and-a-half thousand million times?'

'That's nothing to a heart.'

'You would worry if you were 71,' he said, darkly. 'You're young. I wouldn't worry if I was young. I enjoy myself but I know the clock has got to stop.'

'It's worry that kills the heart,' I said.

'I worry about my liver, too.'

'Feed your liver. Protect your heart. Good food restores the tissues. If you feel all right, you are all right.'

'What an easy fellow you are,' he said. 'Do they know about you at the ITV?'

I took the Cassoulet from the oven and brought it to the dining-room. I took off the lid and the steam swelled and filled the room with a smell that's like no other; the magical combination of meats and sausage and beans (warning: always get rid of the oxide potassium in the beans — flatulence spoils the meal and embarrasses good wine).

'Ah,' he said.

'Any amount of minerals in here,' I said. 'It's as good as a winter cruise.'

The beans were very hot. He ate noisily and drank huge draughts of wine which he swilled round his teeth.

'Tell me,' he asked suddenly, 'do you get it up?'

I replied: 'Usually I do.'

'I haven't had it up for four years,' he said.

'That's a long time,' I said.

'You're telling me.'

I said: 'My girl would soon let me know if I didn't get it up.'

'What's she like?'

'I don't know. Blonde, greedy, sentimental.'

'She sounds all right,' he said. 'What school did you go to?'

89

'Beaumont. Do you know it?'

'You're a Catholic. I say, you're a man of many parts. What were we talking about? You are an awful ass. I think you're possibly a clever man but you haven't done anything with it.'

I said: 'I didn't think you watched TV.'

'My publisher gave me one. I watch it in bed. You say you're a failure. Are you too bright for them? I don't think you bite the bullet. Is that very rude?'

'I believe it's true,' I said.

'Rubbish,' he said. 'You could do what you liked. Shall I give you a word of advice? Give up the booze. If I didn't drink I'd be a millionaire today.'

'You are a millionaire, aren't you?'

'Yes, I think I am. I say, this is jolly good Cassoulet.'

On the cheese, he said: 'You've reassured me about my liver and so forth. Now, what about this other business. D'you know how to feed that? Knew a Jap, an appalling man but very vigorous. He swore by bull testicle pie. Will you look into it for me?'

'Yes, sir.'

His face sagged on to his chest. The spark had gone from his eyes. Suddenly he'd become very sad. 'You see, my dear, there are many of us who are much older that we want to be.'

He pushed back his chair and stood up, throwing his napkin on the table. 'I'm going to kick you out. I want to work.'

I got on to a psychiatrist who'd once had an affair with my wife.

'I've got just the thing,' he said. 'Two hundred aphrodisiac recipes by Pilaff Bey. Good food and they work. I know. I was up and down like a railway signal.'

Elsie was very taken with a Love Drink (endorsed by Baron de M).

This is the version we made:

Into a Sherry glass pour;
A quarter glass of Cherry brandy.
A yolk of an egg.
A quarter glass of double cream.
A quarter glass of dry fino sherry.
The whole is swallowed in one gulp.

It worked. But then it always does with Elsie.

I found Mister B dozing on the chesterfield in the library. He had the bleary look of a bad night and wasn't as enthusiastic as I had expected.

'I suppose all the dishes are like bad curry,' he said. 'To chivvy up the prostate.'

'I think you'll get a pleasant surprise,' I said.

I avoided anything fanciful or impractical (clean and truss a young crane . . .).

He dined alone in the library, reading *Portrait Of A Lady*, propped up on a portable lectern.

I gave him scrambled eggs and kidney (lambs' kidneys cooked in butter with fresh tomatoes and parsley, adding beaten eggs). Roast loin of pork (skinned and 'larded' with fresh rosemary and garlic). Potatoes gratin, three-minute cabbage.

By the time I served the savoury (grilled prawns on toast with a sprinkling of cayenne) the spark was back in his eye and the old, mauve lips were moist again.

'I adore kidneys,' he said. 'Splendid food. But was it really aphrodisiac?'

'The master claims so,' I said. 'But not for people of cold temperament.'

'You don't think I have a cold temperament?' He grinned. 'Has she gone? Go and see. Ask her up for a gin.'

To my relief she had. The washing up was done. The draining board was dry and clean.

When I returned he was trouserless, warming his bottom at the open fire.

'Pity,' he said, 'I thought I felt a twitch.' He didn't move to replace his trousers.

'Tell you what.' He flexed his knees. A large dong hung slack on his leg inside the striped shorts. 'Let's have a party.'

'Tonight?'

'Don't be an ass. How could you lay on a party tonight? At the weekend. Let's have a good, old fashioned orgy. Nothing too louche or vulgar. Something to give the chaps a chance. Put your dishes to the test. Make a night of it. Can I leave the girls to you?'

He saw I was feeling out of my depth.

'My dear fellow, you're a director of the ITV.'

Elsie thought it was all rather sweet.

She said: 'I'll help you set it up.'

She gave me the number of an assistant director, Light

Entertainment, called Bernie.

'Six girls,' Bernie said. 'No trouble. Presents or cash? Cash is favourite. Any special tastes? Old fellas you say. Can be choosey. They don't all want showgirls, you'll be surprised. Nice to do it right, John.'

I suggested looking through *Spotlight* (the actresses photographic directory) so Mister B could choose his friends' best types.

'Let your man surprise us,' he said. 'I've enjoyed many forms of sex, all over the world. My best times were with Korean girls, the Irish of the Orient. They were always fun.'

He gave me a cheque for a thousand pounds.

'Not much of a budget,' Bernie said. 'My girls will want half of that.'

Elsie said: 'Seventy-five pounds each!'

'Got to do it right,' Bernie said. 'These are professional girls. They won't faint if the old fella's got a wart on it.'

We were having a planning meeting in the dining-room. Next door, in the library, Mister B rattled away at his typewriter.

Chalky, the designer, said: 'An orgy has to have a theme.'

Bernie wanted rubber. 'Wet suits, lots of zips, John.'

Then Chalky said: 'If that geezer's name is Pilaff Bey, let's make it A Turkish Delight.'

The best location was the billiard room in the basement.

'Low tables, Roman couches, drapes on the walls and bags of cushions,' I said.

'Everything in satin,' Elsie said.

Bernie said: 'And don't forget the Chinese screens.' He put a paternal arm round my shoulders. 'I think we've got a good show here, John.'

I had two days to plan and prepare the meal. Drink was easy: Champagne and a cask of old brandy from the cellar. But I kept thinking about the old dong. I was the alchemist. What if I was making a terrible mess?

The butcher cheered me with a superb 22lb turkey. This was to be the centre of my meal: roast turkey stuffed with pickled pork and onions. Around this a series of small, tasty dishes to be picked at like tapas. Everything prepared to be eaten with the fingers, Moorish style. Tasty morsels to be popped into the mouth. Rolls of smoked salmon. Kidneys cooked in Champagne. Sweetbreads with truffles and cream. Oyster cocktails. Baked eel pie. Mushrooms Bordelaise. Cold squares of Tortilla Espanola sprinkled with caviar and parsley.

Whole leaves of Cos lettuce in anchovy vinaigrette. Prawns with aioli. Canteloupe melon on Parma ham. Cold, rolled sirloin of beef (marinated in Malmsey Madeira with pepper, salt, cinnamon, powdered ginger, nutmeg, and roasted, basted with the marinade). Crispy French sticks from my bakery in Hammersmith. Hot garlic bread. Stilton with celery. Fresh pineapples with Kirsch. Marrons glacé. Peaches in brandy. Glacé oranges d'Apt. Two bowls of displayed fresh fruit.

I told the housekeeper's sister she could go when the action started.

'Take more than that to shock me,' she said. 'So long as he doesn't ask me to join in.'

Mister B, wearing a bottle-green smoking jacket and a claret bow tie, inspected the orgy room where Chalky, in plimsoles, was putting the last touches to the dressing.

Bernie, got up in his idea of formal dress, adjusted the focus of a projector reflecting slides of erotic, Oriental pictures on to an ornate, Victorian mirror.

The room was rich and dim. A fountain (BBC props, *I Claudius*) played in a lovers' patio, backed by vines supporting bunches of practical grapes.

Distant strains of an evening raga came from an artfully wired loudspeaker beneath the billiard table, which, transformed by drapes and covered with the cold food and Chalky's fruit display was now the banqueting table. And very beautiful it was.

Elsie chirped and danced about Mister B like a TV quiz show hostess. One moment she was whispering in his ear, the next she was touching his arm to show him the phallic motif on a finger bowl.

She ate a grape from the vine and gave him a grape from the vine. The old lips glistened in the lamplight.

The housekeeper's sister and I watched the arrival of the whores from the kitchen doorway, like servants in a genre painting.

The first three, obviously pals, came together in the same mini-cab. They were exotic creatures who wore fur coats and smelled powerfully of expensive perfume. They talked loudly in polyglot accents.

Bernie received them like sisters, hugging and kissing.

They squeaked. Their fingernails were painted. Their hands flashed with bracelets and rings as they undid their coats and shook out their hair.

I didn't see what they had under their coats; the turkey needed basting.

The old boys who'd been winding themselves up with brandy and ginger ale became lively.

'Toby this is Gwen. Gwen this is Robert. Charlie this is Dawn . . .'

'They're lovely girls,' the housekeeper's sister told me breathlessly. 'But you got to laugh. The Taffy's shaved the feathers off her whatsit.'

The champagne popped and popped.

Bernie rushed in with a cigar in his mouth. 'Grub up when you like, John. They're well pissed and the judge is wearing a mask.'

The panic was on. Kidneys sizzled. The sweetbreads wanted boiled cream. I knocked over the Bordelaise sauce. I burnt my thumb on the eels.

A tiny girl came in with a drink for the cook. She wore transparent chiffon pantaloons and a pop-out bra. I gave her a spoonful of caviar.

I was whacked.

The housekeeper's sister made a cup of tea.

'Happy days and lonely nights,' she said.

I remembered Elsie, I hadn't seen her since she took the mushrooms in.

There was a crash of dishes. A shriek. Then a chorus of cheers.

An old fellow, in the full dress uniform of the 17th/21st lancers, stood on the billiard table, legs astride my turkey. Pineapples and nectarines rolled on the floor. His face was flushed, his flies gaped wide. He waved a bottle of champagne in his right hand.

'Time for verse,' he cried.

'Bravo.'

I asked Chalky if he'd seen Elsie.

'No, sorry, old man,' he said, 'but then I've been kept pretty busy.'

The Welsh girl sniggered lewdly.

Bernie remonstrated: 'Shhh.' And cued the Colonel.

'Twas on the good ship Venus.

FEEDING THE OLD MAN

By God! You should have seen us.

The figurehead was a whore in bed . . .'

They stamped and shouted. The party had degenerated. But what did Mister B expect with six free whores and four dozen bottles of champagne?

As for the food. They'd hardly bothered with the food, except for the oysters and the smoked salmon. The eel pie was untouched. The aioli was on the floor with the fruit.

Nobody really complimented me. A couple of slaps on the back and a kiss from the black girl. Not a word from Mister B.

They weren't interested in aphrodisiac dishes and sexual pleasure. They wanted horseplay and Eskimo Nell.

The housekeeper's sister had her hat on. 'Good luck to whoever has to clean that lot up,' she said.

I rescued my favourite poelon casserole from a vulnerable place at the foot of the stairs. It was empty. I wondered who had eaten the kidneys; perhaps it was Mister B?

I went upstairs to the ground floor. They were in the library. I heard the little whoops Elsie makes when she's excited or interested in anything. Mister B was talking urgently. The words were pouring out but I couldn't hear what he was saying. I waited for a pause so I could go in. Should I knock?

I left by the front door, still holding the casserole.

I awoke in the rocking chair at twenty to four. My leek and potato soup was untouched on the table. Elsie still hadn't come home so I drank a glass of mineral water and went to bed.

Eventually I signed my new contract and went back to the work I suppose I think I'm best at, the only work I think I can do.

Elsie married Mister B in the West Indies.

I missed her terribly but what hurt me most was the way she sneaked her passport from the flat and left without even saying goodbye.

One black night when nothing tasted right I telephoned Mister B's villa in St. Kitts.

Elsie was called from the beach by a servant.

'The kidneys?' She said puzzled, far away. 'Yes, we ate them. They were delicious.'

'And?' I asked.

She was silent. The line hummed and scratched.

'Come on Elsie,' I shouted. 'I have to know.'

'Well, darling,' she said. 'He took a bit of time. But when he did, Oh boy!'

———————

The dish that did the trick:

Kidneys with Champagne

4 lambs kidneys
2oz mushrooms
Pinch of flour
Salt, pepper, nutmeg
Round tablespoon of butter
A full glass of champagne
A squeeze of lemon

Skin and core kidneys. Slice thinly.
Peel mushrooms and slice.
Sauté kidneys and mushrooms (adding seasoning) in most of the butter over gentle heat for five minutes.
Sprinkle in flour, stir with wooden spoon.
Pour in champagne and stir as it bubbles up for one minute. (You may want to increase heat here). Add remaining butter and squeeze of lemon before serving. Drink the rest of the champagne while you're cooking it and eating it and tally-ho!

Pilaff Bey's aphrodisiac recipes were published by William Heinemann Ltd in a book called *Venus In The Kitchen* by Norman Douglas (1952).

Poems/Raymond Carver

MY BOAT

My boat is being made to order. Right now it's about to leave
the hands of its builders. I've reserved a special place
for it down at the marina. It's going to have plenty of
room
on it for all my friends: Richard, Bill, Chuck, Toby,
Jim, Dan,
Gary, George, Bob, Michael, Don, Dick, Scott,
Geoffrey, Jack,
Paul, Jay, Morris, and Alfredo. All my friends! They
know who they are.
Tess, of course. I wouldn't go anyplace without her.
And Kristina, Merry, Catherine, Diane, Sally, Annick,
Pat, Judith, Susie.
Doug and Amy! They're family, but they're also my
friends,
and they like a good time. There's room on my boat for
just about everyone. I'm serious about this!
There'll be a place on board for everyone's stories.
My own, but also the ones belonging to my friends.
Short stories, and the ones that go on and on. The true
and the made-up. The ones already finished, and the
ones still being written.
Poems, too! Lyric poems, and the longer, darker
narratives.
For my painter friends, paints and canvases will be on
board my boat.
We'll have fried chicken, lunch meats, cheeses, rolls,
French bread. Every good thing that my friends and I
like.
And a big basket of fruit, in case anyone wants fruit.
In case anyone wants to say he or she ate an apple,
or some grapes, on my boat. Whatever my friends want,
name it, and it'll be there. Soda pop of all kinds.

Beer and wine, sure. No one will be denied anything,
   on my boat.
We'll go out into the sunny harbor and have fun, that's
   the idea.
Just have a good time all around. Not thinking
about this or that or getting ahead or falling behind.
Fishing poles if anyone wants to fish. The fish are out
   there!
We may even go a little way down the coast, on my
   boat.
But nothing dangerous, nothing too serious.
The idea is simply to enjoy ourselves and not get scared.
We'll eat and drink and laugh a lot, on my boat.
I've always wanted to take at least one trip like this,
with my friends, on my boat. If we want to
we'll listen to Schumann on the CBC.
But if that doesn't work out, okay,
we'll switch to KRAB, The Who, and the Rolling
   Stones.
Whatever makes my friends happy! Maybe everyone
will have their own radio, on my boat. In any case,
we're going to have a big time. People are going to have
   fun,
and do what they want to do, on my boat.

WHERE WATER COMES TOGETHER WITH OTHER WATER

I love creeks and the music they make.
And rills, in glades and meadows, before
they have a chance to become creeks.
I may even love them best of all
for their secrecy. I almost forgot
to say something about the source!
Can anything be more wonderful than a spring?
But the big streams have my heart too.
And the places streams flow into rivers.

The open mouths of rivers where they join the sea.
The places where water comes together
with other water. Those places stand out
in my mind like holy places.
But these coastal rivers!
I love them the way some men love horses
or glamorous women. I have a thing
for this cold swift water.
Just looking at it makes my blood run
and my skin tingle. I could sit
and watch these rivers for hours.
Not one of them like any other.
I'm forty-five years old today.
Would anyone believe it if I said
I was once thirty-five?
My heart empty and sere at thirty-five!
Five more years had to pass
before it began to flow again.
I'll take all the time I please this afternoon
before leaving my place alongside this river.
It pleases me, loving rivers.
Loving them all the way back
to their source.
Loving everything that increases me.

A wildly funny new novel from the
author of *Mr Scobie's Riddle* and *Miss
Peabody's Inheritance.*

Elizabeth Jolley
FOXYBABY

'Her fiction shines and shines and
shines, like a good deed in a naughty
world'
– Angela Carter
'A new, true, original' – Susan Hill

£9.95

Just published in America to tremendous
critical acclaim: a beautifully crafted first
novel set in Kenya at the time of
independence

Louisa Dawkins
NATIVES AND
STRANGERS

'This story has a magical appeal'
– *Publishers' Weekly*
'In this novel, more than any other I have
read for some time, there is a sense that
people can decide how to act. It seems to
me that it is this very combination of
dislocation and possibility that takes
Natives and Strangers out of the territory of
the 'colonial' novel and gives it a larger
authority' – *New York Times Book Review*

£9.95

VIKING  FICTION

Show Me Yours

Russell Hoban

I usually stay up till three or four in the morning; those small hours are the door to so much, they open out into everything. I use an Apple II computer instead of a typewriter and I've got a Drake R7 receiver for listening to All India Radio or Radio Moscow or the Voice of Israel or RIAS in Berlin or whoever's transmitting the music I crave at the time. I seldom listen to broadcasts in English; I don't want to understand what they're saying or singing – I just want to hear those voices coming from far away in the night, coming round the curving ionosphere and the great globe-encircling miles, night miles, ocean miles where the deep fish glide in the deep, deep dark and the kraken waits in the uttermost deep with its dark mind wild with the terror of itself.

I almost always record what's coming in; the radio and a cassette deck are hooked up to a timer; when I go to bed I put in a fresh cassette and the timer turns everything off an hour later. In the morning when I sit down to work I listen to the music I've caught.

I seldom get a really clean recording of Bismallah Khan or Tatiana Petrova or whoever it might be but when I buy a perfectly clean commercial recording of a favourite artist I find it's nothing I want to listen to very much; it simply doesn't do it for me: I've got to hear the crackling, the twittering and tweetling and whispering, the sudden storms and surges of that particular transmission as it comes to me in the night. Far, far away in the night are live human beings whose breathing can be heard as they speak, and they're looking at their illuminated dials as I look at mine at this end of the thousands of great globe-encircling miles, ocean miles in the night, the heave and swell and the deep fish gliding in the dark. And always on the night air sweet women singing in all the tongues of humankind, singing to the accompaniment of strange instruments, strange rhythms in places unseen but existing at this very moment, perhaps with dry dust rising on the plains or with monsoon rains beating down or with snow on mountain peaks impassable. And while I hear those sweet voices singing words that I cannot understand I watch my thoughts appear letter by letter in the green dancing of the phosphors on the monitor screen.

One night quite late I was listening to RIAS broadcasting from Berlin; reception was very poor and I wasn't paying close attention to what I was hearing; RIAS is mostly difficult, it hasn't got a strong transmitter; it's often overlapped by the BBC World Service and the ionosphere seldom seems favourably inclined to it; through

103

the fading and the surging and the interference, through the buzz, the crackle, and the roar there burst out suddenly a breathy chorus of young female voices, schoolgirl voices they sounded like because of what they sang: *Show me yours, I'll show you mine!* There were other words but they were indistinct, the only words that I heard clearly were those same ones repeated: *Show me yours, I'll show you mine! Show me!*

What? Who? I waited for the woman at the microphone to say who it was that had sung this invitation that I remembered so well from my childhood, this offer to show and be shown the primal secrets of the flesh. Almost I smelled the sweet and feral smell of the little girls of so many years ago, almost I smelled the sun-warmed wood of barns, the musty-sweet warmth of haylofts, almost I saw glinting in the sunbeams the dust-motes of childhood like golden particles of time lost, time like gold dust trickled from a purse with a hole in it.

But there was more to it, it was not simply the smells, the lights and colours and images of childhood that came to me with those words out of the night: this was a real cosmic message, yes, a message from the universe which speaks to us from the clamorous bowl of space not only with the whispering glister of stars but with the voices of owls and frogs and pop groups, with the hiss of rain and the silence of snow.

Show me yours and I'll show you mine, it was saying, and I knew that if I could tune myself in to it I could show and be shown not in the manner of a man drowning in the sea but as whales do and green turtles on their paths of perception, as the albatross that's never lost, as the shark without fear, and as the kraken whose task is to endure the terror that created it.

The breathy schoolgirls were re-absorbed into the interference, other music followed. After a time the announcer identified the records she had played; I heard her say, *Show Me Yours* but the name of the group was lost in the buzz, the crackle, and the roar. I'd taped what I heard, and I assumed that any shop that sold pop records would be able to identify it for me. Most of them thought that it sounded like a group called Blondie but none could find such a track or single. By the time I got round to phoning RIAS I was no longer certain which night I'd heard it on; they couldn't find it in their library, nor could the Armed Forces Network, nor could Capital Radio.

I thought about it for a while and on reflection all seemed as it should be; the message had come once and was not to be repeated.

Paul Cox

SCREAM WHEN YOU BURN

Charles Bukowski

Henry poured a drink and looked out the window at the hot and bare Hollywood street. Jesus Christ, it had been a long haul and he was still up against the wall. Death was next, death was always there. He'd made a dumb mistake and bought an underground newspaper and they were still idolising Lenny Bruce. There was a photo of him, dead, right after the bad fix. All right, Lenny had been funny at times: 'I can't come!' – that bit had been a masterpiece but Lenny really hadn't been all that good. Persecuted, all right, sure, physically and spiritually. Well, we all ended up dead, that was just mathematics. Nothing new. It was waiting around that was the problem. The phone rang. It was his girlfriend.

'Listen, you son of a bitch, I'm tired of your drinking. I had enough of that with my father . . .'

'Oh hell, it's not all that bad.'

'It is, and I'm not going through it again.'

'I tell you, you're making too much of it.'

'No, I've had it, I tell you, I've had it. I saw you at the party, sending out for more whisky, that's when I left. I've had it, I'm not going to take any more . . .'

She hung up. He walked over and poured a scotch and water. He walked into the bedroom with it, took off his shirt, pants, shoes, stockings. In his shorts he went to bed with the drink. It was fifteen minutes to noon. No ambition, no talent, no chance. What kept him off the row was raw luck and luck never lasted. Well, it was too bad about Lu, but Lu wanted a winner. He emptied the glass and stretched out. He picked up Camus' *Resistance, Rebellion and Death* . . . read some pages. Camus talked about anguish and terror and the miserable condition of Man but he talked about it in such a comfortable and flowery way . . . his language . . . that one got the feeling that things neither affected him *nor* his writing. In other words, things might as well have been fine. Camus wrote like a man who had just finished a large dinner of steak and french fries, salad, and had topped it with a bottle of good French wine. Humanity may have been suffering but not him. A wise man, perhaps, but Henry preferred somebody who screamed when they burned. He dropped the book to the floor and tried to sleep. Sleep was always difficult. If he could sleep three hours in twenty-four he was satisfied. Well, he thought, the walls are still here, give a man four walls and he had a chance. Out on the streets, nothing could be done.

The doorbell rang. 'Hank!' somebody screamed. 'Hey, Hank!'

What the shit? he thought. Now what?

'Yeah?' He asked, lying there in his shorts.

'Hey! What are you doing?'

'Wait a minute . . .'

He got up, picked up his shirt and pants and walked into the front room.

'What are you doing?'

'Getting dressed . . .'

'Getting dressed?'

'Yeah.'

It was ten minutes after twelve. He opened the door. It was the professor from Pasadena who taught English Lit. He had a looker with him. The prof introduced the looker. She was an editor in one of the large New York publishing houses.

'Oh you sweet thing,' he said, and walked up and squeezed her right thigh. 'I love you.'

'You're fast,' she said.

'Well, you know writers have always had to kiss the asses of publishers.'

'I thought it was the other way around.'

'It isn't. It's the writer who's starving.'

'She wants to see your novel.'

'All I have is a hardcover. I can't give her a hardcover.'

'Let her have one. They might buy it,' said the prof.

They were talking about his novel, *Nightmare*. He figured she just wanted a free copy of the novel.

'We were going to Del Mar but Pat wanted to see you in the flesh.'

'How nice.'

'Hank read his poems to my class. We gave him $50. He was frightened and crying. I had to push him out in front of my class.'

'I was indignant. Only $50. Auden used to get $2000. I don't think he's that much better than I am. In fact . . .'

'Yes, we know what you think.'

Henry gathered up the old Racing Forms from around the editor's feet.

'People owe me $1100. I can't collect. The sex mags have become impossible. I've gotten to know the girl in the front office.

One Clara. "Hello, Clara," I phone her, "did you have a nice breakfast?" "Oh yes, Hank, did you?" "Sure," I tell her, "two hard-boiled eggs." "I know what you're phoning about," she answers. "Sure," I tell her, "the same thing." "Well, we have it right here, our p.o. 984765 for $85." "And there's another one, Clara, your p.o. 973895 for five stories, $570." "Oh yes, well I'll try to get these signed by Mr. Masters." "Thank you, Clara," I tell her. "Oh that's all right," she says, "you fellows deserve your money." "Sure," I say. And then she says, "And if you don't get your money you'll phone again, won't you? Ha, ha, ha." "Yes, Clara," I tell her, "I'll phone again." '

The professor and the editor laughed.

'I can't make it, god damn it, anybody want a drink?'

They didn't answer so Henry poured himself one. 'I even tried to make it playing the horses. I started well but I hit a slump. I had to stop. I can only afford to win.'

The professor started to explain his system for beating twenty-one at Vegas. Henry walked over to the editor.

'Let's go to bed,' he said.

'You're funny,' she said.

'Yeah,' he said, 'like Lenny Bruce. Almost. He's dead and I'm dying.'

'You're still funny.'

'Yeah, I'm the hero. The myth. I'm the unspoiled one, the one who hasn't sold out. My letters are auctioning for $250 back east. I can't buy a bag of farts.'

'All you writers are always hollering "wolf".'

'Maybe the wolf has finally arrived. You can't live off your soul. You can't pay the rent with your soul. Try it some time.'

'Maybe I ought to go to bed with you,' she said.

'Come on, Pat,' said the prof, standing up, 'we've got to make Del Mar.'

They walked to the door. 'It was good to see you.'

'Sure,' Henry said.

'You'll make it.'

'Sure,' he said, 'goodbye.'

He walked back to the bedroom, took off his clothing and got back into bed. Maybe he could sleep. Sleep was something like death. Then he was asleep. He was at the track. The man at the window was giving him money and he was putting it into his wallet.

It was a lot of money.

'You ought to get a new wallet,' said the man, 'that one's torn.'

'No,' he said, 'I don't want people to know I'm rich.'

The doorbell rang. 'Hey Hank! Hank!'

'All right, all right . . . wait a minute . . .'

He put his clothes back on and opened the door. It was Harry Stobbs. Stobbs was another writer. He knew too many writers.

Stobbs walked in.

'You got any money, Stobbs?'

'Hell no.'

'All right, I'll buy the beer. I thought you were rich.'

'No, I was living with this gal in Malibu. She dressed me well, fed me. She booted me out. I'm living in a shower now.'

'A shower?'

'Yes, it's nice. Real glass sliding doors.'

'All right, let's go. You got a car?'

'No.'

'We'll take mine.'

They got into his '62 Comet and drove up toward Hollywood and Normandy.

'I sold an article to *Time*. Man, I thought I was in the big money. I got their check today. I haven't cashed it yet. Guess what it reads?' asked Stobbs.

'$800?'

'No, $165.'

'What? *Time* magazine? 165 dollars?'

'That's right.'

They parked and went in to a small liquor store for the beer. 'My woman dumped me,' Henry told Stobbs. 'She claims I drink too much. A bare-ass lie.' He reached into the cooler for two six-packs. 'I'm tapering off. Bad party last night. Nothing but starving writers, and professors who were about to lose their jobs. Shop talk. Very wearing.'

'Writers are whores,' said Stobbs, 'writers are the whores of the universe.'

'The whores of the universe do much better, my friend.'

They walked to the counter.

' "Wings of Song",' said the owner of the liquor store.

' "Wings of Song",' Henry answered.

The owner had read an article in the *L.A. Times* a year ago about

Henry's poetry and had never forgotten. It was their Wings of Song routine. At first he had hated it, and now he found it amusing. Wings of Song, by god.

They got into the car and drove back. The mailman had been by. There was something in the box.

'Maybe it's a cheque,' Henry said.

He took the letter inside, opened two beers and opened the letter. It said,

'Dear Mr. Chinaski, I just finished reading your novel, *Nightmare*, and your book of poems, *Photographs From Hell*, and I think you're a great writer. I am a married woman, 52 years old, and my children are grown. I would very much like to hear from you. Respectfully, Doris Anderson.'

The letter was from a small town in Maine.

'I didn't know that people still live in Maine,' he told Stobbs.

'I don't think they do,' Stobbs said.

'They do. This one does.'

Henry threw the letter in the trash sack. The beer was good. The nurses were coming home to the highrise apartment across the street. Many nurses lived there. Most of them wore see-through uniforms and the afternoon sun did the rest. He stood there with Stobbs watching them get out of their cars and walk through the glass entrance, to vanish to their showers and their TV sets and their closed doors.

'Look at that one,' said Stobbs.

'Uh huh.'

'There's another one.'

'Oh my!'

We're acting like fifteen-year-olds, Henry thought. We don't deserve to live. I'll bet Camus never peeked out of windows.

'How are you going to make it, Stobbs?'

'Well, as long as I've got that shower, I've got it made.'

'Why don't you get a job?'

'A job? Don't talk like a crazy man.'

'I guess you're right.'

'Look at that one! Look at the ass on that one!'

'Yes, indeed.'

They sat down and worked at the beer.

'Mason,' he told Stobbs, mentioning a young unpublished poet,

111

'has gone to Mexico to live. He hunts meat with his bow and arrow, catches fish. He's got his wife and a servant girl. He's got four books out looking. Even wrote a Western. The problem is that when you're out of the country it's almost impossible to collect your money. The only way to collect your money is to threaten them with death. I'm good at those letters. But if you're a thousand miles away they know you'll cool off before you get to their door. I like hunting your own meat, though. It beats going to the A & P. You pretend those animals are editors and publishers. It's great.'

Stobbs stayed around until 5 p.m. They bitched about writing, about how the top guys really stank. Guys like Mailer, guys like Capote. Then Stobbs left, and Henry took off his shirt, his pants, his shoes and stockings and went back to bed. The phone rang. It was on the floor near the bed. He reached down and picked it up. It was Lu.

'What are you doing? Writing?'

'I seldom write.'

'Are you drinking'

'Tapering off.'

'I think you need a nurse.'

'Let's go to the track tonight.'

'All right. When will you be by?'

'6.30 O.K?'

'6.30's O.K.'

'Goodbye, then.'

He stretched out in bed. Well, it was good to be back with Lu. She was good for him. She was right, he drank too much. If Lu drank like he did, he wouldn't want her. Be fair, man, be fair. Look what happened to Hemingway, always sitting with a drink in his hand. Look at Faulkner, look at them all. Well, shit.

The phone rang again. He picked it up.

'Chinaski?'

'Yeah?'

It was the poetess, Janessa Teel. She had a nice body but he'd never been to bed with her.

'I'd like you to come to dinner tomorrow night.'

'I'm going steady with Lu,' he said. God, he thought, I'm loyal. God, he thought, I'm a nice guy. God.

'Bring her with you.'

'Do you think that would be wise?'

'It'll be all right with me.'

'Listen, let me phone you tomorrow. I'll let you know.'

He hung up and stretched out again. For thirty years, he thought, I wanted to be a writer and now I'm a writer and what does it mean?

The phone rang again. It was Doug Eshlesham, the poet.

'Hank, baby . . . '

'Yeah, Doug?'

'I'm tapped, baby, I need a five, baby. Lemme have a fiver.'

'Doug, the horses have smashed me. I'm flat, absolutely.'

'Oh,' said Doug.

'Sorry, baby.'

'Well, all right.'

Doug hung up. Doug owed him fifteen right then. But he did have the fiver. He should have given Doug the fiver. Doug was probably eating dog food. I'm not a very nice guy, he thought. God, I'm not a very nice guy after all.

He stretched out in bed, full, in his unglory.

Prend Ce Sac, Mendiant!

Here is the earthquake
In a slump of stones:
The jar put down, jig-sawn
For archaeology.
The statue, decanted
And disorderly,
Lowers its guard:
The bronze sentinel
Greens at his post,
Jacketed for keeps.
Minos?
        Silent,
Speaks Daedal's flight,
Who stitched the maze
In wilful pedantry,
The feathered father flew.

Sprung upwards into the blue
Bucket of his sky,
Plumbing crazily, his son,
The sun, plumbed the heights.
So much is widely known.
Fathers and sons: see under
Stories, very old indeed.
Icarus, the index adds,
Heedless death of;
Glory, moment of, brief;
Mythology, his place in;
Grief, his father's;
Youth of.
      Momentary
Mote in the sun's hot eye,
Boiling bubble of a boy.

Report a sole survivor,
Blanket-shouldered, Cumae.
Message ends.
Between the chatting lines,
Another story bleeds.
Hear the buzz? Old saws.
Fools survive; masters die.
So synopsise the world,
Its catastrophe.
      Here
Is the mortal flaw, the line's
Caesura, an oracle's cleft
Palate, syllables bent
To tricks and tropes,
Eclectics' paradise,
Mad ivy in the jaws,
Meaningful spit, the word.
Fear ages boys, brings out
The father's face.

      Minos
Calls for minions; tickets;
Maps, provisions, lists
Of enemies. Rich men
Always write cheques
Where others send their love:
Crossed ultimata.
There must be futures
Money can buy.
      The king
Commands his D. to life;
Franks coins, heads and tails,
The winner's right:
Ungreying profiles.
Goggled, M. gears himself
For all pursuits.
He is going

Frederic Raphael

                    To get him back.
As I am the judge,
Condemned to life.
Begin with the end:
Autocrats derive their means
From that. And who'll be king
Of the dead, after all, after all?
For tyrants, the forest
Has no other parts.
Holists admit variety?
One size fits all.
Spot the father;
Hang the son.
                    Myth

Give us a clue?
First person, kept
From ourselves by auto?
Seven letters
I something something us.
Daedalus won't fit;
Icarus always will.
Survivor, skipped reefs
Of nimble cloud, ploughed
And passed, solo,
In an unwalled maze
Of sky, fell, the boy,
To soft safety,
Made his splash, declared,
'I am all right.'
Dead, alas, the man.
Luck and management;
Separate chapters.

Minos will not wear it:
He can rig the press
And wants results.
Can he not pay?
A king has access
To sweet funds, calls
After-hours numbers.
Generosity?
You can count on it.
Nothing for himself:
Art, art, art.
                    Art,
The rubble promises,
Began in roast accountancy,
Sheets in balancing acts.
Next time roof that maze
And seal a catacomb.
He'll not – – –   – – – – again (
And now? There's paper-
work to do.
                    Nothing
Is lost, save what is found.
And
        Here is the earthquake.
Here lies

1975/1985.
Ten years without Michael Ayrton

TRAIN TALK

Allan Massie

'Oh no,' the girl said, 'Brewster's dead.' She looked up at Lake. 'It shatters you, reading it like that in the paper as if it was an ordinary piece of news.'

Her voice drifted into the flat fields they were passing through at a speed and with a smoothness that made them seem like a dull travelogue filling those blank stuffy minutes before the main feature.

'What a marvellous life,' she said, 'and now I've missed my chance. You know he was one of the few people I'd have liked to meet. I'd have been scared of course.' She stopped and lit a cigarette. The hand that held the lighter shook just a little. 'I revered him.'

She was very young and she had written some poems, in short lines with jagged endings. Lake looked at her, sadly. It was an accident they were eating breakfast together on this north-bound train. She was very pretty too, with a pale face, a little square-jawed but still neat and cool and vulnerable in its youth, and dark smudgy eyes. He had noticed as she came towards him from the other end of the train that her skirt was short, almost a mini, and showed off nice legs, not showgirl's legs, but what he classified as nice tennis-playing, bottle-party, bedworthy legs. He smiled to himself as he framed his silent description and was a little ashamed too.

They'd met before, once, at the BBC. Then she'd said achingly silly things, such as he could imagine his daughter mouthing. It was natural they should smile now when they met, by chance, on a train, in travellers' limbo, and should sit down to have breakfast together. Why, he'd even read some of her poems, found them out in a little magazine. The jagged endings had interrupted anything she was saying before it became too dangerous.

And now she said again, 'Brewster's dead, Brewster.'

He nodded.

'Did you ever know him?' she said.

Lake, waiting for his kipper, looked out of the window again to avoid those dark smudgy eyes; puppy's eyes.

But she persisted.

'You'll think I'm naive', she said, 'but people like Brewster, not that there are many like him, have real glamour for me.'

'He wrote some good stuff,' Lake said, admiring her defensive irony, the inverted commas she so audibly placed around the words 'real glamour'.

117

We all have those figures, he might have consoled her. Hemingway was one of mine, and I could give you a whole list. Poor old Lowry and Dylan and a host of them. I remember Connolly's sad moon of a face as I once saw it plain – very plain – in the Ritz Bar; Mailer came in then, and Connolly collected a bottle of champagne, and they retired to a table in one of the pink alcoves. Later, when I knew of his tax problems, I thought of the champagne and hoped The Sunday Times paid for it. Oh yes, glamour.

He might have said all that or he might have spoken differently. 'You should have been content to remain simply a reader,' he was tempted to say. 'That way you could have kept the illusions you are going to find dimming . . .'

In fact he said, 'You remember Auden, don't you?' He was a bit ashamed again to be talking of Auden while he was waiting for his kipper. 'Poetry makes nothing happen . . .'

It hurt her hearing those words. She was so sure they shouldn't be true. She only used those timid lines and jagged endings because she didn't yet really know what the poem was going to make happen; when she found out she would change the world.

'But he was wrong,' she said.

And he almost replied: 'People who make things happen don't read. Nobody who makes things happen reads after he is twenty-five. We talk to babies and to other writers who may therefore actually be babies too. . In a certain sense they undoubtedly are. Now I grant you of course that what we say may be true and beautiful and even sublime, but it doesn't matter to anyone except ourselves. I don't think it ever did. It's as significant as making jigsaws. Nobody but a poet ever thought poets were the unacknowledged legislators of mankind. And anyway what's the point of a legislator who isn't acknowledged? Making up laws in a vacuum – it's like Aesop's bullfrog.'

Instead he told her that, yes, he had known Brewster. Her lip trembled like a girl opening a love-letter; she looks like a camellia, he thought.

'I can't believe he's dead. Of course for me and for so many others he never will be . . .'

John Lennon lives, he thought, John Lennon also.

'I don't know that he had much liked living for a long time back . . .' he said.

You can't, he thought, save people pain, not if they have any awareness, and this girl has. The pale spire of a fourteenth century church rose into view across the fields of beets; a tractor chugged over the mud-grey land towards a Dutch barn under a huge pearly sky. They passed a pond half-choked with weeds, and there was a swan on the little water.

'He was discontented,' he couldn't help saying. 'I met him when he came back from the States to that Oxford fellowship. He hated Oxford.'

'It couldn't ever have been the right place for him,' she said. She sounded Edinburgh for the first time as she said this.

'Oh I don't know,' he said. 'He'd got round to disliking anywhere except hotel rooms. He once said to me, I'm a middle-aged child of the motel revolution. I don't think it meant much, it was just something to say, and he'd said it before. Time and again I shouldn't wonder.'

'He was a drinker, wasn't he?' she said, sipping her coffee and not seeming to notice how bad it must be – he had ordered tea himself.

'A good deal of gin. Tumblers of gin and water at all his readings, a tumbler by his bedside, he used to say. He liked to wake in the night and listen to the silence and ease the shadows away with a good swig of the old reliable. Or at least he liked saying that. I must have heard him say that a dozen times.'

'You knew him well then?'

'No, not well.'

'What did he like, what gave him happiness?'

She had shed two years since they started talking. His kipper arrived. He busied himself separating the flesh from the bone and skin; rather messily.

He liked having people around him and making a fuss of him. He was a lonely man. He liked Westerns and a good cry; Gary Cooper alone in that empty street at high noon. A proud man who was ashamed of being as he was and flaunted what he was. A very frightened man, frightened of the police, frightened of being beaten up, frightened, God help us, of the critics. He had very few interests left when I knew him and was happiest on a bar stool for the two hours before he began to weep. You see, all he had in life was the facility for moving words around on paper, shuffle, shuffle, like a pack of cards, and dealing a poem.

Again of course he hadn't spoken; what was the point? The swan was long out of sight and the landscape was not quite featureless, not even a tree, no human habitation, only a tiny speck in the far distance, another tractor, as it might have been an insect. After all, the girl dealt poems herself.

'There's always a gap between the public life and the private one,' he said, 'unless you become the mask you have adopted. If you do that, well, you may exist in contentment, but your soul fattens like a pig in a sty. If you don't, if at night you take off the mask with the rest of your make-up, well then, the writer disappears. He is no longer what the reader who is often anyway only a fan has imagined. Instead all you have is a person with aches and pains and fears and tax problems. Poor Brewster had terrible tax problems, worse than Connolly's even. He almost had to go to prison once you know.'

Yes, he had actually said that.

'It's monstrous,' she replied, 'we ought to be like Ireland or Sweden.'

He looked out of the window again. The grey shimmered.

'Going north,' he said. 'Going north. How do you feel about going north?'

She looked at him with a faint mist in her eye, like a sea mist. Maybe she was still thinking of Brewster and his fear of buff envelopes; maybe his question had no meaning for her. For himself, going north meant the return to duty and all too often, especially in his youth, the acknowledgement of failure; it was a journey back, a return to the wire perimeter of judgement and obligation. A voyage south on the other hand, the night train to King's Cross or the boarding of an express at the Gare de Lyon which would allow him to wake to Provence or Italy, led always away from himself to a future he could hope to fashion. The South never disappointed; he saw colours only in the South. Brewster of course had sought whatever he was looking for in the West. And that hadn't worked.

'It's like the food in American women's magazines, my dear. That's California; it looks marvellous and tastes of nothing.'

So he'd come back also, to Thames Valley fog and now finally to a small hotel in Berlin where he had died in a bedroom that looked out on the Wall that had marked the inescapable defeat of his sort of Europe. Poor Brewster, child of illusion; like the rest of us, he thought.

Another church, this time abandoned; or rather, he saw now, converted into a shed for machinery. The churchyard which must once have surrounded it, probably not so very long ago, had been ploughed up; and the Church, a mediocre example of Decorated Gothic (to judge from the windows, now empty of glass and boarded up) stood like a rocky outcrop in a sea of sugar-beet.

The girl said, 'And I was feeling so happy. I've just been seeing my publisher.'

The words came in a rush as if she felt she was doing something immodest, boasting of having a publisher of her own.

'There's going to be a book, is there?' he said, keeping a smile back in case she thought it was patronizing. And it would have been, though in its way loving too.

'Yes,' she said, 'in the Spring.'

'Who's doing it?'

She named a firm he had never heard of.

'Good,' he said, 'you're happy with them, I hope.'

'Oh yes,' she said, 'they're very enthusiastic. I was lucky with the timing,' she said, 'I've to be back in school to-morrow.'

'School?'

'Yes, I teach, you know. It's my first year of teaching.'

It made him sad that she was old enough to be employed, that she had already started on the treadmill; he would have liked her to be even younger than that.

The train, he became aware, had stopped; opposite the church. A skein of geese flew over, heading for the sea.

'What do you make of that?' he said.

She looked, first blankly, then in surprise: 'Oh the birds,' she said, 'nothing really.'

'I meant that church,' he said.

'The church?'

'Yes.'

'Nothing particular. Should I? It looks sort of forlorn, I suppose.'

'Forlorn?' he said. 'Is that a word you could use in a poem?'

'Oh no,' she said, 'it wouldn't be right. You couldn't use a word like that, could you?'

'No,' he said, 'I suppose not, and yet, you're right, aren't you, forlorn's just what it is. So why couldn't you use the word?'

She smiled and lit another cigarette.

'What is this, a seminar?'

He shook his head. 'All the same, if it's what it is but you couldn't use the word, isn't that strange?'

'It's been used too often,' she said, 'so it's a dead word. Make something new, Pound said that. Brewster whom we've been talking about, that's what he always tried to do. You can't use dead words . . .'

'Even when we're in agreement that it's the right one. The right one in this instance. Forlorn. It's what that church is, forlorn.'

And more sentences started in his head, sketching out a whole theory of how religion and God were both dead, taking much of our vocabulary to the grave with them, so that what we were left with was something altogether diminished, a starved imagination, a hollow heart. He saw Brewster in his Berlin hotel bedroom, gazing at the Wall.

He looked at the girl, no longer wanting to make love to her.

'Of course you're quite right,' he said. 'You couldn't put a word like forlorn in a poem. That earth's been stopped for a long time. And as you say Brewster knew it very well too.'

He signalled to the waiter and asked for his bill. The train began to move, with slow jerks. The church shuddered out of his sight though for some moments the girl kept her smudged eyes on it as it receded into the past of their journey. She put the cigarette between her soft lips and puffed.

'Forlorn,' he said. 'It's like the knell of parting day, isn't it? Look at that landscape. It's a long time since any ploughman plodded homeward over those fields. Nowadays he gets into his Cortina. Anyway you'll have to excuse me. I must go and do some work. I've a book to read for review. Deadline you know. It's been nice seeing you again. Best of luck with the book.'

She smiled at him and he read the smile like a lost opportunity; not, he knew, that she'd meant it that way. Instead she took a paperback from her bag as though she had been waiting for him to go. She held it up: a volume of Brewster's Essays.

'I feel a bit sick having chosen this,' she said.

'He'd appreciate it, I'm sure,' he said.

She lowered her eyes to the printed page and he began his journey back up the swaying train.

Jonathan Cape

Information on forthcoming books is available
from the Publicity Department (FM)
32 Bedford Square, London WC1B 3EL

Fairy Tale

JANICE ELLIOTT

*O*nce upon a time there was a good woman who took her children for a walk in the forest and told them a story.

The good woman Caresse looks up from her typewriter and sighs. She looks at the blue cornflower in the white pot on her desk. She looks around her white room – O, the room of her dreams, in the house of her dreams: the high white room (Max calls it her cell) with the rough pine table, the sanded floor, the view of the ocean and the forest, and the plain day-bed. Yes, very like a cell.

Not that Caresse is cut off from the world, indeed. When she is working (especially when she is working well) her mind travels comfortably around the rooms of her house, observing the curve of a banister, counting her children, pausing to gossip with Max in his workshop among the motes of golden dust.

They might have some people in this evening or they might be alone. Sometimes the Millichamps come over, sometimes Caresse and Max go over to the Millichamps. Sometimes they take the children, sometimes they leave them, since the oldest Millichamp and the oldest Stungo are both sensible children and the houses are close enough, with no road to cross between.

Caresse puts aside her neat pile of typing paper, secures it against the breeze from the open window with her owl paperweight carved for their fifth anniversary by Max and weighted at the base with lead. She walks around her room touching her magic objects: the paperweight, the bladder-wrack seaweed they found on the beach, a blue glass bottle they dug up in the garden, and, best of all, the children's offerings: drawings of stick-people (Mummy and Daddy) on the notice-board; a polished pebble, wobbly paper-knife, pigeon's feather and jam-jar holding one expiring tadpole – all talismans, lares and penates, bless them.

Caresse smiles, leaves the room, closes the door behind her and calls out: Come on, children, I'll tell you a story.

Once upon a time, says Caresse – walking through the forest telling her children a story – *there was a good woman who took her children for a walk in the forest and told them a fairy story.*

This is an old deep forest – not one of your new conifer conservancies of fire-breaks and nature trails and neat birds. Here are still the tracks and monuments of the dark ages: forest rides like cathedral aisles, towering beeches whose tops are lost in a semblance of infinity. Underfoot the soundless loam of great age

125

and decay and here and there a reredos of brighter green larch or birch. In the black heart of the forest no birds sing.

Wearing her ankle-length sprigged dress, Caresse enters the forest barefoot with her children tugging at her hand. Tell us a story they cry, tell us a story; then they are distracted and run away, for there is a flash of red squirrel, almost extinct. The red squirrel has survived here, Caresse tells her children, because this is a forest on an island. But England is an island? (the planet is an island in space, for that matter). But even islands have islands: to the mainland which is also an island came seafaring grey squirrels who are very sweet eating corn on a bird-table but wiped out the red, gobbled up their dinners. Or the grey squirrel may be an innocent scapegoat. Some species are simply inadequately equipped for change and do not survive.

Tell us the story, they say, so the good woman tells them: *as they walked through the forest she told them a story of the woodcutter and his wife and his children.*

O, it's a *woodcutter* story.

Tell us a swineherd story!

Tell us a princess story!

Princess stories are yuk!

Still on the outskirts of the forest, Caresse's children dance in the falling flakes of light, squeal and chase and run back to their mother for a story.

Hush, be still, chides the good woman, or I will not tell you a story at all. Look at that greenfinch! A dash of gold then Caresse hugs the smallest to her and steps on into the wood.

In any case, this is not a woodcutter story. It is a story about a good woman, who lived with her husband and her children in a house on the edge of a forest: so close was their house to the woods they could hear a weasel cough or a badger scratch. Deer grazed almost at the front door and on a dusky evening the great white owl flew low past their open window and warned: Watch out, watch out.

(Have you written this story already or are you making it up?

All stories have already been made up. You only have to listen and tell.)

They were a happy family. Every day the husband went off to work, mending chairs, and every day he kissed his wife and all his children; every day he said, as he strode off with his tools in a bag on his shoulder and a good cheese with a whole onion in his pocket: mind your mother and do not go into the black heart of the forest.

They were a happy family but just sometimes the children quarrelled, as children do. Then their mother wrapped up a goat-cheese and apples from the loft. She looked at the hearth to be swept and the beds to be made, yet she knew that beds get made sometime and hearths can be swept any day, and instead she took her children into the forest and told them a story of a woodcutter and his wife and children.

This is the story the good woman told.

A woodcutter and a good woman and their children lived in a hut in a forest. One day the woodcutter's wife took the children for a walk in the forest and told them a story.

Wrapped in a muslin cloth in a basket, the mother, who was a good woman, carried a goat cheese and in the basket too was fresh-baked bread. One of the children carried the bag of apples and sometimes he slipped behind his mother's back and ate one. His mother knew what he was doing but pretended not to notice.

Once upon a time, said he woodcutter's wife, there was an old wood where children played. You may play there every day, their father said, provided you do not go into the black heart of the forest. (Was he a woodcutter asked the children? Yes, he was a woodcutter like your father, said their mother).

(There could be too many woodcutters in this story.)

However. Mostly they minded their father and stayed within sound of the ring of his axe. But one day (said the carpenter's wife telling the story the woodcutter's wife told to her children), the woodcutter's children were so busy playing they did not notice how deep into the forest they had strayed.

What did they meet in the forest, asked the carpenter's children?

They met a talking squirrel who cried come, come on, into the heart of the forest, where a goatherd diguised as a prince languishes by a stream and two black knights fight forever to the death for love of a lady they will never free for she belongs to the forest.

(Neither the woodcutter's wife nor the carpenter's wife knew that what the talking squirrel actually said was: I hate woodcutter stories.)

The strange thing, said the carpenter's wife, is that as the woodcutter's wife told her story, and as she walked through the forest with her children, they came upon a talking squirrel and a goatherd disguised as a prince, and two black knights fighting forever to the death for love of a lady.

Real? Absolutely real? asked the carpenter's children.

O, yes. As real as you or I or your father mending chairs and the onion in his pocket.

Caresse's children are hungry. They want to peel the story like an onion and gobble it up, all gone. If they were not such good and cheerful children they might eat up their mother for the story inside her.

Was the lady in the wood a princess? A yuk princess?

No, she was not a princess. She was a woman who worked for a living.

Now, says Caresse, spreading her skirt and settling beneath one of those heaven-seeking trees, we will eat our bread and cheese, then you play hide and seek or sleep perhaps. And later I will tell you the rest of the story the carpenter's wife told her children.

But it was the *woodcutter's* wife's story!

O, my loves – it was the carpenter's wife's story *about* the woodcutter's wife's story.

(Perhaps I should never have brought in this woodcutter.)

Caresse spread goat-cheese for the youngest and hands the others their bread, to spread themselves. Then she tells them: the lady in the wood, you see, worked for her living by singing songs she made herself. And everything she sang of came true – the talking squirrel, the goatherd disguised as a prince and the two black knights fighting forever to the death for love of the lady.

The good woman Caresse kisses each child as it sleeps. While they sleep she walks on, in her sprigged dress, barefoot, deeper into the dark heart of the forest where no birds sing. The deeper she goes, the more she is drawn on, brambles snag her skirts and wild roses prick her cheek. There is a flash of red.

About these woodcutter stories, says the talking squirrel.

About these talking squirrel stories, says Caresse.

She hears the ring of iron as the two black knights fight forever to the death for love of a lady, and decides to give them a miss. Deep in the black heart of the forest she meets a lad in princely gear moaning by a stream. He is her secret lover and falls upon her at once, having seen her reflection in a stream.

I am good woman! she cries, bounding beneath him.

I am your secret lover! he gasps, bouncing upon her.

You are a prince! A prince disguised as a goatherd! Or a goatherd disguised as a prince! You know my secret heart and all my desires! You are all I have ever wished!

Actually, he says, I'm a woodcutter.

Caresse sits up and brushes the leaves from her skirt, the twigs from her hair. She is sitting on a mossy mound, neat as a velvet pincushion. Her secret lover sprawls on his stomach, chewing a straw and grinning. Insolently, she would say, if they had not been one moment before in boundless ecstasy.

You are definitely a goatherd, she says.

If I'm a goatherd you're a princess.

Who's story is this anyway?

It's a lousy story, says the talking squirrel.

Of an even and sunny temperament – known for her common sense – Caresse has rarely felt so put out. Her hair, she knows, looks a fright and when she bends to check her face in the stream, there is no reflection. Only the dark eye of the forest stares back.

What happened next? ask her children, roused from sleep by their mother's return. Normally she loves them like this, warm and sweet from sleep, but today she is edgy as a hedge.

The carpenter's wife – she tells her children – told how the woodcutter's wife and her children played a game with the talking squirrel and the goathered disguised as a prince and the two black knights, and then they went home. The carpenter's wife and her children went home too. And now we're going home.

What game did they play?

Stud poker. The talking squirrel cheated.

So Caresse and her children leave the forest, which seems no longer so enchanting but a nuisancy place. Caresses sends the children to play with the Millichamps. She drops her ankle-length sprigged dress into the Ali-Baba laundry basket and takes a warm bath followed by a short sharp shower. Then she lies on the day-bed in her white room, her cell, with a sympathetic but not intoxicating yellow drink in her left hand, and her right forefinger resting lightly on her forehead to clear her mind of forests. After a while she calls her husband, Max, on the inter-house telephone and says: the Millichamps are coming over tonight. We'll have a quiet evening and we may or may not play mah-jong. I have had a tiresome afternoon but I'm fine now.

You see, the tiniest adjustment, and equilibrium is restored.

Caresse walks through her evening house, counting and naming the rooms, followed by a sweet trail of thyme and rosemary, roasting with the breast of lamb. In every room she snaps on every light until the house blazes to defy the forest.

And here come Dymphna and Hereward Millichamp — exactly the friends she would have chosen – crossing the clearing to dine with Caresse, who thinks she is talking brilliantly tonight, though actually she is a little drunk (and who can blame her; talking squirrels are a pain in the neck).

Caresse says: O, we are so lucky. When I look at the rest of the world and see the things going on, the hijacking and the brain-damaged children and the sexual assaults upon grand-mothers and the bad architecture and the divorce rate and the death of the whale. I think we are so fortunate to be together like this without cancer. Do you think there was a touch too much garlic in the marinade? That is such a pretty dress, Dymphna, though I like your blue best, I always like you in blue, I have some blue beads you shall have. I don't think I shall ever leave here. I don't think I shall ever go to the city again. Why people have to run around so in such herds, I cannot imagine, it's no wonder they get trampled. There is, after all, the life of the mind and there are some very good films on television. Why go to the cinema and catch cancer? Max, pour the wine, Hereward, have some more syllabub. Give me your hands! Let us make a vow. I had a silly afternoon in the forest today.

Even in her present state, Caresse's sensibilities are sharp and she can see there is something funny going on. Max is looking at the table. Hereward is looking at Dymphna. Dymphna says: Caresse, we have to tell you that we're moving.

Moving! But you can't move!

I'm sorry, Caresse.

But why are you moving? Caresse is suddenly sober. She sees that her hands are red and puts them under the table. She may take up smoking again. She may drink a lot more or nothing at all.

Dymphna says, as gently as she can: we simply don't feel, Caresse, that there is room in this story for our characters to develop.

This doesn't *have* to be a short story –

I'm afraid that has nothing to do with it.

Dymphna. I have never before begged anyone for anything in my life. A novel? A triology?

Thank you for a lovely dinner, Caresse. The lamb was perfect.

But you won't know where to go – where will you go without me?

To tell you the truth, we fancied the theatre.

You idiots! Caresse howls. You'll see, she yells after them – it'll be a woodcutter play!

Towards dawn Max comes to her in her white room. He is faint already, fading fast.

Caresse is cried out. You too? she says.

He takes her hand. They sit side by side on the narrow bed. She always loved his hands.

I would have built with them such wonderful things.

But I was never a carpenter.

Who has custody of the children in such cases?

I don't believe this has ever come up before. I don't know.

When even Max has gone, in search of a novella about a novelist trying to write a novella – when he has, alas, at last, slipped hrough her fingers into the blue morning – Caresse sits down at her typewriter, sighs, dashes away a tear and begins to write:

Once upon a time there was a good woman who took her children for a walk in the forest and told them a story.

The Local Reporter

George Macbeth

Into our orbit there has come,
To live in Norfolk, someone rum.
A poet. What? A poet, yes,
And married to a poet-ess.
Their house itself, a Gothic sort,
Resembles an embattled fort.
The chimneys twist in Tudor height,
The windows glow, pre-Raphaelite.

Both write. The poet in his room
Develops verses bathed in gloom.
Three thousand words he does each day
In his inimitable way.
Meanwhile, his lady fair disposes
Things for the babe, and then composes.
Novels of which one might be proud
Are written, and then read aloud.

No lunch they take. They work right through
From twelve o'clock till well past two.
The poet then, lest arteries harden,
Goes for a stroll around the garden.
The poet's wife prefers indoors.
After all, she has household chores.
Bills for the roofing and the plumbing
Require attention, and keep coming.

Both rise at eight and eat in style
A breakfast far from stale or vile.
An egg, perhaps, then marmalade
And toast, which their nice maid has made.
At ten or earlier come the letters
Which frame their time, and forge their fetters.
The lady sighs, the husband copes
With cast-off bills, and envelopes.

GEORGE MACBETH

Up in the library she stands
Warming her bottom and her hands
Like some traditional country squire
In riding boots before her fire.
The poet strikes a graver mood.
With spaniel at his heels, well-cued,
Slowly he strolls, and does his rounds,
And spares the moles to raise their mounds.

Tea, though, is near. A graceful time
When crumpets rise to the sublime,
Plates pass, and conversation flows,
And all is poetry and prose.
The family daughter, home from school,
Floats in, and finds the cakes 'too cool'.
Delightful, and so full of fun,
She washes up when tea is done.

THE LOCAL REPORTER

Winter suppose the season. Now
The robin shivers on the bough
And hungry puppies must be fed
And Alexander put to bed.
Dear little fellow! Rich in joys
Across the floor he hurls his toys
And blinks his darling, screwed-up eyes
And vomits messes down his flies.

In summer it will be the same,
The evening wash, the ritual game,
Then nanny settling, work well done,
Beside her horlicks, and a bun.
All done now, television freed,
The poet can withdraw to read,
And through the floor and falling sleet
Feel safe from Coronation Street.

Drawings by Paul Cox

FLYING INJURIES

Helen Harris

Every year, hundreds of children in this country break arms and legs because they imagine that they can fly. You ask any casualty officer; he'll tell you. Little Johnny climbs up onto the garden wall, looks down into the dizzy depths of the rose beds and, under the sudden illusion that he can fly, launches off into space. Crash; fractured radius or ulna and dreadful humiliation. What went wrong? He never lets on, of course. Never. We see him brought into Cas, white with shock and pain, his lower lip trembling with holding back his tears, but what hurts him most of all is the disappointment. It didn't work. But it should have; he was convinced as he stood up on the wall, that he could do it. It was so simple; he could feel the right muscles ready to carry him through the air, he could already imagine what it would feel like to flap away. He *knew* what movements he would need to make and how expertly he would make them. What had gone wrong? For he is still convinced underneath, although shaken, that in theory it should work. He must have done something slightly wrong or chosen the wrong moment to try it out. There is absolutely no doubt that it should. His conviction on the wall, and in the nights of dreams which led up to it, was so profound, so powerful that it is impossible that it could be a mistake. And even after the Plaster of Paris and the telling off, his belief remains, secret, unspoken, and the danger remains too that one day he will try out the whole performance again.

I have worked in Casualty for nearly twenty years now and they never fail to move me, these phantom flying injuries. For that is what they are, little phantom pilots of the imagination. I find it uplifting that their faith is so deeply rooted and so enduring, despite all the obstacles which life puts in their way.

I flew myself once. I was a pilot of Wellingtons in the War and I experienced the swooping elation which possesses these children before they hurl themselves down to the tender mercies of my housemen. True, the nature of our missions did not prompt one to soar and sing. We flew low and in deadly earnest in the dark. True, the racket in those planes destroyed any passing illusion of self-powered flight. But later, after the War, I found I missed flying and took to weekend joy-rides from our local airfield. I flew over the sun-dappled fields of Kent on a summer's day and I knew what it was to have wings. Yes, I have experienced the crescendo of conviction that makes the children jump.

April 19th. We had another one in today; Berry, Charles, aged six, a stout and sturdy child of solidly respectable upper middle class parents, whom I would not have credited with the fantasy to try to fly. He was brought in by his mother, a fat and forceful woman, as baleful as a consultant's wife, who was naturally convinced that his injury was the result of some foolishness. She harangued the wretched child in front of me, at such length and in such relentlessly unimaginative terms, that eventually I felt obliged to speak up in his defence and informed Mrs Berry rather coldly that her son's spirit was a credit to her and she would do better to console him with chocolate or ice cream. The look of indignation on her large face was gratifying.

Of course, this warm weather encourages them; the first fine days of yellow spring, which rouse us all to groundless elation.

May 11th. A dubious case. For can one accept as an attempt to fly, a jump hand in hand? Two charming little girls, sisters, and a mother distraught at this simultaneous injury to both her offspring; two little girls, sobered, their right and left arms respectively in slings. Surely they must have realized that they would require both arms to fly? It was silly of them to launch themselves from their treehouse holding hands, however blue the sky and sweet the wind. I was not as kind as I usually am to these cases, especially to the elder one, whom I suspect of having encouraged the younger, even though she had her doubts. I told them quite sternly that, just as they would not try to run on one leg, they could not expect to fly with only one hand free. They both looked up at me, quite shocked that I had penetrated their secret.

June 3rd. A dreadful factory accident, the sort of wanton devastation of lives, which the pursuit of a completely pedestrian objective can produce. It is this sort of accident which I hate most about my work in Casualty; hands of apprentice mechanics severed as they clumsily manipulate malfunctioning machines, feet of Tube train drivers crushed in crass collisions. Compared with injuries like these, a flying injury seems a noble, one might almost say, a beautiful injury.

There had been some sort of chemical incident at a plastics factory, we were told, and minutes later the ambulances were in the courtyard, bringing in their human wreckage. Five fine young men had been horribly burnt and blasted when a vat of molten ugliness had somehow ignited. Three of them will carry today's scars for life in the form of some disfigurement, the fourth escaped more lightly, the fifth is dead.

Found the whole thing so distressing that afterwards I wanted to get right away from the hospital and town and functioning society and rush headlong somewhere wide open and pure. I suggested to Meg that we drove to the coast on Sunday for a breath of fresh air.

June 5th. Praise the Lord for our day at the seaside! Meg and I walked on the cliffs after a pleasant lunch at the old Bayview Hotel and the wind spanked the waves with the affectionate blows of a loving hand. It was not quite sunny, but dry and clear. I felt a weight lift from my shoulders as I looked down at the misbehaving waves. Away from town and Cas, I felt freed from the crushing responsibility to be serious; Dr Midwinter, the one you can turn to in trouble. (I once overheard one of the nurses say something quite astonishing about me: 'He's like a landmark left over from the olden days, Dr Midwinter, isn't he? So dependable and familiar and down to earth.' Judgements like these condemn me to immobility.) Meg must have caught my irresponsible holiday mood; she skipped a few steps on the chalky path and gambolled in her heavy lace-ups like a little girl. On the headland, we stopped and surveyed the view. The wind made us feel almost weightless, as if, given a stronger puff, we might soar out over the waves, up into the empty white sky.

July 9th. I thought about writing a paper on the flying injuries, but then thought better of it. A droll little submission to the *BMJ* or *The Lancet* would be a betrayal of my child pilots, make them open to ridicule.

When we had two in on the one day and Sister Gardener (there are, thank God, only few Sister Gardeners) commented acidly, 'Anyone would think these wretched children imagine they can fly,' I was filled with a longing to stand up for the children, champion their case in a cynical world.

August 1st. There is too much cynicism in the world and never worse than when expressed by children. We are currently playing hosts to my little nephew and neice, while their parents take a

139

week's holiday in the Canaries. Being my sister Beatrice's children, they are, needless to say, as depressingly sensible and sceptical as could be. They reproved Meg for having bought brightly iced 'zoo' biscuits for tea on their first day here, saying, 'We're not *babies*, you know' and when they went up to bed and found the surprise gift pyjamas under their pillows, an owl and a penguin costume respectively, they rejected them with derision. I overheard them discussing Meg and me out in the garden on their second day with us. 'We should feel sorry for them, I think,' Belinda was saying to Roland. 'It's so obvious they're just trying to use us as substitutes for children of their own.'

August 4th. Tomorrow will be the crunch. I have decided to take Belinda and Roland to the seaside, as a last resort. Meg and I have been appalled by their lack of levity. I cannot stand to see them playing solemnly with their computers and video games. 'Playing' is almost the wrong word; given bigger desks and shorter tea breaks, they would be model office employees. Still, I have never yet met a child who did not respond to the wild elation of the seaside.

August 5th. I know just what Bea's reaction will be. I can hear her now, rounding on her husband, as though he were to blame, poor Basil, and crying, 'I *knew* we should never have left the children with Michael! I *told* you something would go wrong!'

We set off for the coast bright and early. It was going to be a classically splendid August day. In the back of the car, Roland and Belinda were politely excited. It was hard to tell whether they were genuinely enthusiastic about going to the seaside or just putting it on to humour us. The first sight of the sea reassured me; they 'oohed' in chorus and even began to jostle and bounce in their eagerness.

We found ourselves a good spot on the beach and set up our enclave of towels, rugs, beach umbrella and picnic things. Then it was wonderful to see Belinda and Roland spurt off into the distance, running like little freed zoo creatures, over the sand to the sea.

After their swim, we had lunch and after lunch, Meg and I napped. Roland and Belinda played industriously a little way away, building themselves a slab-like prison of a sandcastle. Round about three o'clock, it must have been, I decided it was time they did something a little livelier, so I suggested a walk along the cliffs to view the view. Meg stayed down below to guard our belongings. A little unwillingly at first, the children came away from the beach and followed me to the cliff path. Their faces brightened, however, at the sight of the rickety steps which led up the cliff face. Even sedentary children have a spark of spirit in them.

I climbed first, telling them to copy where I put my feet, since the steps were not all safe. We had only gone a little way up, luckily, when I stopped to make sure that they were both managing alright. (Belinda was climbing in much too dainty sandals). They had fallen a little way behind, climbing with almost caricatured care, and as a I waited for them to catch up with me, I looked out at the view. It was superbly bright and breezy, the sunlight playing games on the shimmering surface of the sea.

The children caught up with me. They were a little puffed from the climb, a little dazzled. The stood uncertainly on the wobbly steps, waiting to see what escapade their eccentric uncle would come up with next. I turned to them and I exclaimed, a trifle foolishly, I might now concede, 'Isn't it magnificent? Isn't it magic? Doesn't it make you feel you could fly?'

The Green Boy

Lisa St Aubin De Terán

Antonio didn't like the child to be talked of as 'the green boy'. To him, he was always El Capino, his son. On the second day he had sent the child down in advance, led like a sick lizard by his sister. He had hoped that the Doña would cure him. He watched from above as his daughter, Mary, picked her way over the stream and weeds to the courtyard of the Big House. El Capino was his favourite, but Capino was sick.

Mary had crossed the bridge, following the willow-lined track past the machine house and mill and on through the gates and garden to the Doña's house. She tried to leave Capino by the barn, but he clung to her, frightened to stay alone. A bad man lived in the gallery of the barn. He shrank back from its double doors. He didn't want to be left. Mary pushed him back firmly against the wall, whispering, 'Just wait a minute, Capino, I'll be back. Hush, and the bad man won't get you.'

Capino leaned heavily against the wall, unreassured by these words, but too limp to move. He was five years old. He was in trouble and very afraid. Mary ran into the yard and called, 'Doña, Doña, where are you?'

A voice answered, 'I'm upstairs, I'll come.'

Lydia, as the Doña was called, appeared, glad to see Mary. She always liked to see the girl and her little brother. Lydia was new on the hacienda, and a foreigner, and the two children kept her company, childless as she was, and they kept her informed about all that happened in the valley. Mary had a genius for never coming empty handed. She would bring strange flowers for the garden, or a clothful of rose-scented plums. She brought snail shells and seeds, or mottled beans to pod. There was hardly a day when Mary didn't come with some little offering or surprise. So that when she said, 'I've brought something to show you,' Lydia said, 'Thank you,' without really thinking.

Then Mary brought her brother forward and stood him in the courtyard in the sun. His pale skin was green, as were his limp hands by his sides. The whites of his eyes were marbled green and even his fair hair, which gave him the name of Capino, which means blond, was spiky green in the sun. Lydia was at a loss. He seemed so dull and lifeless that she reached out to touch him to see if he was real.

Mary said, 'Mother says to help him.'

Lydia looked from the girl to the sad little boy, wondering how he could possibly have been dyed so thoroughly.

'What is it?' she asked.

'He's taken a paper,' Mary said.

'A paper of what?' asked Lydia.

'Will he die?' Mary answered simply.

The implications of the boy's colour crossed Lydia's mind for the first time. She wondered if it could be some generalised gangrene, but it clearly wasn't. There was no smell and the boy's skin was not a dark rotten colour; it was clearer, like bean leaves or the tendrils of a vine. El Capino was hauntingly strange, he was very definitely green, more green even than the bloated underbelly of a dead fish. His colour and listlessness were reptilian.

Mary was asking, 'Will he die?'

'Loosen the wheel,' Lydia ordered, and the girl ran away, relieved to have something to do.

'Will I die?' Capino whimpered, his green fingers clawing at her skirt. 'Will I die?' he pleaded, echoing his sister's words. She tried to reassure him and then left him standing in the yard while she beat together egg whites and water. She could hear the slow clanking of the wheel, and then the rumble as it gathered speed. Its empty rumbling, out of harvest time, was the signal for all and sundry to gather at the Big House. It was only ever used in emergencies. Its sound was loud enough to carry through all the lands of the hacienda. Its rush and thud began to ring through the valley, tolling alarm. She covered the child's head with a towel.

'Will I die?' he murmured.

'You'll be all right,' she said. 'Drink this, it will help you.'

His voice continued as monotonous as the mill wheel turning, 'Will I die? Will I die?'

Lydia realised that the boy could neither hear nor understand her any more. She left him standing. She could see him turning to the colour of weathered bronze, and he looked slightly absurd with the cloth on his head to shield him from the sun. She fetched Mary back.

'Make him drink this,' she said, handing her the glass of egg and water. Mary held the glass to his dry lips and tipped; it spilled slimy down his chin and chest, but he swallowed a little, shuddering.

High on the hill, Antonio had heard the wheel turn that day, and the idle clanking of the mill had frightened him. He knew from long experience that the thud and clatter of the massive wheel always announced bad news. It had called him down for over sixty years now. And that day it turned to spread the news of his son's disease. He had hoped for a miracle from the Doña, but none had come. Antonio thought that if a miracle would come to save this child of his old age, he would even believe in God. But then the mill wheel had turned, sounding her failure and its own alarm across the hills, summoning everyone to the Big House.

He saw people begin to stir and stop in their tracks. As the noise continued, he saw them heading for the Big House and the courtyard and his son. By the time he reached the gates, quite a crowd had gathered. They stopped him as he went in, quizzing him, but Antonio was in no mood to speak, and he brushed past them to the house itself.

Lydia said, 'I'm sorry, Antonio, but we'll have to take him into town . . . to the hospital.'

Antonio turned to fetch the lorry. The very word 'hospital' was like death itself to him. He backed the old lorry to as near the courtyard as he could get, while Mary and Lydia carried El Capino to him. The workers at the gates craned forward to see, starting back in disbelief. Lydia asked them to take care of the house in her absence, and thanked them for coming so promptly. As the lorry lurched on its way to town, the crowd behind them began to disperse. They seemed disappointed by the lack of action.

Lydia watched the fields of sugar cane stretching out on either side and rising into the thickly wooded hills. All the different greens seemed to glare forward that day, comparing themselves to El Capino's vivid skin. He was the colour of lettuce leaves and young banana palms, of marsh grass and ripe passion fruits. His cheekbones and knuckles seemed almost as dark as the cane itself and the convolvulus that grew around it. And his thin eyebrows were like dull lichen. El Capino himself didn't heed or even hear his sister's words, or bother that she fussed and buttoned him. Twice he sicked up the albuminous water transformed to pond weed by his poisoned stomach. The mess slid on the floor of the truck in a deep green mass.

Lydia half-sensed that there was something to hide. They were still five miles from the hospital. Antonio was driving, and his son was saying: 'Will I die will I die?' all rolled into one.

She knew that someone was going to ask, and it may as well be her, so she plucked up the courage and said, 'What has he taken,

Antonio?'

Antonio looked away and murmured, 'Copper sulphate.'

'What?'

'Copper sulphate,' he repeated.

'But that's rat poison,' she said. 'How did he come by it?'

'It was in the chemist's paper.'

'How much did he take?'

'All of it.'

Lydia was silent. She hardly dared ask how Capino could have swallowed such a quantity of poison.

'But the taste,' she argued. 'It's even disguised for rats.'

'He didn't like it,' Antonio faltered.

Capino's head had lolled against the glass, he was gripping his stomach as though disembowelled under his torn shirt, and he was whispering at the window: 'Will I die? Will I die?'

'When did he take it?' Lydia asked.

'Last night,' Antonio answered and his face was blank with grief.

'Why didn't you bring him to me before?'

'We were afraid,' he said simply.

Lydia brooded as the lorry jogged along. Capino repeated his sing-song to the glass. He was sick once more before he fainted.

'What will you say at the hospital, Doña?'

'What will you say, Antonio?'

'I'll say that it was an accident.'

'Then so will I,' she said.

The lorry pulled up outside the hospital. It looked like an open air concert. Row upon row of women and children sat in folding chairs surrounded by siege-like quantities of provisions. They only ever came in desperation and they had little hope of recovery. To them the hospital was a grim last resort. Nothing that happened there surprised them. It ate into their families, reducing their numbers with its neglect. At one time or another they had all heard the standard 'come back in three months'. It was like the ducking of witches. Those who lasted three months could usually last more, and those who died in the interim wouldn't need that later appointment. However, some cases always defied delay, and the green boy was one of them. Antonio gathered up his son and pushed his way past the trollied heaps of stab wounds, gun wounds and burns. Then he carried him on past the waiting queues and a murmur rose up behind him. A green boy had come down from the hills. A nurse came up to Capino, she took a look at him and asked a few questions. Then an orderly wheeled him away in the direction of the dressing room and the stomach pump. A trickle of brown blood was running down his leg.

Antonio and Lydia were left alone in the corridor. Lydia had never been in the hospital before and she didn't know what to do.

'He hasn't got a chance like this,' Antonio said. 'The only way to survive this place is to use your influence. Have all the wards paged, Doña, use your name. It will bring some good doctors to us. There have to be people with a special interest in a patient here, because if they don't die of neglect they just die of the general disorder. And the children's ward is the worst of the lot.'

Antonio had taken off his hat and he was fingering the brim, nervously. His eyes were slightly bleary from the residue of years of direct midday sun, and drink, and old age edging over them.

'Ramón,' he continued, 'who works in the mill, had a little boy in here last year, before you came. He was just a baby. They couldn't deal with his fever at home, so they had to bring him in. It was pneumonia. The doctors wouldn't let them stay, but Ramón came back early the next morning, and they told him he'd died of the fever. Well, he had in a way, you see, they'd put the baby on a great high bed and not bothered to draw up the side, so he rolled over with his fever and broke his head. Ramón said they hadn't even bothered to wipe away the blood from the floor; and all the bones were broken in his face.'

Lydia squeezed Antonio's sleeve and then stood up. At the desk she just gave her name and address, twice, to make sure it had sunk in. Within minutes the gloomy lobby seemed to come to life. One of the trolleys was wheeled off to the morgue, and a general air of activity bristled about the place. Notes were being taken about Capino's case. Soon Capino himself reappeared, greener than ever, swamped in a regulation gown. He had a drip rigged in to his arm, and a bag hanging from the edge of the trolley collecting his trickle of poisoned urine. He had come round, and was wheeled through the arch of expectant doctors as though through a guard of honour, and as he passed, he left a trail of questions like confetti.

'Will I die? Will I die? Will I die?'

Lydia recognised one or two of the men there, and entrusted the sick child to their care. Mary would be able to stay by his bedside while she and Antonio returned for the child's mother. The armed guard at the door was asking Antonio, 'Who bought the poison?'

'I did,' said Lydia firmly and followed this statement with such a hard look that the guard merely stood to attention and forebore to ask the other questions that he had in mind.

They rode the bumpy journey back together and neither of them spoke. They took the lorry along the dirt track of the plantation to the foot of the hill where Antonio lived, and then they left it to go on foot. Lydia felt herself come of age in the mile's distance that they climbed that day. Antonio spoke to her most of the way.

'We don't like doctors here,' he began. 'We don't trust them.'

They walked on a little, and then he continued: 'There's a witch doctor who lives over the hill, Doña, who has a way with ailments. I've known him all my life, and he has been a help to us many times. Some of his cures are famous hereabouts.'

'And is that where you took Capino?' Lydia asked.

'Yes, he'd been ailing all year. He's my favourite, you know, and it hurt me to see him pine. This witch doctor used to be a simple man like me. I had faith in him. There is little left to have faith in.'

Antonio strode ahead, jabbing the path bitterly with his woven shoes.

'But even he has changed now,' he continued. 'He has taken to writing down his remedies. He has grown too proud to speak his cures anymore.'

Lydia looked at Antonio's gaunt face. He was labouring to tell his tale. And she listened, following his words as best she could.

'So when he sent his medicine for Capino's stomach pains, he wrote it down on a scrap of paper.'

Lydia listened in silence. She knew that Antonio couldn't read, and she realised that he must have bought the poison himself and forced it down the child.

'Didn't they ask what it was for at the chemist's?' she asked.

'Yes,' he said, 'I told them it was for the hacienda, and they let me have it. They must have known,' he murmured. 'They must have thought it was for bait.'

Lydia felt for him as never before. There was nothing she could do or say to ease his pain, so she just let him talk on.

'You see,' he explained, 'you don't expect medicine to taste nice. When Capino wouldn't take it, we held him down, and I

148

made him drink it. Some of the powder was like little granules and I crushed them up for him.

'We thought he would stop crying soon, but when he cried all through the night we were afraid. The women said it was the evil eye, but I knew that it was the paper.

'From the day they built a box of old fruit crates to bury my mother in, denying her a proper coffin, I have known what shame is. But I never thought I'd live to see the day when I'd kill my own boy.'

They had reached the bend in the path that curled around the dead lemon tree in Antonio's yard. He finished what he was saying almost hurriedly.

'The witch doctor made a mistake, Doña. He's not used to fancy names. I don't know what he meant to write. . . .'

Lydia interrupted him. She was furious.

'I know what he meant to write,' she hissed. 'He meant to write Epsom Salts. But, like you said,' she added savagely, 'he's not used to fancy names, and he must have written copper for magnesium sulphate.' She paused. 'And now it's tearing through your Capino. What are to going to do about it, Antonio?'

Antonio sucked in his cheeks.

'I can see you think I should denounce him,' he said, 'but he's one of us, and he's the only help we've got. And this boy, Capino, was all I had, and now I must tell his mother to go and watch him die.'

Antonio stared down at the ground, and Lydia felt too sick to speak, so they both just steered their way through the milk tins of geraniums and the fallen pods of Antonio's yard.

Over the next five days they went to and fro, Antonio ageing daily, and Lydia doing everything within her power to save the child. And it was then that she realised for the first time the extent and the limitations of this power. The blood bank was filled up by radio appeals for El Capino's rhesus negative transfusions. He was given every medical aid available in the hospital, where ultra modern equipment and neglect bulged side by side. Each day new lengths were reached in treatment and diagnosis. Ambulances were brought and cancelled, a fully-equipped military plane stood by to move the child to Maracaibo, if necessary. Plasma was flown in in frozen containers. His old kidneys were linked to a kidney

149

machine, his heart and lungs to life support, and a transplant surgeon was hired to take the case on at the military hospital. But the little plastic bag that trailed by Capino's side defied all efforts. It slowly filled with a darker and darker blood, until a thick black paste was all that came. And the child's thin voice calling out to the host of staff that towered over his bed asked,

'Will I die? Will I die?'
and seemed almost to mock their sudden concern.

On the fifth day, he did die, and his bowels were removed as is the custom, and in respect of his patron, he was sewn up neatly and filled with straw, and not with newspaper as is the custom. And he lay at home in his father's hut for his wake. And the children from the neighbourhood sang over his still green face. And his eyes were propped open with thorns so that he might see his god when he entered heaven, because, they said, children were innocent. And there was no weeping either at the wake or the funeral. Even Antonio held back his tears, because, they all agreed, that children were well out of this life, and what hope could there ever be for a green boy?

SNAKES &
LOVERS

LUCY PINNEY

Lisa was sitting on the high stone wall separating the garden from the wood. She was picking grey lichen off the warm brick with a piece of fir-cone. Miniscule scarlet spiders swarmed in the sun. Above her a pine branch rocked to and fro in the breeze coming off the sea. Her parents had friends to stay; their son, Dan, was twelve like her, but over the last week he had avoided her company. From her vantage point she could see him coming round the back of the house with a plastic bucket in his hand and two old tennis rackets under his arm. As he passed beside her wall she called down to him.

'What are you doing?'

'I'm going hunting.' He looked up at her in an unfriendly way.

'What are you going to catch?'

He glanced round to make sure no parents were listening. 'Snakes.' Lisa leapt off the wall. Her ankles stung when she hit the ground, but that wasn't the highest she'd jumped. She spent a lot of time practising jumping from high places, and could now manage the top of the garage roof, although she felt sick afterwards.

'Where are these snakes?'

'They're in that marshy bit where the river flows into the sea.'

Beyond the wood was a neglected field, often flooded by spring tides. They walked singly down a path trampled out by grazing sheep. The tall vegetation made Lisa uneasy about insects dropping down the back of her neck, and her canvas shoes filled unpleasantly with mud. Dan walked ahead, obviously familiar with the route. They parted a clump of reeds and came out into a grassy, hillocky area, steaming in the strong afternoon sun.

'They sunbathe here,' said Dan, putting down the bucket and one of the rackets and creeping cautiously forward. Lisa peered around but saw nothing. In the distance she could hear the sea breathing in and out, and the jumbled shouting of bathers. She sat on a tussock and watched a flat triangular insect struggle over the blonde hairs on her arm. On the periphery of her vision she was aware of the pale blue blur of Dan's tee-shirt and his black hair as he crouched in the grass. The tennis racket thwacked down.

'I've got one! Quick, get the other racket!'

She leapt up and ran over to help him. A large snake was in mid-writhe in the grass, pressed firmly by the catgut mesh. Dan slipped the second racket under the first, enclosing the snake in a kind of flat oval cage. It flicked its tongue evilly. Lisa was enraptured by the glowing patterns on its back and the dull gleam of its skin. As Dan walked rapidly along she ran beside him, trying to look into the snake's eyes. He stopped by the bucket and tipped the snake in. Lisa tore off some coarse grass, cutting the side of her hand painfully on the spiky blades, and stuffed it into the bucket to protect the snake.

'How did you know how to catch it?' she said admiringly, looking up at Dan's impassive face, with its long eyelashes and strong cheekbones.

'I've been trying to catch one every afternoon, but I couldn't do it before. It's the first time I've tried tennis rackets. I started with a fishing-net, but they got away when I lifted it to pick them up.'

It was Sunday. As they walked with their catch past the drawing-room windows, bent over so their heads couldn't be seen, Lisa heard her father's voice, enriched by expense-account dinners, read something out from a newspaper and then convulse with merriment. There was the chunk of a coffee-cup against a saucer, and then the breathless voice of Dan's mother, Biddy. In her imagination Lisa could smell her perfume and see her glossy mouth. She had thick black curls and wore very new white canvas shoes which set off the deep tan of her legs. Lisa looked down at her own shoes, chosen to resemble Biddy's. They were encrusted with black slime and grass. There was no way she could copy Biddy's expensive freshness.

Dan stopped by the window of the downstairs lavatory.

'If we climb in here no one will see us.'

Lisa nodded. He put his hands on the windowsill and pulled himself up with practised ease. Lisa smiled to herself. She knew how proud he was of his muscley stomach. She'd even seen him through the half-open door, admiring it in his mother's dressing-table mirror. She passed up the bucket and rackets and then stuck out her hand. He had to take it and help her up, and she tried to make the contact last as long as possible, to memorise the feel of his warm, hard palm. They walked quietly up the stairs. Lisa heard her mother cough in her bedroom above. She used a cough as a bird uses a song: to inform others where she was, and establish her territorial rights.

'We'll have to go in your room,' Lisa whispered, 'or my mother will hear us.'

They closed the door and tipped the bucket out on the carpet. The snake lay inert for a moment and then lifted its head uneasily. Dan stretched full-length on his unmade bed and watched it. Lisa unthreaded a lace from her shoe and dangled it in front of the snake, teasing it as if it was a kitten. It stared at the plastic-coated tip of the lace and then struck in one alarmingly swift movement. Lisa leapt back.

'What kind is it?' she asked.

'It's either a grass-snake or a slow-worm.'

'It's pretty frightening when it strikes, isn't it?'

Her courage returned, Lisa dangled the lace again, but she still flinched when the snake struck.

'Leave it alone.' Dan rested his chin on the bed and studied the snake as it rippled across the floor and slipped under the wardrobe.

'Are you going to keep it?'

'No. I'll put it back in a minute.'

Lisa lay flat on the carpet and peered into the pool of darkness under the wardrobe.

'I can't see it. I don't know how you're going to get it out.'

She climbed on to the bed beside him and sat with her arms around her knees. She could see the ends of her hair on her shoulders. When she touched it it didn't feel like a part of herself; it felt coarse and strange, like a horse's tail or a wig. A piano started up downstairs. Jason, Dan's father, was practising for his next concert.

'Do you like staying here?' she asked. Dan was gazing at the foot of the wardrobe. Lisa wondered whether to put her hand out and touch him, but she was sure he didn't want her to, and it would be really hurtful if he pushed her away. He got up from the bed without replying and rummaged in his suitcase. He found a torch and snapped it on, then shone it under the wardrobe.

'It's gone!'

The wardrobe stood alone at one side of the room. It was hard to imagine where the snake could have escaped to. Lisa stood up on the bed.

'It must be there! Perhaps it's climbed up the sides.'

'I'll see if I can drive it out.' Dan picked up a coathanger and pushed it in sideways under the wardrobe.

'I can't feel anything.' He dropped the hanger abruptly. 'It bit me!' There was a red mark on his hand, where the thumb went into its socket.

'Does it hurt?'

'Yes. Like a wasp sting.' The flesh was swelling up round the bite.

'I thought grass-snakes didn't bite.'

'Well they obviously do.' Dan's voice was tearful and he held his wrist, trembling violently.

'You know what you're supposed to do,' said Lisa excitedly, 'I've read about it. You're supposed to suck the poison out.'

'You can suck it out if you want.' Dan stretched out his hand, the wrist puffy and red, and she lifted it to her mouth and sucked as vigorously as she could. She tasted salt, but no poison. It didn't work.

'It looks bad,' she said, examining the wrist. 'We'd better tell your parents.'

'We can't. They'll go mad if I tell them we took a snake into the bedroom.' Sweat was trickling down Dan's face.

'We don't have to tell them that. If we go back outside through the loo window we can say it happened in the garden.'

They crept downstairs to the lavatory. Lisa climbed out first, and helped Dan as he slipped awkwardly off the sill. She took his good hand confidently, and led him to the drawing-room window. She stood on tiptoe and looked in. There didn't seem to be anyone there. She hammered on the glass and shouted.

'Dad! Biddy! Dan's been bitten by a snake!'

Something moved in the depths of the room, and then the window banged open and Biddy, very pink in the face, stared out.

'What?'

'It's Dan. Look, he's been bitten on the wrist. It was a snake, down in the field by the river.'

'My God!' shrieked Biddy, and Lisa saw her father loom up like a shadow behind her. 'Dan's been bitten by a snake!'

'Did you see it?' Lisa's father was calm and serious.

'It was green, with a zigzag on its back.'

'An adder. It was an adder.' He turned to Biddy. 'You'd better take him to the hospital right away. I'll drive you if Jason won't.'

As Lisa helped Dan round to the car she heard the piano stop abruptly.

It was dark blue outside the kitchen window before the car

returned. A moth bounced backwards and forwards inside the big yellow lampshade. A bottle of wine stood open on the table. Lisa's father had his spectacles on and was reading. Her mother was rolling dough into sausages and then tying it into knots. In moments of anxiety she always baked. Her fine blonde hair was pinned up, and a streak of flour crossed her cheek. As she put each roll on the tray Lisa, sitting sideways on the table, brushed it with beaten egg and sprinkled it with poppy seeds.

'Do you think we should ring the hospital?' Lisa's mother turned to her husband.

'I'm sure it's all right. They'll be back soon. Don't worry.' His voice was weary and he didn't look up. His feet, in thick leather boots, rested on a corner of the table. Lisa's mother walked round him irritably and set the rolls to rise by the Aga. A car drew up outside.

'It's them! They're back!' Lisa ran to open the door. Dan looked pale and was pressing a bulky bandage to his wrist, but he smiled at her. His parents fussed over him, settling him in a chair.

'Is there some ice?' Biddy asked. 'The doctor said if we kept the bite cold the swelling would go down.'

'We've got lots.' Lisa's mother opened the fridge. 'What else did he say about Dan?'

'He gave him an anti-histamine injection; apparently there's not much else they can do for an adder-bite,' replied Jason, pouring himself a glass of wine. 'Luckily it's not at all serious at his age. It would be different if he was a toddler. It's the shock to the heart that can be fatal.'

Biddy turned to Lisa's father and her face became animated.

'The doctor had the most amazing thick German accent, like a really overplayed camp commandant in a Colditz film.'

While the adults talked Lisa and Dan glanced shyly at each other, Dan nursing his swollen arm and gently rocking himself. Biddy hugged him.

'You'd better have an early night tonight.'

Lisa shuddered at the thought of the snake waiting upstairs in Dan's bedroom. She looked anxiously across at him.

'Mum,' he said with diffidence, 'I know this sounds pathetic, but could I sleep in your room with you and Dad tonight? Please? I'm sure I'll have nightmares about the snake. I'd feel so much safer.'

Biddy stroked his face affectionately.

'You'd be a bit uncomfortable on the floor. Why don't you share the double bed with Jason and I'll sleep in your room?'

Dan opened his mouth and shut it again. Lisa bent over her ragout, the aroma mingling with Biddy's expensive perfume.

Lisa woke from a troubled dream to the sound of a car door slamming and footsteps on the gravel. The darkness was just starting to fade, but the dawn chorus hadn't yet begun. She heard the warning buoy strike its note out across the sea, and the curtains shift in the breeze. She sat up. Outside, in the corridor, her mother coughed, like the coo of a dove.

'Mum!'

The door opened.

'Go back to sleep,' came her mother's voice softly.

'What's all the noise outside?'

'There's nothing to worry about. Your father's just been to the hospital, but he's back now, and he's all right.'

'What happened?'

'He couldn't sleep. He went for a walk in the garden and an adder bit him.'

Fiction from John Murray

A Shadow in the Weave
MICHAEL HUMFREY

A compelling story of love, racial hatred, disinheritance and shattered ideals, set in the Caribbean in the first half of this century. The power and sensitivity of the writing creates and sustains the atmosphere of the West Indies and there is a magical quality to the descriptions of the islands and the sea. This is Michael Humfrey's second novel. His first, A Kind of Armour, *was described by* Books and Bookmen *as 'An outstanding first novel ... a remarkable combination of powerful writing, sensitivity and passion.'* £8.95

White Poppy
MARGARET GAAN

The second novel in this major Opium War trilogy, eminently bearing out the promise of its predecessor, Red Barbarian. £9.95

The Nathaniel Drinkwater novels
by Richard Woodman

'This author has quietly stolen the weather gauge from most of his rivals in the Hornblower stakes.' The Observer

Available in this series: **An Eye of the Fleet; A King's Cutter; A Brig of War; The Bomb Vessel; The Corvette; 1805.**

For full details of all our Fiction list please write to
50 Albemarle Street, London W1X 4BD.

FEET

Duncan Bush

It has been just a Saturday afternoon in September: 1 of the hectic, dragging 4 – sometimes, 5 – that each month bought.

Then that beautiful, youthful pair of feet – still brown as if from the athleticism of a summer holiday under the white, frayed hems of jeans, in ramshackle sandals of cheap leather (bought, presumably, from a seller of gewgaws on some probably Greek island) and white on the straps still with an efflorescence of the summer's salt – had come into the shop.

He went to her.

She spoke.

He listened. Went.

The girl sat down.

He reemerged with boxes.

He'd put the boxes down. And dropped upon 1 knee in order, finally, to remove the left sandal of the pair and fit on that cool naked foot a short succession of highheeled dancingshoes like those the girl had noticed in the window.

'This style's quite nice.'

She'd extended her leg and, putting her head on 1 side, considered the gold slingback on her foot – as he'd seen women extend an arm to appraise the varnish not yet dry upon their nails.

'Can I try the other on?'

Willingly he'd fitted, on the right foot in its turn, the 2nd shoe: just a stillettoheel, the curved slope of a sole, and narrow braided thongs across the toes and instep. Then relinquished the foot and stood with her, to watch the pair stride up and down the green and yellow carpeting, along the crowded row of chairs, the column ashtrays, and before the uptilted, anklelevel mirrors.

'Do they' – he'd asked almost tragically – 'fit comfortably?'

'Yes,' the girl had said. 'They're fine.'

They had both watched her feet – the instep arched now and thrown forward by the 4-inch heels, the tender little toes gripped at the open end – stroll on a few more steps, pivot, return.

The girl had disappointed him with her decisiveness.

'Yes,' she said. 'I'll take them.'

She'd sat down on the chair again and, lifting her right foot, then the left, onto the angled ramp of ribbed rubber, suffered him first to unbuckle at the topmost strap and then, almost too reverently, take off each shoe in turn.

These intimate personal services were, naturally, dissimulated into the oldfashioned but still permissible courtesies associated with his job. But when he had disclosed the 2nd naked foot and while he still retained it lightly in his palm for what he knew would be the final time, he'd been unable to resist the opportunity of surreptitiously fondling it and lightly fingering the wrinkles of its sole.

The girl had squealed with what might almost have been delight, and snatched the foot away.

'Forgive me,' he had said, knelt at her feet – or to them – and lifting his face to hers in polite remorse.

She giggled.

'It tickled,' she said, apologising – for the abruptness of the movement – in her turn.

They'd exchanged smiles, in a moment of awkward (but, he knew, incompatible) complicities.

And suddenly there'd been nothing more to do but climb to his feet and repack those gold shoes for her – side by side, and toe to end – among the tissuepaper in their box.

Then he'd led her to the salesdesk, where he sellotaped the lid at either end and slipped the box into a plastic carrierbag bearing the shop's name on its side.

He'd made out the receipt.

He'd checked her cheque and verified the number on her Visa card: and learnt – with a shock almost of anguish at the vista of her life that this quotidian information opened up for him – that her name was Rosemary M. Wilson and her bank was in the Fulham Road.

He'd handed here the chequecard back and given her the carrierbag.

Had smiled and said:

'Thank you. Goodbye.'

And then had watched those feet, now once more sandalled, leave the shop, pause on the mat before the automatic doors of glass, and pass out to the crowded pavement: walking, as so many pairs had done, out of his life for good, leaving him with no more than her name, a bank-address, the hand that risked the momentary caress.

And once again there had been nothing more to do but turn back to the shop, towards some other customer. And spend the last hours of that tedious, badgered Saturdayafternoon in futile,

nervous, halfdelighted speculation as to whether – if that bare foot
had not been torn so quickly from his cradling hand – he might not
finally have bowed his head still further in subjection to it; have
kissed that smooth, brown, sinewed instep as devoutly as the
faithful have been seen to kiss St Peter's toe of bronze; or even
taken full into his mouth that perfect, sapid hallux with its clean,
neat, tiny crescentnail that he could so easily, heartbreakingly,
imagine being painted with the chipped and flaking vestiges of
crimson . . .

It was probably fortunate, then, that the remainder of the
working day gave him little chance to indulge his thoughts in
wistfulnesses and regrets. In fact, he'd been almost grateful for the
continual, harrying distraction of the rush. And – as always in the
equivocally shameful and selfcongratulatory aftermath of his
indiscretions, his velleities – he had been even more attentive,
courteous and uncomplaining with his ordinary customers than
usual. For that, perhaps, was in the nature of his job and of his vice
itself: he redeemed his debt to those furtive pleasures he yearned
for, and occasionally stole, through the more penitential aspects of
politeness, service – almost, he might intermittently have thought,
of servitude.

He stood.

He stopped.

He knelt.

Humbly all afternoon he fitted footwear on the most unaphrodi-
siac of feet: the lumpy, stockinged feet of sadistically irresolute old
ladies with swollen ankles and veined legs; the feet of bored and
irritable children overseen by economical and watchful mothers;
the feet of men in rancid socks worn since the day before.

He ran, time after time, into the storeroom, climbed up to the
top rung of the mobile aluminium steps and found a halfsize in the
permanentlytoppling wall of stackedup label ends.

He gathered up, to patiently repack, the detritus of mingled
pairs and tissuepaper, lids and boxes, in the wake of customers who
tried a dozen styles or sizes on and, after half an hour, walked out
with nothing but the pair that had first brought them there.

He sold, with pleasure or commendation, pair after pair of the
cheap and provisionally fashionable platformsoles – a style as ugly
as, he always thought, surgical boots.

Pair after pair of models tricked out with a large gilt buckle or a cellular polythene heel.

Pair after pair of Adidas-imitation trainingshoes with coloured stripes of PVC down either side, made in the sweatshops of Taiwan.

All afternoon – he was, let it be said, a snob about such things – he hardly sold a single shoe of solid, fragrant English leather. He hardly sold a classic, handmade Oxford or a sturdy rural brogue.

He sold instead – as if only to confirm the epiphanic memory of that single pair of feet shod in the simple elegance of the expensive slingback shoes of tinselgold – all afternoon, till closingtime, a series of imported fashions: all, he thought, as meretricious and as badly made as fairground trinkets, and to individuals entirely lacking in what he would have considered charm of foot or taste.

He sold Cubanheeled cowboyboots to stunted youths.

Shoes with sharp points to women with cramped toes.

Sandals with manmade uppers to men who would in all probability, he knew, wear socks with them.

Only the once did he find himself looking jealousy across to where another of the assistants was attending a young woman trying on numerous pairs of all the cheaper styles – he thought of them, excitedly, as whorish – of highheeled boots: tall boots of supple glossy hide; in lavender and oxblood; beige and black and cream; once, even, in the style that had the straps and metal studs, as if for spurs.

He watched her draw them on and pull them off.

He saw her tug their zippers up and down, and felt his heart catch in the teeth.

He saw her wellshaped legs, ankles and toes, sheer in tan hose in which already he had dreamed the sordid charm of ladderings.

But, obscurely, he was by now relieved to do no more than furtively look on, sidelong, as this, while serving someone else. For a long time he had wondered if, 1 day, 1 of his ostensibly incidental caresses might not be immediately transparent to its victim, who would cause a scandal in a shop thronged with suddenly indignant witnesses. Sometimes he had even had ambiguous waking dreams of that humiliating moment of discovery.

And today he felt strangely impulsive, reckless almost . . .

His craving was not sated – what, after all, can sate abjection? – but the theft of that earlier intimacy, the touch of dry cool skin under the hand's subtlety, was enough at least to calm his vice: if

164

only by way of his delighted fear of having once again surrendered to his urge.

The fluorescentlighting was on inside the shop, as it had been all of that sunlit Saturday of confinement. It was too hot: the dead, unventilated heat of shopinteriors. All the assistants had grown dazed in that unremitting light, that enervating warmth. By 5, as on every Saturday, they no longer uttered a word to each other, and could only bring themselves back to the brink of politeness for a customer out of a kind of doggedness. They have grown desperate, were threadbare with indifference, with impatience for the time when everyone – then they themselves – were gone.

His socks were sticking to his insoles. The damp appendages he fitted brandnew shoes upon had had all day to sweat in theirs as they had hurried all over the city on the treadmill of the Saturday: the weekly shoppingspree, compulsive as migration.

Lateafternoon ran down to closingtime. The sun sank low above the buildings on the farside of the street: a dazzled edge of roofs that had not yet attained the clarity of silhouette. Its last rays slanted in among the stands and trees of footwear in the window, stretched a mournful orange light across the patterned carpeting.

He had a headache.

At 5.20, one of the assistants locked the plateglass door and waited by it, to release the few lastminute customers who still remained, seated to flex their feet in unfamiliar shoes or stamping up and down before the mirrors in the final throes of choice.

He sold a pair of imported tennisshoes to a young male in cracked, shabby and downatheel slipons – who, having threaded through and tied both laces, asked with uncouth assurance if he could simply leave behind, to be discarded in the bin, the shoes he'd taken off; who paid from few, soft, and crumpled 1-pound notes; then walked out of the shop in the astonishingly, insolently white pair he had just bought.

He dutifully collected odds and ends of string, cardboard and tissuepaper from the floor. There was now only a single customer left in the shop a bulky woman in a litter of wedgeheels sat in the corner of the room.

He stood and waited by the window, looking out. He felt suddenly sick – the familiar ennui of another vacuous, completed Saturday: a feeling of distantiation and disgust induced by exhaustion.

The pavements were full. The empty Saturday evening stretched out ahead of him: a view of roofs outside the window of his room, the radio, a darkening sky.

He stared out at the crowds caught in the fenzy of impending closingtime, the jostling fight for busqueues or a tube jammed to the doors – encumbered by their plastic carrierbags of purchases, burdened by whining and exhausted children. Soon it would be time for him to go out too – into the metropolis, into the swarming press and hurry and anxiety, compulsive and ubiquitous, of all those ceaseless, countless feet.

The Love Object

Gillian Tindall

When she went away from home for a few days to stay with her widowed sister in Richmond and do some shopping, Mrs Lacey always made a number of dishes beforehand and left them in the freezer for her husband. She also arranged for various neighbours, in the small village in Cambridgeshire where they lived, to invite him in for meals, sherry, coffee or bridge 'so that', as she explained, 'he won't feel too lonely.' Some of the neighbours regarded this as a touching and commendable expression of marital concern: others secretly thought it a little patronising, as if Mr Lacey had been a pet dog or cat, but they did not say so even to each other. The established fact in the village was that Mr and Mrs Lacey, in spite of the difference in age, were a devoted couple.

Actually the age-gap was not so very great, but since the trouble with ulcers that had caused his early retirement Mr Lacey did look rather gaunt and grey, whereas Mrs Lacey, according to popular concensus, 'did not look her age', which was in fact fifty-two. Particularly she did not look her age when she put away her gardening apron, had her hair done and her work-roughened hands manicured by Maison Francis in Grantchester, and dressed carefully for her expedition to London.

So, one April morning when the daffodils were making a fine show in the garden, Mrs Lacey kissed her husband affectionately and set off, wearing the becoming misty-blue tweed jacket she had acquired on her last little holiday away, in November, and had hardly worn since. She carried the very nice pigskin shoulder-bag that had been brought back from an earlier holiday, and a matching suitcase. It was, one might have thought, rather a large suitcase for a lady simply planning to stay in her sister's suburban house for a few nights, but, as Mr Lacey knew, his wife did like to shop, when she had the opportunity. She also, for the same reason, had quite a lot of money with her, though actually it was a larger sum than Mr Lacey guessed. Probably, as a 'mere male' (one of his ready, genial phrases) he did not know how expensive ladies' clothes could be, and perhaps Mrs Lacey did not like to tell him. They had a joint bank account – Mr Lacey had never really considered any other arrangement – but he had always been generous with the house-keeping and Mrs Lacey was a skilful manager: perhaps she had managed to save quite a bit out of the house-keeping, over the years.

She caught the bus to Cambridge and the train to London, and that evening she rang from her sister's house to say she had arrived safely. 'Lulu sends her love', she said, and Mr Lacey replied, 'Please give her mine' with the usual touch of irony that was in his voice whenever his sister-in-law was mentioned. Poor Lulu, it was tacitly agreed between the Laceys, was rather a mess. Her husband had been a well-to-do businessman, and, unlike the Laceys, the couple had been fortunate enough to have two children – two strapping daughters. But one was now in Aberdeen and the other in Arizona, and poor Lulu, widowed in her forties, seemed to have become disheartened about life. That was partly, as Mr Lacey explained to friends and neighbours, why Boo – Mrs Lacey – went every few months to visit her. Boo Lacey's gaiety and decisiveness were good for Lulu. Privately he thought harder things about his sister-in-law – that she was a born muddler, and spineless, and would have made a poor hand of whatever life she had. She was, he thought, just the sort of rich, empty-headed widow who gets exploited by some bounder, or worse, and is found one day in a cupboard with her throat cut . . . There was no doubt about it (such tough, philosophical reflections had become more habitual to him since his illness) life was what you made of it. Why, look at what a good, satisfying life he and Boo had managed to make all these years, in spite of that long ago disappointment about a family, and then that business of him being passed over for promotion, and, more recently, his ill-health and enforced retirement.

Early the following evening Mr Lacey was sipping a small sherry in his neighbour's house and desultorily watching television. They had switched it on only after the news had started, but there seemed to have been another of those awful plane crashes. In France. Mr Lacey had heard some rumour of this during the afternoon, when he had turned his wireless on to get the three o'clock time signal, but he had not listened further because he made a point of not having wireless or television on during the day. It was, he believed, important when one was retired to keep oneself up to the mark, to establish a regular routine of chores and stick to it. That day, he had hoed the vegetable garden (his wife's province was the flower garden), changed his library book at the travelling van, and done the accounts for the Parish Council of which he was Treasurer. Tomorrow he was planning to hoover the whole house, go into Grantchester in the afternoon to pick up some fertiliser he had ordered, and perhaps have tea in that nice shop near the church . . .

. . . The shots of the aircraft wreckage, when they came on again at the end of the news, really were awful: colour television had a lot to answer for. The plane had apparently crashed in a field just as it was coming in to land at Charles de Gaulle airport: no one yet knew why. In the alien French sunlight on the small screen, wreckage, seats, bits of luggage and other bits of what one could only suppose disgustedly must be bodies, were scattered far and wide. Dust seemed to hang over everything, mercifully obscuring the worst, but Mr Lacey noticed a dead cow. Really! Alien French officials stood about in flat-topped hats and cloaks, like Ruritanian toys; after a moment one of them seemed to be shooing the camera-team away with exaggerated, theatrical gestures.

'Shouldn't have let them on the scene in the first place', muttered Mr Lacey. 'Wouldn't happen in this country.'

'Typical', agreed his neighbour – though he, like Mr Lacey, had rarely been abroad, and then only to Majorca or Malta.

A policeman tapped on the french windows.

But this one was not a French policeman. He was in fact the village constable, in uniform, but without his helmet, and well-known to both Mr Lacey and his hosts. He apologised heavily for coming round by the garden path: he had stood at the front door for a while, but as the bell didn't seem to be working and he could hear the television on . . . the three in the living room could all tell that the young man was upset about something.

'What is it, officer?' said the neighbour testily. His wife's hand was at her throat, fingering her pearls and his own stomach was suddenly uneasy, recalling their son who was in the Navy, even as he told himself it was probably just about the cricket pitch or the right-of-way or Mr Wagstaff's Alsatian.

But it was not the hosts the constable wanted but Mr Lacey, whom he had guessed might be there, and it was not on Parish Council business either. It was to tell Mr Lacey the station had just received a call from Area HQ, and that Area HQ had had notification from British Airways that Mrs Barbara Lacey, address supplied, had been listed among the passengers on the plane that, at that moment, was in many pieces in the field near Charles de Gaulle airport, France.

'What nonsense!' said Mr Lacey, with absolute conviction.

He went on to explain that he and his wife had a joint passport, and that he had happened to notice it this afternoon in its usual place in the third pigeonhole from the left, when he was working at his desk at the Parish Accounts. 'So naturally there must be some mistake, eh constable? Tell you what, I'll fetch it now to prove to you.' And he set off out of the french windows.

But a mind, even a well-controlled one like Mr Lacey's, can move through a great arc of thought in a few minutes. And Mr Lacey had not even reached his own house, and his own desk, before his racing mind had reached the fact that his gesture was quite futile. You did not need a full passport to visit France, an EEC one from the post office would do. And, while it still seemed utterly incredible, if – if – if Boo had actually deceived him to the point of letting him think she was in Richmond with Lulu when she was in fact on a plane to Paris – then the mere obtaining of a travel document without his knowledge would have been nothing. *Nothing*, his careering, incredulous mind told him, as it vainly tried to scale further heights, or depths, of possibility, as hitherto inconceivable ideas presented themselves to him.

When he returned to the others, more slowly and empty-handed, it was evident that they had been thinking rapidly also. His neighbour was doing inconclusive things with a decanter of brandy, the wife was talking about strong, sweet tea being better for shock, and the constable had got out his note-book and was preparing himself to ask Mr Lacey some questions in a special, tactful voice.

So Mr Lacey had spoken to his wife in London only the night before? But had she said nothing about her plans? Was it just possible that the two sisters had decided to take a little jaunt together without telling anyone, as women sometimes do?

'Is *her* name on the passenger list too?' asked Mr Lacey grimly. Of course the Constable did not know. A thought passed through Mr Lacey's mind that this ghastly muddle was much more like Lulu than it was Boo. He would not be a bit surprised if that damn fool Lulu had set off on some hare-brained trip without telling anyone and had come to grief because of it. Could Lulu indeed possibly have been *posing* as Boo, and that was why Boo's name was on the list . . .? His head seemed to be spinning.

At this point it became apparent to all those present that a call had to be put through to Richmond and there was no point in delay. The Constable dialled the number at Mr Lacey's tight-lipped direction, got through, and handed the receiver to him:

'Your sister-in-law's on the line, Mr Lacey'.

Lulu was in a terrible state. This, to be sure, was not infrequent with her, but now Mr Lacey realised, with fresh horror, that it was warranted.

She too had seen the television news. She had no idea whether or not Boo had been on that actual plane – but she confirmed that, towards the end of the morning, Boo had indeed kissed her goodbye and set off in her becoming blue jacket, with her suitcase, for Heathrow. Her destination had been Paris, and she had been fussed because she was a little late. She had been doing her nails, time had run on, and then they heard there was a go-slow on the tube . . .

'But why, in God's name?' Mr Lacey interrupted savagely. '*Why?*'

'She always does – did – that.' Lulu was weeping copiously.

'You mean she stayed only one night with you and then – went off.'

'Yes. Oh yes. Nearly always.'

'But – why?'

But so rapidly can all previous assumptions be overturned once a key one crashes and disintegrates, that already Mr Lacey thought he could guess the answer. When Lulu began to sob out a long, semi-coherent story about Boo having someone she met in Paris, Mr Lacey listened with the weary, bitter resignation of a man who had long known it – even one who had always known.

But suddenly Lulu stopped, with a muffled exclamation. Momentarily, she seemed to leave the phone. 'Lulu?' said Mr Lacey sharply. Then: '*Lulu!*' he bellowed with rage down the empty receiver.

'I'm back – it's alright! *She's* back. It's all OK, John – all a mistake. Oh, don't listen to a word I said. It's all nonsense –'

'What the hell do you mean now?'

'I mean she's just walked in the door.'

By late that night John Lacey had decided that his situation was intolerable. On the face of it, all was much as it had ever been. His wife was not dead in a field in France, but alive in Richmond. She had come on the line to him and she was alright. And yes, she would be in Richmond for the rest of the week. No, she was not coming straight home again. What an extraordinary idea. Why should she?

Then Lulu, in tears still, God rot her, had come on the line again and reiterated that it had all been a silly misunderstanding – that she'd made a muddle as usual, that everything was perfectly alright, that she was dreadfully sorry to have been so silly, that John must please stop worrying.

Everything was perfectly alright.

But nothing was as it had been that morning, and he felt it never would be again. His wife of twenty-seven years, his Boo who shared his bed and grew him roses and had been sorry for him when he had not been promoted to head office, and had left him six suppers in the freezer – his wife had a lover in Paris. Had had for ages, apparently. Probably for years. That idiot Lulu had told him so, in so many words – and was now even more idiotically imagining she could unsay it. It could never be unsaid.

How she must have been laughing at him all these years . . . Probably, he told himself masochistically, she and Lulu had laughed about it together. Poor John, such a fool . . .

He ground his teeth as if in physical pain. What a fool indeed he had been.

And was he now supposed to sit docilely in Cambridgeshire till the end of the week, eating his suppers, fertilising his beans, an object of covert pity and surmise to the neighbours, waiting obediently for further explanations till she chose to come home on her appointed day? . . . And what, in God's name, would she now *do* in London for five days. Go shopping, as she had originally said? Oh, ha, ha. Make another attempt to get to Paris successfully? . . . Call her lover to her in London . . . His thoughts raced.

After a near sleepless night, he did something entirely untypical of him. He made no more phone calls, but he shut the house up, got into the car and drove to Cambridge. There, he caught the same train to London that Boo had taken two days earlier.

The air smelt stale and used up, and it seemed to take him a long time to make his way to Richmond. He had rarely visited Lulu's house himself in recent years. He found her there alone, as his imagination had morbidly predicted. Boo, she said, had gone to the West End to shop. Oh yes? She brought him a cup of coffee, in her lounge where the carpet was too deep and purple and the cushions and photographs were seldom, these days, disturbed.

THE LOVE OBJECT

At first she hesitated and prevaricated, telling little, flustered stories about having stupidly misunderstood something Boo had said, but he soon put a stop to that. Soft – she had always been soft, this failed female, this has-been comforting herself with chocolates, light romances, living disgustingly on the dregs of other people's dramas . . . Discovering in himself a toughness he had hardly known he possessed, he soon ground her, metaphorically, into her own purple fitted carpet. She was not a pretty sight. Crying again, she presently told him the whole story.

Two years earlier, on one of her visits, Boo had suddenly announced she was off to Paris for the middle of the week, had left, and had returned serene and smiling. She had asked Lulu not to tell John about her absence; Lulu, had of course complied. Then, on every subsequent visit, the same pattern had been repeated.

The becoming clothes she had brought back to Cambridgeshire had mostly not been bought in London at all, but in Paris. That lovely blue tweed, for instance. John, said Lulu, crying harder, had probably not noticed, but Boo had cut the labels out before taking them home. She was always so careful . . .

'Not careful enough', said John Lacey bitterly. He was reduced, now, to the low point of feeling that, yes, everything would have been alright forever if only he had not known.

Oh, she was careful, Lulu insisted, she really was. For instance, she had always left the name of the hotel she would be at in Paris. In case anything should happen to John . . . With cold politeness John Lacey requested the name.

It was – let's see, now: it was the Hotel Moderne, Place de la Sorbonne. Even as Lulu's foolish pink mouth uttered it, John could tell how deeply romantic she had thought the whole thing was.

As he had now got what he came for, he turned to go. Almost as an afterthought, he said:

'I suppose you don't know the name of the man involved?'

Lulu shook her head mournfully. Boo had never mentioned it, and she had never quite liked to ask. Of course she had perfectly understood there was someone. But there had never been any details. Boo had always been very reticent in that way, even when they had been girls together . . .

As John Lacey left the over-heated, still house, resisting Lulu's almost panic-stricken entreaty that he at least stay for lunch, he

vaguely perceived that poor Lulu had been so impressed and
star-struck by the whole business that his own position in it had
been something quite beyond her calculations. She deserved to be a
widow, he thought with deliberate ruthlessness, She really did.

He took the Underground to Heathrow. It was surprisingly
easy. Then he, who never in his life had travelled anywhere
without making reservations months in advance, without insurance and hotel vouchers and the blessing of some reassuring,
intermediary travel agent – he, John Lacey, went to the British
Airways desk, took out his chequebook and bought himself a ticket
on the next flight to Paris. There seemed to be plenty of seats and
that surprised him faintly, accustomed as he was only to
package-travel. Once in the air, it occurred to him that it was
probably this very flight, twenty-four hours earlier, that had
crashed, and that maybe this had put off prospective travellers. But
the thought caused no tremor of personal anxiety in him, for being
beyond hope he was beyond anxiety also.

Not hungry, he refused lunch, with a lingering abstract regret
for its ingenious, plastic-wrapped dishes, but drank a whisky and
soda.

From the futuristic confines of Charles de Gaulle airport, no
wreckage was visible. He was directed to a coach, which took him
on motorways till the green fields changed into a townscape of
international high-rise blocks and incessant traffic, and then into
one of those foreign looking boulevards with unwelcoming grey
buildings. At the terminal, exhaustion suddenly descended on
him: he forced himself to a money-changing desk, then down into a
Metro Station and into a struggle with maps and turnstiles,
unfamiliar trains and unfamiliar signs. To his consternation, there
was no station called 'Sorbonne', but a fellow map-studier to whom
he appealed in desperation silently pointed to the name 'Cluny'.

Once there, and up in the street, vague memory returned to
him. Not for this quarter as such – he did not think he had ever
been there in his life – but a generalised, boiled-down memory for
Paris, a concentrate of paved streets, cafés, plane trees, as if all
Paris were the same half-acre, endlessly replicated. He had been
only once before in this city, nearly twenty years ago, on an
away-from-it-all week when he had been getting over shingles. He
and Boo . . .

But of course (his mind somersaulted again) all this must be familiar to her now, known and loved . . . Up this animated boulevard, thronged with students, she must have walked often, noting shops in whose windows she liked to look, singling out *her* (or *their?*) favourite cafés and restaurants. Across this square — for he had found Place de la Sorbonne, now — she must have hurried uncounted times, sometimes alone, sometimes arm in arm or hand in hand, running laughing through the sunshine, or the November chill, or (as now) through the beginnings of a spring shower, running towards that tall hotel with its name across the façade that he could already see ahead, running towards a narrow hallway, a flight of winding French stairs, a room, a bed, love . . .

Love. Was love for him, for John Lacey, now over forever as an experience? It seemed impossible to believe. Yet of course it must be so. Of course. Weighted with sadness, he walked resolutely to the hotel and into its narrow hall.

Naturally the elderly women at the desk with the keys spoke no English. But she summoned a young man – son, night porter, passing guest? – who did. Clearly, thought John Lacey grimly, his luck was in. If 'luck' was the word.

Even as an enquiry for a Mrs Lacey had left his lips, he realised its futility. Of course. Boo would have registered under the name of the man, that man, the man in the case . . . He should simply have referred to 'an English lady' and then described her. But already the young man, having exchanged remarks with the lady, was replying: yes, Meesees Lacee was known to them. She was a regular client. They had indeed expected her yesterday, but she had telephoned from England to say she would not be coming after all. They thought, perhaps, the air crash had discouraged her . . . Such tragedies were bad for the hotel trade: Monsieur would understand.

John Lacey acknowledged the tiny, poor taste joke with a twitch of his lips.

And the gentleman?

He waited, breath drawn in, for all to be confirmed.

But, after another exchange, the young man turned back to him in apparently genuine puzzlement. Gentleman? There had been no gentleman, that they could recall. Meesees Lacee always came alone. She took a single room without a bathroom, the cheapest room in the hotel in fact, and used to book it a long time in advance to be sure of having it.

'Then perhaps', he said, after a pause and in great pain, 'she was out a lot?'

When this was retailed to the lady it produced quite a long response. At last the boy turned back to John Lacey and translated:

'On the contrary, my aunt says, Meesees Lacee only went out in the days, never in the evenings. She says – and I remember this myself – that Meesees Lacee does not like to be out late on her own. For her evening meal she has brought in cheese and fruit and a *yaourt* and a bottle of Perrier . . . We do not normally encourage the bringing of food to rooms, because it causes problems you understand, but we have tolerated it with Meesees Lacee because she is a very nice lady.'

A further long remark in French intervened. Finally the young man turned back again to John:

'My aunt says that she has always felt a little sad for Meesees Lacee because she is alone. She likes to go shopping, and when she comes back to the hotel she shows my aunt what clothes she has bought. From Galleries Lafayette and Printemps and such big stores. She seems such a friendly lady, but without a companion. She never received any calls . . . We do not want to be indiscreet, Monsieur, but who are you? What is your business with Meesees Lacee?'

John Lacey flew out of Charles de Gaulle on the last plane of the evening for London. Paris and its hinterland – motorways, boulevards, Metro, streets, Metro, boulevards, motorways – danced behind his tired eyes.

'*She was alone . . . Such a friendly lady, but without a companion . . . She never received any calls . . .*'

At Heathrow he took the Underground direct to Kings Cross and just caught the last train back to Cambridge. He should, he reckoned, be home in bed soon after one-thirty a.m. It had been the longest day of his life.

He could, of course, have broken his journey at Richmond and spent the night there, with Boo, in Lulu's ornate spare room. But he felt too exhausted and confused to see Boo yet. Tomorrow . . . tomorrow he would ring her and have a long chat . . . Tomorrow he might be his old self again.

As he put his car in the garage just after one a.m. startling the cans and ladders and old paint pots in the headlights with the unaccustomed lateness of the hour, it occurred to him that, as he had driven in, the house had not looked entirely dark. He had seen the scullery light which they normally left on, on the rare occasions when they went out in the evenings, to discourage burglars. Could he have providentially left it on himself since early that morning? But he knew he had not.

With a mixture of apprehension and incredulous hope, he let himself in and climbed the stairs.

In their bed, as he had hoped and dreaded, lay Boo. The light was off, but as soon as he came in she sat up and switched on the bedside lamp. She looked dishevelled. Was she angry? He was not sure.

'Where on earth *were* you? I was worried . . . Were you at the Hodgsons or the Millers? . . . No, you can't have been: John, it's after *one*.

He almost answered, in the same tone of domestic realism, 'No, no – in Paris, actually', but could not bring himself to do so. Never, never should she know he had tracked her in this way.

'I – I was in London. I got the late train back . . . I expect Lulu told you I'd called.'

'Yes, she did. That's why I came home.

'You said you were going to stay in London for the rest of the week', he said, in the tone of restrained reproach suitable to a wife who had merely been too busy with her committees lately to keep the house tidy; and in the same reluctantly apologetic tone she answered:

'Yes, I know I did. But when I heard you'd come to Richmond I thought you must be worried and would like me home . . . Anyway, I wasn't enjoying myself.'

'*Not enjoying myself . . .*'

'*My aunt says she has always felt a little sad for Mrs Lacey because she is alone . . .*'

He went to the bathroom, came back, got into his pyjamas.

'Did you turn off the scullery light?' she asked, and he said, 'Oh no, I quite forgot', and went downstairs to do so.

When he came back their bedroom too was in darkness. He hesitated another moment, to see if she would speak – then got into bed beside her.

At last, in the silence, he said:

'Boo. Why? *Why*?'

'Oh – You *know* how I've always loved good clothes', she said irritably. 'I know it's a weakness, and vain, and pointless anyway when you don't notice and everyone round here lives in sheepskins and wellies – but I have something in my life, John. I have to have *something*.' Then she began to cry.

'But why – why?' he repeated inadequately. He wanted to say: why go about your weakness in such an extraordinary, secretive way? Why behave so rashly and extravagantly and run such a terrible risk of upsetting me and our whole marriage.

Instead he at last said:

'But why on earth did you tell that story to Lulu? She was imagining you were getting up to – God knows what, in Paris. Stupid cow.'

'I didn't – I didn't, John. Not really. She jumped to the conclusion herself – that I had someone there. Oh, I admit I didn't contradict her, I let her think it . . . Oh I *know* that was wrong of me, but, as you say, she is stupid and it was such a temptation, it really was . . . I'm sorry, I really am.'

She cried some more. A little later she said again, contritely: 'I know it was rather selfish of me. I mean – poor Lulu, she doesn't have much in her life, these days. I know I didn't have to show off to her in that way. But – she was so keen on believing it, you see. And I've never even had a child, let alone a lover, and years ago when she had Amanda and Jennifer and we didn't have one, she used to be so *smug* . . . Oh John, I know I've caused trouble. But you've no idea how awful it can be to have a sister, you've really no idea.'

And that was the last thing she ever said on the subject.

Neither of them referred to her very near miss with death. That, at any rate, could not be considered her fault, he supposed. Or perhaps it was just too serious a subject to mention at all.

Sometimes, in the uncomfortably ample spaces of time that were his in his retirement, John Lacey speculated further on the whole business. Was it herself Boo had been in love with, when she had made those clandestine journeys whose only purpose was self-adornment? Women, he had heard, were like that. But what she had said did not seem quite to fit with that and it bothered him. '*I've never even had a child, let alone a lover* . . .' His confident, pretty, self-possessed Boo, whom everyone liked, how could she be racked by such thoughts? It didn't, to him, make sense.

Once or twice the phrase 'a wasted life' visited his stiff

imagination like a cold hand laid upon him, like a death of another sort, but he shrugged it off. Morbid rubbish. Anyway Boo seemed quite cheerful again now, and was even talking of their *both* going to London to stay with Lulu in the autumn.

Gradually, the trauma they had each suffered faded, if not entirely, from his mind. At any rate they never referred to it again.

IMAGINARY MEADOWS

Aidan Higgins

I was born on March 3rd, 1927, in the old Barony of Salt in the County Kildare in the Province of Leinster, of Catholic parents since deceased, under the watery astrological sign of Pisces. It was the year that Michael MacLiammóir met the compelling stranger, beak-nosed Hilton Edwards on the steps of the Atheneum in Enniscorthy. English archaeologists were making discoveries in Egypt, and Babylonian boundary stones being examined.

A fresh westerly airstream no doubt covered most areas, while a frontal trough of low pressure remained stationary over Ireland, but seemed about ready to move eastward.

Conceived at the tail-end of an early June day, in the year of grace 1926, I was expelled on the following March 3rd, passing into 1927, puffing and choking with mouth half open, the cold being so intense, wellnigh irresistible the compulsion to sink back into the warmer uterine depths with a bubbling groan. Hearing faraway music, moody themes for the good-times-gone. Albinoni's now famous Adagio or a Debussy Arabesque played on the harp. Not yet the wild nocturnal bagpipe music and the wind tipping the scales of the weighing-machine on the bedroom windowsill of a bungalow in Emor Street in the so-called Liberties, just off the South Circular Road in the city of Dublin.

This would be in the '70s when I found myself the ill-dressed recipient of a cheque for $7,000 from the American Irish Foundation – Kennedy bad conscience money – paid out on sole condition that I live for ten months in my erstwhile homeland, which I had not been in a position to do since leaving it twenty five years before. (My father was still knocking them back, delighted to be a father for the third time, his penultimate paternity).

I had just turned fifty.

A group of young lady harpists from New York of surpassing comeliness all, were entertaining the American Ambassador Mr Shannon and his wife and their selected guests at the Vice Regal Lodge in the Phoenix Park. A herd of grazing deer were visible through the elegant long windows as Ambassador Shannon, bald as a coot though a decade younger than your humble, handed over a sealed envelope. Held in close-up for Irish television viewers to admire, it was seen to be clearly addressed to Seamus Heaney, the previous year's winner.

March 3rd in Basho's day was the Festival of the Dolls in 16th

183

century Japan: *hina matsuri*, sometimes called the Festival of Pearl Blossoms. Or simply Girls' Festival, which would suit me fine, backing into the strange withdrawn world of the fish. The Piscean twilight world of the deep fish lost, or just gone astray in the head. Is this why the light still enchants me; the hidden observer remaining a prey to the most giddy kind of guilt? But now, classic-lovers, it's once again diddley diddley time.

All this by way of preamble. Nothing is too clear, of its nature, least of all the limpidities of language. 'The particles of which must be *clear as sand*': I refer you to Diddling. The strange phosphorus of the life, nameless under the misappelation.

I tell you a thing. I could tell it otherwise. A few pictures emerge into the light from the shadows within me. I consider them. Quite often they fail to please me. I call them pictures but you, kind readers, ideal readers suffering from an ideal insomnia, must know otherwise. What I mean to convey is: movements from the past. So, putting as bold a face as I could on it under the circumstances, out I crawled yelling blue bloody murder, mishandled by wet nurses.

Fifty was Basho's age when ill with failing health he began that long last marathon hike in South Japan in 1694. He was six years junior to Jane Bowles – if you'd kindly be good enough to move on nearly three centuries – when she died in hospital in Malaga, capital of sorrow. In a snail-bar near the brothel quarter the shabby ghost of Terry Butler, never so shabby in life, failed to recognise me, darkened by tramping in the Sierra Almijara. Peter Handke's mother was fifty-one when she killed herself in a village in Austria.

Why, there are days when we do not know ourselves, when we do not properly belong to ourselves, as the children know. Assailed by mysterious sundowns and gory red endings of days: the extraordinary clarity of the nocturnal firmament burning above the little pier on Anaghvaughan. Then out went the candle and we were left darkling. Breathe in, breathe out. In the memory of old men it's always June. Were the summers of my childhood as sunny as I seem to recall?

The city certainly had changed. The Grafton Cinema was closed, the ghosts in the toilet departed, the Commissionaire Mr Shakespear dead. It was still raining in Auggier Street on the office of Fanagan the undertaker, the busiest man in Dublin. The estate walls are ridged with glass, the great houses abandoned. Our maid

Lizzy Bolger gave me a Christmas present of a small hinged monkey that when wound up could perform tricks on a swing. He had a red cap and a mad look. This would be in the early 1930s. Lizzy Bolger's smeared red lips alarmed me greatly, more than the sea at Ringsend, as did her overpowering scent, sweat vying against face powder, stronger than civet cat. She had a heart of gold. My mother said: 'Lizzy has a heart of gold.'

The late arrivers wore deerstalker hats. The large men brayed, young wives whinnied, whips were brandished; and off they went. Life was a giddy whirl. My own parents tended to look down on the natives whom they found amusing enough in their ways; as long as they kept themselves to themselves, knew their places. They relished saying in approbation: 'He (or she) knows his (her) place.' Meaning God-given lifelong dependency before the kitchen range, or in the cow-byre, the pig-stye, the butchering yard. My mother was a snob.

My progenitor was a puzzle to himself: a hedonist who took little pleasure in life, a walking (or preferably lying in a summer orchard) contradiction in terms. He was averse to abstract thought. His life was one long struggle against boredom; always defeated by small details. Or else: his life went by in a shot. One day it was over, used up. He suffered from boredom, although he didn't know it, would never admit it. He put in time.

Did not believe in guilt, refused to think of it, tried to cover it up. It didn't exist, although I was often accused of it. 'Look, he's got the guilty look!' I felt myself to be permanently guilty of something or other, and suffered agonies before Confession, the ordeal-by-questioning in the dark. With priests I lost my nerve, became cowed, invisible.

His recourse was to affability, the purest bravado. He shrank as he aged. Finally he became pathetic. He was neither rowdy nor calm but something in between, fidgety, uxorious, a scuffler of gravel, drinker of tea, starer out of windows, gossip. He was the only son in a family of fifteen sisters, which may have explained his furtiveness. His toilet was extravagant; he took hours preparing for town, a Pasha. My three brothers and I, well spaced out walkers, none on speaking terms, arrived at Hazelhatch station, a good two mile walk, with two hours to spare. My father liked to pace up and down the depature platform with the Station Master, a grizzled man with a long lugubrious horse-face who sucked Zubes. My father's intent was to impress him, stopping every now and then to make some telling point, a telling finger on his braced chest. My brothers watched in sullen silence.

The First Class carriage smelt of Edwardian drawing room, or airless hall with antlers. Framed sepia photographs like aquatints were set above the plushy seats, showing joyless seabathers or gentlemen in baggy plus-fours on windy golf links. Parknasilla and Lahinch were the places to go to. An advertisement for Fury's coach tours of Ireland ('in luxrious 20-35 seater Coaches') had it, 'WE LEAD, OTHERS MAY FOLLOW', with decent restraint.

He owned land but it meant nothing to him. He liked to walk in the fields, whistling. His secret enemies broke in hedges, grazed their cattle on his land at night, lifted things. He went in for sunbathing, horse-riding, golfing, in high summer turned rhubarb-red. It was only another way of passing the time. He read five newspapers a day, seven on Sundays, and was the most ill-informed man you could meet on a day's march. My mother studied the obituary notices.

For him, her husband, my father, the hardest thing was to believe in his own existence. He led a phantom life – a foiled poet. He frittered money away, it did not interest him either, he had never worked a day in his life. When it was gone he lived on credit, until one day he had no credit left. He had woken my mother in the night to confess, 'Lil, it's all gone'. In summer he made himself scarce in the long grass of the orchard, braced himself for the Irish sun, covered like a wrestler in cod-liver oil. We, his four sons up in trees or perched on walls, were instructed to say he was 'sick', or 'out', or (as last extremity) 'gone away'. The most trusted formula was 'not in today'. Perhaps he was the reincarnation of a fox? He avoided physical work, invented a stubborn ailment ('the old appendix is at me again'), the longer winters 'took it out of him'. What they could not take out of him was laziness, nothing could remove that. He wanted to be left alone; in him were elements of grasshopper and rook, the rare bird that plays with the air. He was my Da. Batty was the name he was widely known by. He knew everybody.

I have inherited some of his idle day-dreaming nature. Disbelief in one's given life is a common Irish failing, if it be one. You can observe it in the streets of Dublin – incredulous recognition on all sides, some of a theatricality which must be suspect, such as grasping an apparently long-lost friend by the shoulder and loudly expressing disbelief in his corporal existence, his smiling presence, while pumping his hand up and down. 'Is it yourself that's in it?' Odd, you will say, but so frequent an occurrence as to be an undoubted characteristic of the place. Watch yourself any day in the purlieus of the Long Hall in South Great George's Street, or around Stephen's Green.

Who am I? Am I or am I not the same person I have always taken myself to be? In that case, who are you? Is your silence significant or just lack of something to say? Is that significant? Speak up, but kindly confine yourself to the essentials; write on one side of the paper only.

Meanwhile, up in his fine new residence in Rathfarnham, Senator Yeats, impaled upon a fine idea, was just looking at his yellow canaries and saw symbols streaming. He wrote in his fine calligraphy: 'I am a crowd. I am a lonely man. I am nothing.' And all the canaries started singing. He did not name his enemies when corresponding with fine ladies, English and Irish, but designated them thus:

The Tower.
The Wolf Dog.
The Harp.
The Shamrock

and rather finely, 'verdis-green sectaries.'

He was his father's son and no two ways about it. His correspondence with his father is nothing less than heart-warming, not something you expect in such close blood connections. Joyce was still abed, writing The Wake in sinful Paris, or it was writing him. Mr Beckett was abed with what's her name and had just written: 'The sun, having no alternative, shone on the nothing new.' Frank O'Connor was alive. Brendan Behan wasn't yet born. Flann O'Brien, better known as Brian O Nualain, was refusing to learn bad Irish from his Professor Douglas Hyde, the man with the walrus mustache who was later to be first President of Ireland. He whom David Thompson saw crawling on all fours across a drawing room with a bar of chocolate stuck in his mouth, challenging some well-brought-up little colleens to take a bite; he too perhaps impaled upon a dream.

We speak of mistakes we have made, losses we have suffered; but it is not the end, not just yet. Nevertheless a form of paralysis had begun. (And here I begin to bewail that which after followed. 'For now,' said I to myself, 'I am in two dangers, and forced to receive the one of them'). Paralysis of the will. Petrification of the will must follow unless something is done, and done soon. It may be already too late. Beware of Black Heart, a disease of the spirit which attacks with warning all men who put things off.

Where am I? Where was I then? What do you do when memory begins to go? I spend much time looking back into the past. It is no longer there. It has moved. Where?

My father as lame landlord owned three gate lodges, one stood empty, one needy tenant paid no rent for years. Major Brooks hid in a bush when the tax collector called. My father hid in the orchard; the notion of taxes being collected outraged him. He was not a man of uncommon sagacity but a common enough type of landlord in his day, the landed gent who preferred not to work under any circumstances. A sort of absentee landlord perpetually in residence, but inactive. Poor old Ireland, he said, was 'going to the dogs' under the mismanagement of de Valera, his old schoolmate from Blackrock College. He had 'killer's eyes,' and blood on his hands. Ireland was 'going down the drain,' was 'done for.'

His refusal to work was not due to idleness, but a refusal to ape the type of landlord he had supplanted: an English Protestant gent. Springfield went to rack and ruin, was in time sub-let like the land itself. The inebriated sub-tenant, a violent man by the name of Ball, went for my father, who defended himself with a spade – he chanced to be once again scuffling the front yard. I and the aggressor's wild son watched from a yew tree. The Guards were called but very diplomatically did not put in an appearance that day or the next, allowing the matter to blow over.

A monoplane flew over the house, the daring pilot (being known to my father) waved before going through the telegraph wires. The engine coughed. 'By God, he's down!' my father cried, delighted. But he made it over the trees, heading for Baldonnel. When Heinkels and Dorniers flew over, off course, chaser fighters of the Irish Air Force (motto: 'Small but Fierce') took off in the opposite direction, hid in the clouds. The Luftwaffe, playing their Schlägermusick, dropped bombs on Dublin and the pheasants in Killaddon let out a scream. The high explosive earth-tremor came twelve miles to rattle our windows, wake me.

So Springfield went to rack and ruin. The mismanagement was total. My father lost all interest once the inheritance in America dried up. He wore cricket boots in the house, spent much time at windows, picking his ear with a match. Some of the farce I put into a novel called *Langrishe, Go Down*, the name of previous owners, two spinsters who were put to bed drunk by their servants. It was less Cherry Orchard than Strindberg's Miss Julie. I converted my brothers into ageing sisters. The reality had been somewhat grimmer.

One last word: some strange instinct bound my father to inactivity, the uselessness of much effort on this earth. Apathy was masked by bonhomerie — the shield he used against the world. Lax mostly, he could be strict when occasion demanded, even cruel with us. One could not tell what thoughts he was thinking. He was swept by contrary moods like a woman. One part of him was shifty, shallow; he drifted, that was what he liked doing best of all, drifting. My father wanted none of us to leave home, ever. Possibly he was not such a common type after all. At all events he didn't care to reveal himself to me in whom my embittered mother, who had married him for his money, had buried very deeply her disappointments. His access to us was cut off by her by a calculated smear campaign. 'That bloody fool.' So he drifted away. Their graves in Dean's Grange cemetery are not adjacent.

A picture begins to form. Two stout men sit side by side on a collapsing sofa before a roaring fire. One is grossly fat and wheezes like a pekinese. His companion is tall, dark-visaged. The drawing room has a foreign smell as strong tobacco smoke swirls and through it boom unearthly human utterances. They seem to be engaged in noisily clearing their vocal passages; they are conversing in Flemish. The tall dark man is my uncle Juss Moorkens. He was the go-between when my parents were courting in Longford. 'Bart will follow on bicycle.'

In one gloved hand my father, Bartholomew Joseph Higgins, holds the reins; with his free hand he draws a large service revolver from an inside pocket. The moon comes out and shines artfully on the long dangerous barrel. My mother straightens her back, her eyes sparkle as my father cocks the Browning. 'Did you ever see,' he asks waggishly, 'did you ever in your life, Lilian Boyd, see such a large revolver?' No, you can be sure my lovely mother never had. He is protecting her from the Black and Tans, who go about murdering innocent Irish. English troops are garrisoned in Longford Barracks. Brandishing the Browning in one hand and with whip aloft my father drives the high-stepping pony at a brisk pace down the Battery Road. He is deep in one of those day-dreams which can overtake even the shallowest of men. It is like being in the midst of the most tumultous of parties.

Cheering wildly a line of ashen-faced Tommies rise up from a trench and stumble forward into a gas attack. Poison fumes drift over No-Man's-Land. Juss Moorkens prepares to go into action with the Belgian troops. He carries parts of a machine-gun, and wears a strange helmet with a sort of ridged backbone down the crown. Now he stands with arms folded outside a dugout, smoking a pipe. In the background, trees with their tops blown off, shell craters, a shell-pocked wasteland: Flanders fields. His dark eyes stare directly at me.

Speculation about a living person only begins to be legitimate when the ascertainable has been ascertained as far as possible. I see a figure with head hidden in a gas oven. My mother had some intuition of his end but she never told his wife Evelyn, who was her younger sister. Years later she told me her prophetic dream. It was of a windowless room, a stark naked dead man was stretched out on the slab. The corpse was sweating.

Two years later Juss's eldest son was brought by the Guards into the Dublin morgue to identify the body of his father. When he stepped into it he was in my mother's nightmare: for there was the windowless room, the long sweating corpse on the slab. My mother's dream was out.

From his mouth always he had seemed to exhale dangerous fumes. He covered himself with his greatcoat, put his head into the oven, turned on the gas. I see in the heavy family album the carriages with 'Hommes et Chevaux' painted on them. I study it and when I knew what the word meant, could think of it with Juss dead, I thought Abbatoir!

'Poor little Belgium,' my mother sighed, sitting on the window-seat, calmly knitting. Heavy summer rain pelts down. She is probably thinking: 'Poor Juss!' The rain drives at an angle into tea-coloured puddles on the recently scuffed gravel before the house, indenting and pitting it, with little v's running across them like shivers. I thought then: 'When I'm fifty I'll understand this.'

I am fifty-four. I do not understand it.

Carnation petals lie like drops of blood on the green-house cement floor. It smells of ferns and tomatoes. My mother weeds the rockery, wearing gardening gloves and an old hat, smoking Gold Flake to drive the midges away. My mother is cutting flowers for the high altar at Straffan church. She has one bloodshot eye. Her attention is caught by some small rock-flower. She knows all their names. Gardening calmed her nerves. She suffers from nerves, from claustrophobia.

In a field near the Hill of Ardrass the last triangle of wheat is being cut by the reaper-and-binder. The last rabbits hop away before the guns. A limp dead line of them are laid out on sacks. The dogs sniff at their bloody noses, back away licking their chops, looking shifty. I hear the murmur of the little stream. The reaper-and-binder raises its steel teeth and sets them into the wheat.

On an old tandem hired out for the day my brother and I cycle on through woody Kildare. It is one life.

It is a day.

Christmas 1931

Dirk Bogarde

The very first sign of all that it was about to be Christmas was when Lally took down the big mixing bowl and she and our mother started to make the pudding. It took a long time because all the fruit had to be cut up into little bits, and my sister and I had to de-seed the sultanas which had been steeping in warm rum, which was fearfully boring even though we were allowed to eat a few, without making pigs of ourselves, as they said.

And then it all got lumped together, somehow, by our mother who was very particular about that part, and everybody had to have a stir with the wooden spoon for luck, and then the best moment of all was when we scattered the lucky charms into the mixture. They were made of silver, because otherwise you had to wrap them in a titchy bit of paper and you could quite easily swallow them unknowing and they'd pass right through you, Lally said, and then you wouldn't have any luck in the New Year: which was what it was all about.

There was a thimble, and if you got that it meant you'd be a spinster, and a button which if you found that meant that you'd be a bachelor, and a pig for greed, and a horse-shoe for extra luck and so on, and best of all two threepenny pieces which were real silver and boiled and polished so there weren't any germs or anything. And then we all stirred each once more.

It took ages and smelled lovely and we didn't see it again until Christmas Day, which was years away. Well: a long time. Because our mother always made the pudding in October, and it was kept in a dark place to get ripe.

That was the first sign. But it was so early that sometimes we forgot all about it until the next sign: which was the Photograph.

Every year our father had a special half-page photograph taken somewhere very beautiful in the snow for the Christmas edition of *The Times*. Quite near the time he would be fussing like anything about where there was a good fall of snow that year. Or even a really heavy hoar-frost would do; because the picture had to have snow, or anyway a very wintry feeling about it for Christmas: but the trouble was it didn't always snow at that time and he got into a terrible fuss and kept on telephoning people all over the British Isles asking them how their snow was: and quite often there wasn't. And that made him very jumpy indeed so he kept on sending his photographers everywhere just to sit and wait until something happened. And they got jolly fed up, they said, sitting about in the

Pennines or up in the Shetlands or down in Land's End. Because
nothing much ever happened, and if it did it wasn't enough.

But if we were down at the cottage for a weekend, and it
suddenly got very frosty, he'd rush down to the village and
telephone The Office to get someone down quick sharp before it all
went away and the weather changed.

We were sometimes allowed to go out with him when this
happened, which wasn't very often because Sussex was too mild,
he said, and we usually went with a very nice photographer we
called Uncle Bill. Of course, he wasn't really an Uncle, not kith and
kin or anything, but we had known him for ever and ever, anyway
long before my sister was born even, and we liked him very much
and he was called Mr Warhurst. Well: such a fussing. We went off
in the OM with cameras and tripods and maps and things, and
climbed hills, stamped through woods, and went to quite far places
like Herstmonceaux, where there was a beautiful castle, or
Ashdown Forest, or Rye, and wherever we found 'somewhere
suitable' we'd stop and have a terrific picnic with thermos flasks of
hot tea or soup, sausage rolls, meat pies, or cold chicken and
hard-boiled eggs, and waited for the light to be right. We always
had to do this. It never seemed to be just right when we got there.
And all the time we were eating or drinking they were looking at
the sky through little glass things and shouting numbers at each
other and looking for the cloud to be just exactly right. There had
to be clouds too, that was very important, because you just had to
have them with the sun slanting through. The readers liked that,
my father said, especially if they were miles away in places like
Africa or India or Ceylon or somewhere very far, and the
photograph would remind them of England in all the heat, and
among all the black men.

When the light was exactly right there was a terrific rushing
about and sometimes my sister and I had to go and actually be in
the picture to give it 'interest'. Only never our faces or fronts . . .
just our backs, and we'd have to drag a big log about, or perhaps
carry a heavy bundle of twigs, through the frost or the snow. It was
really quite exciting in a way: anyway it was for them. My sister got
a bit fed up dragging bits of wood about and got cold, and started
moaning, and I got a bit tired with it all too, but remembered the
poor people being terribly hot in Africa or India and in a way that
cheered me up: and it cheered us both up to remember that the

Photograph was the second sign, which was rather good because it reminded us, you see, of the first sign, the pudding. And that meant Christmas was on its way. Which was even better.

Of course, about the pudding time, we started to save up for presents. Which was a bit boring to begin with, but quite nice when you got to the shopping part. I mean it was boring to have to put half your pocket money (and we only got fourpence each a week) into an empty Vim tin to buy other people things. But it had to be done, so we did it. And it was quite a good feeling when the tin got heavier and you began to think what you'd buy everyone. The trouble was that you couldn't buy people what *you* wanted. You had to buy them what they wanted. And Lally, or our mother, was very particular about that when we came to the shopping part. I didn't know *why* our father wouldn't have liked a very pretty glass goldfish in a little bowl, with waterlilies painted round it, but our mother said he'd detest it, and much prefer a pair of dull old socks. So I just let them choose in the end. You really couldn't fight them. And once my sister wanted to buy a rather nice little clockwork bird for Lally, which wound up and went rushing about pecking things. But she had to get her a stupid bottle of bath salts in the end. It wasn't worth fighting, you see. Nothing we really liked was 'suitable' they said.

Of course the main thing about Christmas was the Presents. I mean, we knew it was about the day that Jesus was born and everything, and the presents were supposed to be the ones the kings all brought to the manger that time. But we got a bit muddly about Santa Claus who seemed quite different from Holy Things. And it was quite hard to understand. Anyway it didn't matter much because I knew, ages ago, it wasn't Santa Claus but our father, because I watched one night and saw him with our mother creep in and put the stockings at the end of our bed. And years ago, when we were really quite small, Lally took us for the day to Mrs Jane's at Walnut Cottages and, as a special treat, we went to a big shop in Kingston to see the Goblins' Grotto and Father Christmas. And it was a bit worrying because we had seen him at Selfridges the week before: only he was at the North Pole there. We stood in a long line waiting to have a word with him, and when it was my sister's turn, she went rather red in the face, and he put her on his knee and was being quite decent to her when she suddenly hit him and screamed and screamed so that Lally and Mrs Jane had to rush and take her away. And she sobbed and snivelled all the way through the Lampshade Department and even through the Corset one. It was awful really: and people kept turning round.

We went down in the lift and when we got to Soft Furnishings Lally made us sit down, dried my sister's eyes and asked what on earth was all the fuss about.

'He had terrible red eyes!' said my sister.

'Nonsense!' said Lally. 'Red eyes indeed.'

'Red . . .' she wailed. 'And awful long whiskers and he made rumbling noises at me and said if I hadn't been a good child in the year he'd come down the chimney and sort me out.'

It took a long time to get her all right, and they only did it at the ABC Tea Shop when Lally let her have first choose of the cakes. So then she shut up. But we never mentioned Santa Claus again, really. And every time she saw one, and there seemed to be hundreds everywhere, she grabbed Lally's hand and hid herself in her skirts. And she was very relieved that we had a gas-fire in the nursery so he couldn't get down the chimney anyway.

So we knew that presents really came from family and from kind people we knew.

Because we hadn't much kith and kin of our own, we had to invent Uncles and Aunts, which was quite good in a way, because you only had the ones you really liked as Uncle or Aunt. The rest you just called Mr or Mrs and they didn't count.

Of course we did have some real kith and kin up in Scotland, who belonged to our mother, but we didn't see them often because they lived so far away in the cold and mists, and although they were quite nice, I suppose, they weren't a bit like us. The one bad mark against them was the presents they sent, and they were awful. I mean you always knew exactly what the present was long before you even opened it.

Flat.

Just flat.

No lovely bumps and lumps and poky bits sticking through the paper which made it really exciting, just flat.

So I mean you just knew it was a box of Edinburgh Rock or a pair of gloves, or a jigsaw puzzle, or worse still, a book. I mean whoever sent anyone a book for Christmas? You'd have to read it before you could write the Thank You Letter and you never read a book at holidays. Only at school. Forced.

There was no fun in books or gloves or Edinburgh Rock. Even though the rock was quite nice, especially the cinnamon bits, but sweets aren't very interesting even in tartan boxes with pictures of Prince's Street on the back. I mean boring. And gloves. Whoever wants gloves when you've got your own anyway?

So we just knew by the *flatness* what we were in for and left them to the last to open. But we still had to write Thank You's and Lally kept all the labels and wrote on them saying who they were from and what they had been, because things did get into a bit of a mess on Christmas Morning round the tree. So she wrote 'rock' or 'Book (*Kidnapped*)' or 'gloves' or 'long, knitted stockings' to help out at the Thanking time.

Long, knitted stockings. I mean, honestly.

But some people sent marvellous presents like another borrowed Aunt. She was French, and a famous actress and we called her Aunt Yvonne and she sent the best presents ever. All bumps and knobs and poky things sticking out. And huge. Once I got a sort of Hobby Horse with a head and a real grey and white speckly mane, and once a butcher's shop with a butcher, sides of meat, sausages in long pink rows. All in plaster of course, but it was a lovely present. And she always remembered Lally as well and sent her soap, which was very interesting because each piece had a picture of a different dog or a horse on it, and they never wore off, even when the soap got to a little thin sliver of a thing. It was called RSPCA Soap, because that's what it had on the box, which made it sound pretty important, and our mother said that Aunt Yvonne had probably bought it at one of the Charity Bazaars she always had to open, but it was a very kind thought anyway. And Lally said she had enough soap to open a laundry: but she was quite pleased, you could tell.

We always had Christmas together, either at the London house, which was all right but not quite such fun, or the cottage. Which was the very best. But once, on a dreadful occasion we had to go and have it with some real kith and kin that my father had found who belonged to him. It was a bit of a shock I can tell you. They were what he called his Second Cousins Twice Removed or something. But we still had to go. And even if it sounded quite interesting it wasn't. It was dreadful.

Aunt, well we had to call her Aunt of course, because even if she was Twice Removed and we didn't like her all that much at first sight, she was 'blood' or something silly. Anyway Aunt Phyllis was terrible. I mean she was quite nice but just didn't understand children, our mother said. And she was married to a man called Digby, who was just as bad but worse really. Because he never spoke to us at all except to say 'Herrumph' or 'Now; I'm quite sure you'd like to go for a splendid health-giving walk over our Common. Lots of fascinating things to see, you know.' And we didn't want to go at all because it was freezing outside, and anyway there wasn't anything to see except awful old dead heather and big, gloomy, pine trees. They lived in a most peculiar house. Our mother said they designed it themselves and it was very modern and advanced. It was jolly uncomfortable; huge glass windows and no fireplace and all the chairs were made of shiny metal and even the dining table was made of thick glass and silvery iron stuff.

I ask you.

And they didn't even have a Christmas tree because Uncle (we had to call *him* Uncle too) Digby had asthma or something, and anyway, Aunt Phyllis said they were very dangerous and shed their needles everywhere and made a mess, and in any case it was all nonsense because it was invented by the Hun. Our mother said that was her name for the Germans. Which was a bit peculiar.

So we just had our presents up in our bedroom, which our parents had brought with them in the car; and that was pretty horrible too because it had bunks like on a ship, and my sister had the lower one and I had to climb an iron ladder to get into mine, and she was under me and was terrified all night that I would want to do a pee and wouldn't bother to go: and then where would she be?

Well I mean, I did see, but I didn't go, so that was all right.

There were no flowers anywhere in the house; just prickly cactus things in big china bowls or square pots, and a ghastly shiny lady made of brass with her arms round a sort of clock, sitting on a tiger or something. And they had a fearful dog, an Alsatian called 'Hamilcar' which had to wear felt bootees on its feet in the house because it might scratch Aunt Phyllis's parquet floors. Which were dreadfully cold and you skidded on.

They didn't eat meat, another bad mark; so my sister and I had a titchy little chicken which she especially cooked for us, which was kind I suppose, except it was quite cold and had bloody legs inside, but there were about fifty different sorts of vegetables like swedes and parsnips and things, and loaves of bread, dark brown, with bits of corn sticking in them. It was all pretty dreadful. And after dinner Uncle Digby started to play his gramophone but not with Christmas things like Elsie and Doris Waters or Stanley Holloway, but dreadful serious music which you had to listen to: at least he did: lying back in his iron chair with leather sides, and his eyes closed, and Aunt Phyllis sitting on a pouf working away at something she said was a rug for the fireplace. Only there wasn't one. I mean, it was just all wonky.

And then Uncle Digby looked at his pocket watch and said, 'Isn't it about time that our young guests were on their way to slumber-land? Too much excitement in one day is not a good thing, is it?'

Too much excitement!

Thank goodness we went home quite early the next day and our father said never again because he'd only been given two measly watered whiskies before dinner, two glasses of thin Australian wine with, and nothing after but a mug of cocoa. And our mother said it wasn't her fault, because they were his relations, and perhaps the next time he was intent on discovering his family he'd have a thought for his own, and if he ever did it again it would be over her dead body: which worried us a bit because she looked pretty furious, you could see in the car mirror, and we felt a bit uneasy about the dead body part, but she said she didn't mean it quite like that. We asked her. And she explained. Sort of. So that was the Ghastly Farnham Christmas, and we never forgot it ever.

And when we saw Lally again the day after Boxing Day, she was all smiling and cheerful and didn't even say that she had missed us, but that they'd had a lovely time at Walnut Cottages, Twickenham, with her father and mother, and they'd had a goose and mince pies, a whole bottle of Tonic Wine, and that Brother Harold had played 'Come, all ye faithful!' on his clarinet: which was Mrs Jane's very favourite.

So that was all right.

THE ART OF
STANLEY
MIDDLETON

A. S. Byatt

At first glance, or even at second, Stanley Middleton's world is easily recognisable. His novels are set in the Midlands and his men and women are mostly drawn from the middle classes, schoolmasters, solicitors, businessmen, often with their roots in that older, chapel-going, confined culture described and fulminated against by Lawrence. Some of them are also artists but their art does not have the ferocity or the spirit of opposition that drives Lawrence's visionaries and David Storey's uprooted painters. The excellence of art, for Middleton, is an exact vision of real things as they are. And because he is himself so exact an observer, his world at *third* glance can seem strange and disturbing or newly and brilliantly lit with colour.

His characteristic plot poses his characters a complex moral problem, which character and author then explore, trying to understand. He is particularly interested in marriages suddenly at breaking point. The hero of *Holiday* has left his temperamental wife to think things out at the seaside resort of his childhood holidays. In *The Other Side* Elizabeth is reduced to a state of extremity by her husband's announcements, within days of each other, that he is leaving her for another woman, and then that he has changed his mind. In his latest novel, *Valley of Decision*, David's brilliant young singer wife goes to America to sing in a Handel opera and then suddenly ceases to write to him. In all cases whole families, parents, parents-in-law, children become involved, while the central characters try to sort out how to behave and who the other person is. Middleton feels his way meticulously into the flickering of feelings, analysis, discovery, ignorance that possess his people. He works on the borders between people where the nature of the self of the other is a mystery and a blank. What is, in our time, unusual in him, is not a gift for presenting the inarticulate areas of this experience, but for making his people articulate. They think their problems out, they put them into words, they get somewhere. At the end of *Holiday*, when Edwin Fisher confronts his estranged wife, Meg, baffled, full of goodwill and resentment, she says: 'I don't think, really, that much good comes of talking. Daddy argues it does, and you. Or do you? I don't. We're not rational creatures. Not you and I.' to which he replied: 'I know. But if we don't act with reason, where are we? What standards can we apply? We'd go about knocking one another out with knuckle dusters or bombs.' 'That mightn't be any worse.' 'You know damn

well it would. Blow a man's hands or legs off, where is he? What is
he?' The same belief in reason and proportion, fear of violence,
informs David's choice, at his lowest in *The Valley of Decision*, not
to drown himself:

> 'In spite of loss, the total wreck of happiness, there seemed
> inbuilt inside him a common sense, an everyday rationality, a
> kind of formidable schoolmastery which had refused permis-
> sion. When he had considered this later he had decided that his
> affliction, desperate as it seemed, earth-shattering, must have
> been weak, small, compared with that of men who hacked their
> throats open with cut-throat razors or drove headlong into brick
> walls. Perhaps he was pathologically incapable of such intensity
> of feeling.'

'A kind of formidable schoolmastery' describes another area of
Middleton's moral concern as well, one more peculiarly his own
than incomprehension in marriage. He writes about a society stiff
with conventions about what is done and not done. He knows the
dour Midlands; his mourners do not scream and fling themselves
about but are grimly self-controlled. And yet, perhaps because of
these constrictions, people in his world are always desperately
calling out for help, for advice, for judgment. Fathers and
fathers-in-law in advisory professions like the law and school-
teaching offer advice sought and unsought, pompous and shrewd.
But it goes beyond that. Walter Payne in *In a Strange Land* is called
in from a morning's shopping by a frantic stranger on a doorstep
who fears he has damaged his wife, to whom he leads Payne. She is
totally naked. This encounter leads to further requests for Payne's
family to visit the naked lady's dying Polish father. This involves
the musician hero who has already discovered Mrs Payne's brother
floating dead in a pond, and is in due course required to help with
the disposal of this dead man's effects. It sounds like Kafka, but is
all perfectly decorous English social observation, a kind of
bucket-chain of advice and support in the face of disaster. In *The
Other Side* the wronged wife, Elizabeth, is given the task of
rescuing and advising the woman with whom her husband
intended to run away: she is called in by the woman's husband.
Advice-giving is the pivot of the plot in *The Daysman*, which opens
with a successful headmaster, John Richardson, being called in to
advise the daughter of a neurotic woman writer on choice of

universities. He fails to detect the girl's desperation and she kills herself. He advises, in turn, a member of his staff whose wife has left him for a driving instructor, a boy who cheats in exams, those responsible for four boys who die in an accident, the wife of the suicidal girl's lover, another headmaster who grips his arm like an Ancient Mariner on a pavement and tell him that his school has been burned down by his own pupils and for good measure that his clergyman brother is dying horribly of cancer at 50. The novel is both comic and terrible, as the hero faces up to disaster and tries to be rational and constructive. It is tragi-comedy and yet it is also George Eliot's meliorism; Richardson, a little self-satisifed, full of his own life, *will not let go*, keeps trying for reason, for hope.

I reviewed this novel on Critics' Forum where Clancy Sigal hated it because he saw the hero as pompous and humourless. Paul Bailey in *The Standard* said he was a truly good man, which seemed to me to be much nearer the mark. When I put this point to Stanley Middleton himself, he said, drily, judiciously schoolmasterly: 'He did a little better than I would have done in the circumstances, I think.'

Another aspect of life which Middleton treats with complex accuracy and an unusual respect is the human desire for success. He understands how it drives through a family, through a father's ambition in and for his sons. (He is not so good on daughters – many of his women are clever, but almost all seem to find an adequately demanding destiny in marriage). In *Two Brothers* he describes the relationship of Jack and Francis Weldon, business- man and poet, showing as much curiosity and insight about the drive behind the heavy outgoing businessman as about the private poet. *Entry into Jerusalem*, a novel about a painter whose scope is said, by his mistress and his critics, to be too restricted, explores the territory between mastery and overreaching, haunted as it is by that failed megalomaniac painter, Benjamin Haydon, who cut his throat after the public indifference to his 'masterpiece' *Christ's Entry into Jerusalem*. In *Valley of Decision* the hero's father's genius as a businessman is easily seen to be a force comparable to the young wife's considerable talent as a singer. The characters in Middleton's novels characteristically take a step back from themselves to see where they've got to, what they've made of themselves, if they could have done better. This can take the form of social ambition and express itself in the rhythms of men-of-the-world measuring themselves or each other, in bar conversation. It's a tone one hears constantly in life and not often in fiction, nowadays.

The self-examination can also take the tone of a non-conformist examination of conscience. It is more than competitive drive. It is the need to have made something of oneself. In *Cold Gradations* the retired schoolmaster hero receives the bitter confidences of a neighbour whose life is being worn away by his wife's devotion to a mentally defective grandchild. 'One of these days', he began, 'I am going to to die. Can't be long now. And what shall I have done? Served tons of nails and screws and paraffin across my counter.' His two successful sons are out of touch. The hero responds stiffly: 'You, by your efforts, helped two of your sons to create careers for themselves far beyond the average of children of their class and status in this town.' He recognises the stilted inadequacy of this but goes on, because it is true, and it is something.

In *Blind Understanding* the elderly hero meets another Ancient Mariner, a schoolmaster-poet on a pavement, who describes his habit of remembering little walks, 'short journeys taken years ago.' He generalises from this:

'If I could express this sense of travel, of going towards some good thing, non-existent as that may be, in a poem, that would be sufficient justification for my life. I think this sense of intense purposive activity, the walk, leading generally nowhere, is typical of the human condition, or Western European/North American life. I would also claim that this applies equally, if not more strongly, to people of the highest genius, because their objectives or expectations are so much greater.'

The form of Middleton's novels is deceptively plain. I had imagined that he composed them carefully and self-consciously, since their characteristic virtue is that each little passage of dialogue or meditation, each new incident, illuminates the central problem towards which the novel is addressed. When I met Stanley Middleton he told me that no such planning takes place. On a pre-determined day, in a hard-backed exercise book, he starts writing, with no idea where he is going, only with a problem to work at. When he was in Cambridge Raymond Williams pointed out that this meant his novels were 'books from the beginning'. This means that they are characteristically both tentative and beautifully formed. He does not know what will happen – he was three-quarters through *Entry into Jerusalem* before he realised that Worth was to be a *successful* painter. *Valley of Decision* grew from the story of 'a corporal I had' whose wife didn't write to him. He finds it interesting, he says characteristically, 'when a good person won't do the right thing.' I imagine him listening to his own dialogue, as he might listen to any other conversation, intently, noticing the twists and hesitations, the sudden statements. He also describes his world and his people's actions as though he is seeing them as he writes, noticing the *kind* of kettle or mug, central heating or carpet that is being poured from or walked across or passed, bringing his world into being as he goes.

He gets amazing effects, moral and artistic, from juxtaposition. The most terrible and the most daring is at the end of *Cold Gradations*, where he inserts one chill paragraph into a scene of reconciliation and light to describe the closely approaching sudden death of the hero's powerful and energetic son. Or, in *The Other Side*, in one page, Elizabeth visits a Primitive Methodist Chapel with her father-in-law, a vigorous and delightful old man. 'A serious house on serious earth it is', she quotes. And in the next paragraph she is attending his funeral there. Quietly, quickly, we are shocked.

What Stanley Middleton has is a remarkable combination of an accurate ear for the haphazard movements in life and talk, and a clear sense of overarching poetic or musical form. He writes completely convincingly about artistic activity, the concentration and narrow focus of the painter, the ordered *work* of playing music. When I talked to him he said he would have preferred to be a composer or a poet. A novelist comes 'well down the list'. (He writes poetry but doesn't publish it). He admires Larkin and Tony Harrison, and likes Hardy better than Eliot – the poets who transmute the everyday, not into something rich and strange, but into a clearer, sharper, more significant vision of itself. The poet in *Two Brothers* wrote a mocking self-obituary:

'Provincial. Limitation of subject matter. Some flatness of language. Absence of the larger gestures. Awkwardness. But, but, but. Characterized by a deep sincerity, a single eye, an attachment to reality, a love of humanity and the townscape of his midland home.'

This is self-deprecating irony, as the character of Worth in *Entry into Jerusalem* is self-mockery (and self-justification) in part, inspired by a politically-minded friend who told him he should be trying to change the world. Stanley Middleton, like David in *The Valley of Decision* suspects himself of some inadequacy or failure – he told me that his novels were perhaps a therapy for him. He also quoted Blake's Memorable Fancy (from *The Marriage of Heaven and Hell*). The poet asks the prophet Issaiah: 'Does a firm persuasion that a thing is so make it so?' Isaiah replied: 'All poets believe that it does and in ages of imagination this firm persuasion moved mountains; but *many are not capable of a firm persuasion of anything.*' 'I wonder', Middleton says, 'if this is what troubles me in my novels?'

There is a sense of certainty out of reach, religious or artistic or human, in Middleton's novels and yet this may be simply the human condition, as his poet-character, Potter, said about the short walks leading nowhere. The poet of *Two Brothers* tells an interviewer that he is religious, but not as she would mean it; he doesn't believe in Providence or an after-life. When pressed, he explains: 'I am amazed, baffled beyond bearing by the complexity of matter.' The hero of *Cold Gradations*, another schoolmaster, is baffled by the structure of a flower. He has been 'a man of words', a man to whom

> 'words only brought certainties . . . Poets complained of their imprecision, of their slippery, evasive nature, but they only offered a steady reward to him . . . He was an elderly pedagogue, who'd taught history and literature and Latin, who had now paid the penalty for his bias. But all paid. There were no free gifts, no windfalls from his own God. If one worked, one prospered. He laughed at his own puritanical fancies.'

Middleton's word is the world *after* the Chapel certainties, in which the old man of *The Other Side* could say, 'This is none other than the house of God', firmly persuaded. It is the world of questing morality, without the sanction of religious injunction, upheld only by decency. 'I believe in some sort of God, I think,' Stanley Middleton said to me very soon after we met, as if it was important to get this clear, 'but I have more admiration for the firm atheism of my wife.' His people work and prosper in a world of blind chance. It is the elderly pedagogue to whom words bring certainties who is brought to a standstill by the vision of his dead son in the penultimate paragraph. 'I would be looking for some good, even in the Moors Murderers' Stanley Middleton said. The blows of fate do not cancel virtue, or the power of music and paint. But he records the blows unflinchingly.

Like a Gangster on The Night of the Long Knives, But Somewhat in a Dream

AMOS OZ

When I sit down to write a story I already have the people. What are called the 'characters'. Generally there is a man – or woman – at the centre, and others round about or opposite. I don't know yet what will happen to them, what they will do to each other, but they have converged on me and I am already involved in conversations, arguments, even quarrels with them. There are times when I say to them: Get out of here. Leave me alone. You are not right for me and I am not right for you. It's too difficult for me. I'm not the right man. Go to somebody else.

Sometimes I persist, time passes, they lose interest, perhaps they really do go to some other writers, and I write nothing.

But sometimes *they* persist, like Michael's Hannah, for example: she nagged me for a long time, she wouldn't give up, she said, 'Look, I'm here, I shan't leave you alone, either you write what I tell you or you won't have any peace.'

I argued, I apologised, I said, 'Look, I can't do it, go to someone else, go to some woman writer, I'm not a woman. I can't write you in the first person, let me be.' No. She didn't give up. And then, when I did write, so as to get rid of her and get back somehow to my own life, still every day and every night she was arguing about each line. She wanted me to write in this way or that, she wanted to put more and more things into the story, and I kept saying, 'This won't do, it's bad, it's unnecessary, this is my novel not yours, after all you're my obsession, not the other way round.' I said, 'Look, you don't even exist, you're nothing, only I can – maybe – rescue you from everlasting darkness and put you into words, so don't bother me, stop telling me how to do it, it's hard enough for me without you, that's enough.' (You must not confuse this with something else: I am not talking about a 'model drawn from life'. There's no such thing.)

That is, more or less, how the people in my stories come to me. And they start to bring with them their own way of speaking, their habits, their places. And the things they say or do to one another: their relationships, their troubles. I have the impression that I know what I want to do: the beginning, the middle and the end. There was even a time, when I was writing my first short stories, when I never sat down to write until I knew the whole story by heart, from beginning to end. I had a very good memory. I was twenty, twenty-something. I knew it all by heart, from the first word to the last. And the writing itself was like dictation – six, eight hours and I had a complete story which only needed a few slight corrections here and there. (Perhaps it was because I was in the army then, or working in the cottonfields, or a student, I didn't have a desk or a room of my own and I was obliged to put the whole story together first and then simply copy it out of my head and onto the page).

Nowadays I am much less of a hero. And I have a room, and a desk. And I also write slightly longer, even much longer things than those first short stories. And so often start off thinking that I know what's going to happen, and it turns out that I don't. I decide, I make up my mind that the people in a story will do this or that, and suddenly, they want to do something entirely different. I say, for instance, 'You're both out of your minds. We arranged that you would meet in a small bar on Mount Carmel: what are you doing suddenly meeting in some olive grove in the Judean Hills? It's not right for you, you so obviously belong in bars, not in an olive grove'. And they reply: 'Don't you tell us what's right for us and what isn't. Just shut up and keep writing.' And then I have a quarrel with my 'characters', and sometimes we reach some sort of a compromise. That is the moment when I feel a tremendous sense of relief: my story has come alive. I don't need to stand behind my people any more and push them. They run around of their own accord among my pages, in my notes, on my desk, in my dreams at night, and even in the daytime when I am not writing at all but talking to people about politics or going about my business or reading the newspaper. They have come to life. The difficulty now is how to hold them back, how to stop them running wild and making me do things with them that are beyond my power, how to stop them bursting into hysterics or emotional scenes, how to stop them getting out of control and ruining everything. Sometimes they are stronger than any restraints I can impose on them. Once I was working on a story about two boys and a girl in a kibbutz. In chapter four or five a sort of travelling lecturer from the Labour Council turned up at the kibbutz, an old chatterbox who lectured about Soviet Jewry. I said to him, 'You can speak for half a page here and then we'll see, maybe you can appear again at the end of the story once or twice, briefly, and then I'm finished with you.'

But he hadn't finished with me, that old lecturer. He talked and talked and talked. He got completely out of hand. I said, 'Get out of this story. It's not your story. Stop interfering.' But he went on; lecturing, shouting, sighing. Pouring his heart out. Not just on the page, but aloud, all day long, when I was eating, and even at night in my dreams which were his dreams now, he was afraid of a Russian invasion and I dreamed of a Russian invasion, he was trying to write a long letter to Moshe Dayan and I, for my part, on my lap, in a train between London and Oxford, in the margin of some magazine, wrote out for him this letter of his to Dayan. He kept on lecturing me in a strange Russian syntax, and my acquaintances were beginning to laugh at me because suddenly when I spoke my words had a Russian tune to them. Ludicrously Russian, Russian through and through, to the point where eyebrows were beginning to be raised.

And so I let everything drop, the boys and the girl on the kibbutz, my plans and intentions, and I wrote – against my 'will' and contrary to my intentions – a story about an old Russian from the Labour Council who travels from place to place and speaks about all kinds of troubles and dangers. Only when this story was finished did I return (for a while) to speaking properly and dreaming the dreams I deserved.

People always ask if a story is written 'on purpose', or 'consciously'. What is 'consciousness'? There is nothing whatever perhaps that anyone does while 'being of sound mind', as they say in the law courts: whatever one is doing, even if it is only mending a dripping tap, one's sound mind is mixed up with something which is not 'mind' and not even exactly 'sound'. It is obviously the same if one is making a picture or a statue or a masterplan for a new town, or making a story. If a man sits down to write, let us say, music, he has to be, on the one hand, alert and sharp-witted like a gangster on the night of the long knives, when any split second could be vital, and on the other hand he also has to be somewhat in a dream. If he is alert and nothing more, he cannot write music. But if he entirely in a dream he cannot write music either. Or else he will write rotten music, and the following morning he will be amazed at himself, how on earth could he have written such rubbish.

Hebrew. The Hebrew language is a unique musical instrument. And in any case, a language is never a 'means' or a 'framework' or a 'vehicle' for culture. It *is* culture. If you live in Hebrew, if you think, dream, make love in Hebrew, sing in Hebrew in the shower, tell lies in Hebrew, you are 'inside'. Even if you haven't got the smallest drop of 'Jewish consciousness' or Zionism or anything. If you live in Hebrew you are 'inside'. If a writer writes in Hebrew, even if he rewrites Dostoevski or writes about a Tartar invasion of South America, Hebrew things will always happen in his stories. Things which are ours and which can only happen with us: certain rhythms, moods, combinations, associations, longings, connotations, atavistic attitudes towards the whole of reality, and so forth. (Important reservation: provided it really is Hebrew, and not a garbled mishmash of mistranslations from foreign languages.) In Hebrew even inanimate objects are obliged to relate to each other in a Hebrew way: masculine and feminine, for example, or what the grammarians call the 'construct state'.

Incidentally the whole of Hebrew literature has its own set themes. The exceptions only prove the rule. It deals with Jewish suffering. Jewish suffering in all its various incarnations, settings, reflections, perspectives, rituals. If anyone can write in Hebrew about love for love's sake, about 'the human condition in general', in such a way that no Hebrew echoes intrude on his 'universality', good luck to him. I don't see myself how it can be done. What we are all writing about is Jewish suffering, from Mapu's *Love of Zion*, by way of the agonies of faith and loss of faith and sex and sin and humiliation in Bialik, Berdichevsky, Brenner and Agnon, to the untough tough-guys of the *Palmach* who grappled with their sensitive Jewish souls and found no way out, right down to the latest writers.

Of course, there is also an American Jewish literature, which is in English and also deals with Jewish suffering. And there used to be German Jewish literature dealing with Jewish suffering. There was also Jewish suffering in Yiddish. There are even those who say that Kafka, when all is said and done, was concerned with Jewish suffering. There is no inherent conflict between dealing with Jewish suffering in all its various aspects and soaring to the heights of 'universality'. On the contrary: one can be anything, lyrical, mystical, metaphysical, satirical, symbolic, without departing from the theme of Jewish suffering. After all, Jewish suffering is, in the last analysis, just like any other suffering: the Jews wanted, and still want, something they will never have, and what they do have they despise, and so on. Just like everybody else, only in their own private 'key', and, if they live in Hebrew, whatever they say has a Hebrew tune to it.

I have a family relationship to the Jews and their suffering. You love and belong, and sometimes you also hate. There is no contradiction. Whenever I hate the Jews it is inevitably an intimate hatred, which comes from my heart and is part of it, because I am one of them and they are inside me.

How sick we are. Sometimes I try to take comfort in the thought that others are also sick, that the 'German psyche' and the 'Russian soul' are sick, that the 'Christian mind' is surely sick and poisoned, but this is no comfort at all. Perhaps we are slightly sicker than all the others. We have been so much persecuted. So much hatred has been directed against us, at various times, in various places, under various pretexts, that in the natural course of things we have started to scribble and poke around to find out what is wrong with us, what people hate in us, no doubt we have even internalised some of this hatred, we feel warm and cosy inside it.

Anyone who is misled into supposing that the Jewish sickness is merely the result of dispersal among the nations and lack of territory is mistaken. So is anyone who thinks that now that we have obtained a piece of territory we can settle down peacefully and recuperate. So many victims of oppression and persecution, a Hasid from Poland, a businessman from Brooklyn, a goldsmith from Tunis, a ritual slaughterer from the Yemen, an ex-Komsomolnik from Odessa, all packed into one bus under this sweltering summer sun – can the fact that they are all in the same bus transform them into the 'heroic generation' that will 'emerge into the bright light of a new day'? Abracadabra and 'the Maccabees come back to life'?

We have never been able to settle down. For a thousand, two thousand, three thousand years we have been unable to settle down quietly. Whichever way we have turned, whatever we have put our hands to, we have always caused a mighty stir: sweat, nervousness, fear, aggression, a constant ferment. This is not the place to examine who was responsible: whether we always radiated nervous hysteria because we were persecuted, or whether we were persecuted because of the nervous hysteria we radiated. Or both. The crux of the matter is the restlessness, that irritating, fructifying fever: anxious, eager Jews, always trying to teach everybody else how to live, and how to tell right from wrong. Ideas and ideals. We even have a collection of portraits which we wheel out whenever we have the feeling that we are being slightly undervalued or denigrated: Spinoza, Marx, Freud, Einstein, etc. All the Jewish Nobel prize winners. The proportion of Jewish scientists. The percentage of doctors, of musicians, and so on. Incidentally, most of these geniuses were assimilated Jews who felt burdened by the Jewishness, and some of them we even disowned and excommunicated. But whenever we are on the defensive we wear their names like talismans to protect ourselves against libels or pogroms. Just as it is popular here to boast that we are descended from the heroes of Massada. But the heroes of Massada killed themselves and their children, and we are all descended from the 'defeatist' Jews who chose surrender, exile and survival. Or take our other boast, that we are the 'descendants of the prophets'. Surely we are the descendants of the Jews who stoned the prophets. Never mind: every people has its own boasts. We have had our share of sufferings. If we were to mention just a few of them, a kind of catalogue of selected Jewish woes, it would be evident that our sufferings, by and large, have been neither heroic nor romantic: they have been merely humiliating. The repulsive, sweaty dregs of thousands of years of 'self-discipline' coupled with sexual repression, turning our backs on all the joys of the world, on nature, on sensual pleasures, on everything which is not 'Torah', coupled with fermenting petit-bourgeois hypocrisy, and with alternating fits of self-abasement and exaltation in relation to the rest of the world, with its culture and its fatal charms.

Jews can no longer look gentiles straight in the eye: either they kowtow and fawn on them, or they puff themselves up with a kind of solipsistic megalomania.

I hate the Jews as one can only hate one's own flesh and blood. I hate them with love and with shame. After all, we are not a nation, like the British, the Poles or the French. We are still a tribe, and if anyone bites our thumb, our ear hurts too. If a member of the tribe gets killed on the other side of the world, we feel panic, outrage, fury and sorrow. If some Jewish confidence trickster is arrested in Lower Ruritania the whole tribe shudders at what the world will think. If a functionary or manager is convicted of embezzlement, I personally cringe with shame and embarrassment, as if it had happened to my own family; what will the neighbours say.

Yes, we are a tribe, an extended family, a clan, and there are times when I feel suffocated and wanted to escape to the other side of the world to be alone and not to have to bear the perpetual burden of this Israeli intimacy. But there is no escape. Even at the other end of the world I am bound to come across some foreign newspaper with a report of dirty business in the Israeli army, or a Jewish fraud, or shooting on the border, or manifestations of antisemitism in north-eastern Argentina, and at once I should feel the old constriction in my throat: more trouble. And the feeling of depression inside me: surely I ought to do something about it, at least write a stiff article, sign a petition, startle somebody.

There is a powerful inner truth which must not be concealed: supposing this hysterical Jewish bond were severed, how could I live without it? How could I give up this drug, this addiction to collective excitement, these tribal ties? And if I could kick the habit, what would I have left? Are we really capable of living ordinary, peaceable lives? Could any of us? I couldn't.

Israel is not a fresh leaf or a new chapter. Perhaps, at best, it is a new paragraph on a very old page. The Jews came here to recover, to recuperate, to forget, but they are unable to recuperate, forget or recover and in fact, deep down in their heart of hearts, they don't want to. They didn't even come here out of choice. Half of them were born here. The other half are mostly refugees who drifted here because there was no other escape. And the rest, a handful, a few tens of thousands out of three million, are the only ones who came out of idealism or from choice. And they brought with them a burning ambition to turn over a fresh leaf, to start a totally new chapter: 'There, in the land our fathers loved, all our dreams will be fulfilled.'

There was a hope, which was expressed in several different and conflicting versions, that when we arrived here, as soon as our feet touched this good earth, our hearts would be changed. A recovery. And indeed there have been a few signs of a gradual recovery. A relative recovery.

Only the prolonged quarrel with the Arabs is delaying this recovery, even causing the patient to relapse into his former condition. Perhaps, as some people say, a short war can 'temper' a people, even grant them their 'finest hour'. Perhaps. But one thing that is certain is that a prolonged squabble does not ennoble, it degrades. In our case it is pushing us back into our 'hereditary' depression, into the neuroses, the atavistic tribal madness from which we were trying to escape, back into the megalomania, the paranoia, the traditional nightmares. A bloody conflict which drags on for decades, a conflict which involves isolation, withdrawal into ourselves, mounting condemnation from the international audience which we pretend to despise but which secretly, in the depth of our moaning Jewish hearts, we have an almost hysterical desire and need to be loved and admired by – such a conflict would have driven even a far more sane and resistant people than we are out of its mind by now. All this is 'too much for our medical condition'.

Translated by Nicholas de Lange.

The Arvon Foundation
Courses with Writers

Bernard MacLaverty, Jan Mark, Deborah Moggach, Wendy Perriam, Lynne Reid Banks, Dyan Sheldon, Lorna Tracy, Rose Tremain, Hugo Williams.

These are just some of the writers who will be tutoring Arvon residential writing courses during 1986. If you are interested in writing poetry, novels, short stories, plays, radio and television scripts, stories for children etc then further details can be obtained from either:

<table>
<tr><td>Totleigh Barton</td><td>Lumb Bank</td></tr>
<tr><td>Sheepwash</td><td>Hebden Bridge</td></tr>
<tr><td>Devon</td><td>W Yorks</td></tr>
<tr><td>EX21 5NS</td><td>HX7 6DF</td></tr>
<tr><td>Tel: Black</td><td>Tel: Hebden</td></tr>
<tr><td>Torrington 338</td><td>Bridge 843714</td></tr>
</table>

In Conversation with Alasdair Gray

Frank Delaney &
Chris Swan

Paul Cox

Q. What is your background?

A. If background means surroundings: first 25 years were lived in Riddrie, East Glasgow, a well maintained district of stone-fronted corporation tenements and semi-detached villas. Our neighbours were a nurse, postman, printer and tobacconist, so I was a bit of a snob. I took it for granted that Britain was mainly owned and ruled by Riddrie people – like my father.

If background means family: it was hardworking, well-educated and very sober. My English grandad was a Northampton foreman shoemaker who came north because the southern employers blacklisted him for trade-union activities. My Scottish grandad was an industrial blacksmith and congregational kirk-elder.

Q. What was childhood like?

A. Apart from the attacks of asthma and eczema, mostly painless but frequently boring. My parents' wish for me was that I go to university. They wanted me to get a professional job, you see, because professional people are not so likely to lose their income during a depression. To enter university I had to pass exams in Latin and Mathematics which I hated. So half my school experience was passed in activities which felt to my brain like a meal of sawdust to the mouth. And of course there was homework. My father wanted to relieve the drudgery of learning by taking me cycling and climbing, but I hated enjoying myself in his shadow, and preferred the escapist worlds of comics and films and books: books most of all.

Q. When did you realize you were an artist?

A. I did not realize it. Like all infants who were allowed materials to draw with, I did, and nobody suggested I stop. At school I was even encouraged to do it.

Q. What made you decide to write?

A. The discovery that I could, and the encouragement of teachers. Only half my schooling bored me. When I was seven or eight it occurred to me that if I wrote a story it would be PRINTED one day. This gave me a feeling of deliriously joyful power.

Q. Why did you take such a long time to write *Lanark*?

A. I meant to tell the whole story of a man's life. Before the age of 40 I was too young to do so.

Q. Is *Lanark* autobiographical?

A. Book 1 is wholly so, Book 2 less so, Books 3 and 4 barely so.

Q. Critics have called *Lanark* a blend of science-fiction and realism. What do you think of this description?

A. I'd say they'd just about got it right. It is always a pleasure to recognize the sort of people and places you know in a story – that is why realism stimulates. It is always a relief to see the people and places you know exaggerated to the level of the grotesque and exotic – that is why fantasy stimulates. I wanted my book to engage folk by both modes, since both modes have delighted me.

Q. How are you regarded in Scotland?

A. Scots have bought and commissioned my paintings. An Edinburgh publisher, Canongate, printed *Lanark* after three London publishers refused it because I would not shorten it. The Scottish Arts Council have bought my work and given me money. Scottish writers, some older, some younger (Archie Hind, Tom Leonard, Liz Lochhead, Jim Kelman and others) encouraged me by example and criticism before I was ever in print.

Q. Do you think that Scottish writers are perhaps too obsessed with politics?

A. None that I know. Most writers here agree with the majority of the Scottish people who have an opinion on the matter, and with the findings of the last three parliamentary commissions to investigate us. We think Scotland should be self-governing. But if we were more obsessed with government than with art we could not be artists. At the same time, politics are essential artistic material. All Shakespeare's tragedies happen in the families of leading politicians. Hamlet is a young statesman who prefers making bitter little opposition speeches in private to publicly fighting the murderer in charge of the country. In the end he only acts from private, not public motives, so Denmark is annexed by Norway. A very modern, very British politician.

Q. Did you ever regret being an artist?

A. Yes. My parents did not mind me painting, but they feared, correctly, that living to do it would bring me to dole-queues, and wearing second-hand clothes, and borrowing money, and having my electricity cut off – bring me to the state many respectable working folk are forced into during depressions, for reasons they cannot help. That I should become a seedy parasite in order to make obscure luxury items hardly anybody wanted depressed them, as it would depress me if my son took that course. So till a few years ago I was embarrassed if I had to tell people my profession. But that feeling of shame stopped last year when I earned enough to pay taxes, so it was not important.

Q. What is your political attitude?

A. My childhood and young manhood happened during the war and its aftermath, when Britain was a better state than nowadays, so politically I used to be an optimist. There was less wealth in the country, but it was carefully shared. We had full employment and tight price controls in those days, and a new welfare system operated by a government which wanted it to work. So although people who had been wealthy during the 1930's moaned about *austerity*, and company profits were low, most British people were better off than they'd been before or since. I thought Britain had achieved by peaceful means the democratic near-socialist state Russia had failed to get by violent revolution. I thought, in those days, Britain was an example to the world – in a few years we would be as classless as Denmark or Australia and as stable as Switzerland. Well, we can read in the papers what Britain went on to become. If we don't get a government which deals with the companies running the country as firmly as the coalition government did in the early forties, life here will get fouler and fouler and fouler. So although I am prospering by my work in the luxury trade I am glum about the future. Like most of us.

Q. What do you want to write next?

A. I have the libretto of an opera, *The Rumpus Room*, which I'd love to see put on.

Q. What made you write *1982, Janine?*

A. A wish to show a sort of man everyone recognizes and most can respect: not an artist, not an egoist, not even a radical: a highly skilled workman and technician, dependable, honest and conservative, who should be one of the kings of his age but does not know it, because he has been trained to do what he is told. So he is a plague and pest to himself, and is going mad, quietly, inside.

Q. What are the main themes of that novel?

A. Sex, politics, language and religion again.

Q. What are the main themes of your painting?

A. The Garden of Eden and the triumph of death. All my pictures use one or other or both. This is nothing abnormal. Any good portrait shows someone at a point in the journey from the happy garden to the triumph of death. I don't regard these states as far-fetched fantasies. Any calm place where folk are enjoying each other's company is heavenly. Any place where crowds struggle with each other in a state of dread is a hell, or on the doorstep of hell.

Q. How important to you is religion as a theme?

A. Religion is not a theme, religion – any religion – is a way of seeing the world, a way of linking the near, the ordinary, the temporary with the remote, the fantastic, the eternal. Religion is a perspective device so I use it, of course. I differ from church people in seeing heaven and hell as the material of life itself, not of an afterlife. Intellectually I prefer the Olympian Greek faith. Emotionally I am dominated by the Old Testament. Morally speaking I prefer Jesus, but he sets a standard I'm too selfish to aim for. I'm more comfortable with his daddy, Jehovah, who is nastier but more human. The world is full of wee Jehovahs.

Q. Do you see yourself as a writer who paints or a painter who writes?

A. Neither. Both are ways of showing something imagined at a level which precedes the words or outlines describing it.

Q. The first television programme about you, *Under the Helmet*, implied that you were dead. Why?

A. My friend, Bob Kitts, got a BBC television job and decided to make a film about me. His boss, Huw Wheldon, wanted to film me at home with my family, and painting a picture. He assumed that viewers prefer artists to the things they make, and that Van Gogh has given the world more pleasure by amputating his earlobe than by his pictures of sunflowers. But I was half the age I am now, more proud and honest, and wanted the viewers to be given, not me, but my words and pictures. Painting before a camera is like love-making before a camera – we have photographic proof that painters and lovers can do it, but who will take them seriously afterward? Bob Kitts decided that, since people prefer dead artists, and since I was unknown outside Glasgow, the film would grab the viewers' attention by suggesting – without actually stating – that I was dead: and telling the truth at the end. This would compel the viewers to re-examine their attitude to art and artists. I think the film succeeded, but the viewers disliked having to re-examine their attitudes. Changing your mind involves effort.

Q. You show a grim view of the opposite sex in your novels. Is this your usual attitude?

A. I certainly show the sexes disappointing and hurting each other, but love cannot last without doing and suffering a lot of damage. That does not mean love is a bad job – the pains of it are better in every way than the pains of loneliness. When I was younger I resented women because I seemed to be thinking of them all the time while they hardly ever thought of me. But nowadays half my friends are women. As Carlyle said after his honeymoon: 'I have been mercifully dealt with.'

Q. Do you feel that taking part in an interview like this is a damaging activity?

A. No. You and I are simply collaborating to provide harmless entertainment. We may fail, but that is unimportant because we will get paid all the same. And the large part of me that is sheer vanity is enjoying itself.

In Conversation
with Anthony Burgess
Richard Rayner
& Jonathan Meades

The Fiction Magazine interviewed Burgess when he was in London for the launch of *Enderby's Dark Lady*. He wore a frog-green sports shirt with a grey tie and a spiv's sports jacket – the style of a colour-blind man. He spoke with enthusiasm about England, politics and the novel. He regards his own role as a novelist as that of 'serious entertainer' though he refuses to mystify his craft. 'I start at the beginning,' he has said, 'go to the end, then stop.'

Q. What dictionary do you use?

A. The dictionary I like best is old and American, the 1926 Webster. It's pre-electronic but it's enormous and full of obscure dialect.

Q. Have dictionaries changed?

A. Oh yes, no question of that. I think the best dictionary is the Collins dictionary which came out a couple of years ago. It's very good, with biographic information as well. 'The Rolling Stones' are an entry for example.

Q. Is Anthony Burgess in it?

A. Yes, but with the wrong pronunciation of the name. I'm just above Burgess, Guy.

Q. Did you know him?

A. He's a member of the family, a rather remote Scottish branch.

Q. Did you ever meet him?

A. Never, never, never . . . I would have been seduced if I'd met him. He was a powerful and seductive man. That film *An Englishman Abroad* was very good. Coral Browne particularly. He pissed in our soup and we drank it.

Q. How far do you regard yourself as being an Englishman?

A. An Englishman? I never was English. I am mostly Irish and a bit of Scots. I don't suppose our family have much Anglo-Saxon blood left. We married into Ireland to keep the faith alive, you know the Catholic background. It's only the Catholic converts who have the luxury of being genuine Englishmen. Like Graham Greene.

Q. Do you hold on to your Catholic temperament?

A. I think I probably do. Other people want to become assimilated but I hang on to it chiefly to make a point against Graham Greene who regards himself as the *only* Roman Catholic. Evelyn Waugh was the same. Very rigid. A great writer but very uncharitable. His son is a bloody idiot.

Q. Isn't your solution to that to deny his existence?

ANTHONY BURGESS

A. I did that but Graham Greene assures me that Waugh does have a son. He *does* exist. He used to like my work but then he had to review a book called *The Paris Review Interviews* in which an interviewer asked me for a recipe for Lancashire hotpot. Which I gave. That turned Waugh (*fils*) off me. Of course, Lancashire Hotpot would never have been served in his father's house. Lancashire Hotpot has caused a lot of trouble. In *The Honorary Consul* Greene invented a Latin American restaurant which specialises in English food and they have a hotpot with carrots in it. Greene asked me, '*Are* there carrots in Lancashire Hotpot?' I said, 'No. There are *no* carrots in Lancashire Hotpot.' 'Oh, I see,' he said. 'I've done it again have I?'

Q. Would you ever come back to live in Lancashire? Or anywhere in England?

A. I don't know. I think that once you lose touch as I have, once you lose continuity it's very difficult to start again. I feel like a fool trying to work out how much the types of coins are worth. I don't know television personalities. I don't know who Terry Wogan is.

Q. Does this worry you?

A. It's the currency you see, the daily currency of life and also the currency of the modern English novel. Look at A. N. Wilson. I don't think I'd dare write a novel with a contemporary English setting. You've got a problem. You're doing it in English anyway and your view of English life is only an approximation to the reality. It's a problem. Greene finds this. I keep mentioning Greene because Greene lives not far from me. He's in the same situation as me but he doesn't worry about it. I worry. The *one* thing that we are in contact with is English pop music, that's the only aspect of English culture that I really meet. A lot of people have fallen for the youth culture thing. I suppose the great discovery is that people are no longer sure when middle age starts. They are not sure when they're old. I'm 67 now. I'm *obviously* old.

Q. Why do you write so much journalism still?

A. I enjoy it. I think you need that immediate contact with the audience. I like the deadline.

Q. Do you impose a deadline when you're writing a novel?

A. Not so much. Publishing does involve deadlines to some extent. The book I'm writing now has one because it's tied in with a TV series I've written and which has just finished filming. A ten hour mini-series called AD. So much research was involved I thought why waste it. Do a novel as well.

Q. Do you write films just for the money?

A. I think most British novelists have a financial problem which you don't associate with novelists in America, because of advances and because American novelists are subsidised by councils and universities. Few novelists in this country can afford to write long books. The time came late for me.

Q. Was *Earthly Powers* a deliberate attempt to write a bestseller, to make a lot of money?

A. Only one critic, David Holloway of the Daily Telegraph, spotted that it was supposed to be a *parody* of the bestseller form.

Q. Do you read books like *Princess Daisy*?

A. Yes, indeed. I read *Princess Daisy* with great interest. I read it only once. I read most books twice. It's an incredible work. So mindless. It's a great gift to be able to write like that. The high point of the book, the absolute summit, is where the hero is given the chance to make a 60 second commercial for Coca-Cola. To have one following stuff like this with interest is indeed quite an achievement. It was rather like my old friend Shirley Conran's book *Lace*. That was done, I think, rather more cynically. But it's similar. Human beings do not have brains, they have a large sexual apparatus. That is what it's about. She wrote *Lace* in Monaco and came round to me every evening with it. *That* was an interesting experience.

Q. Is there anything wrong in writing fiction just to make money?

A. I don't think that anyone has worked out the ethics of this kind of thing yet. There's nothing wrong with making a million dollars out of a book. But to pretend that book is a novel . . . I don't know. There's a lot that hasn't been thought out about the ethics and aesthetics of the novel.

Q. Aren't there novelists who have nothing in mind other than to entertain?

A. That's perfectly in order. I've always had a high regard for that. I included *Goldfinger* for instance, in my little squib *Best Novels Since 1939*. That made a lot of people angry. But Ian Fleming knew what he was doing and had no pretentions. Currently I'm very worried about the pornographic element. Alasdair Gray is a man I admire but his recent novel *1982, Janine* raised problems because I found it pornographic.

Q. Why?

ANTHONY BURGESS

A. Because it does excite the glands. And I think we have to avoid being excited in certain areas. I think that in writing fiction you are drawn to two areas – sex and violence – and you feel sometimes corrupted by writing about them. That's why it's a relief for me to get back to music. The climaxes there *suggest* violence only. Music's a safe art. Literature is not safe. I think Evelyn Waugh was aware of that, aware of the ethical and theological problems of writing fiction. Greene, being less intelligent than Waugh, doesn't see it clearly. Do you understand what I mean? Once you set up a scene in which somebody hits somebody, especially with sadistic overtones, you've abetted corruption in some sense.

Q. Isn't that the same argument which Mary Whitehouse directed against *A Clockwork Orange*?

A. That was against the film not the book. And I think she was right. In the book I tried to disguise what was happening – the violence – through language. In the film you saw it directly. It upset me a great deal.

Q. Isn't that underestimating the power of the book?

A. I can't answer that. I don't know.

Q. Do you read your fiction in translation?

A. It's one of the problems you have. One is not just a writer. You have to organise all this – all the translations and so on. I'm delighted when I'm translated well. One doesen't expect translation to be a close reworking of the original. But it must try and capture the original's tone and spirit.

Q. So it's possible for the translation to be better than the original?

A. This is so. And I would say that the German translation of *Earthly Powers* that has just come out *is* better than the original. It's the author's duty to watch the translation. Take Kingsley Amis for instance, an English writer I admire very much. He's better than Golding who I consider a very mediocre writer. But there were some fabulous blunders on the Italian translation of *Jake's Thing*. Kingsley should have watched that.

Q. Do you think your own style has become simpler and therefore more translatable?

A. I don't have a prose style. I don't think that a novelist should. Something the critics never notice is that there's no room for elegance in the novel because you're trying to record the current of life. To bring in Amis again, he's a *clumsy* writer. I am too. A sentence should look like the current of life. Clumsiness is part of it. Waugh in that sense is not a good novelist because he wrote in an Augustan, Gibbonian manner. You can't catch the current of people's feelings if you write elegantly.

Q. You've started a lot of books with dialogue?

A. Yes, dialogue is a help. You get dialogue on paper and it can start things flowing. It's a helluva problem, style. Every book should have its own style.

Q. Do you still go to Mass?

A. I go to Mass in a particular town in Italy because of one priest. But I don't normally. I don't regard myself as a Catholic except in the sense that I was brought up a Catholic.

Q. Yet your preoccupations are Catholic?

A. Bound to be. They have to be either Catholic or Marxist. I don't think there's any other way.

Q. What is your objection to socialism?

A. I don't believe it can work. It's based on a false conception of man. It always tends to tyranny. I don't know why but history shows that it does. In the 1930s I was a great believer in Catalonian anarchism. I was in fact a Communist then, a card carrying member. The Americans found out about that, of course, and made a fuss. But I gave it up in 1939. A lot of us were like that then and especially in the war because the class conflict was sharpened to the point of absurdity in the armed forces. We didn't hate the Germans, we hated our officers. Evelyn Waugh had to be protected from his own men. He was sent off to write *Brideshead Revisited* in *uniform*. He was a sensitive man, an artist, but he adopted the persona of the officer class.

Q. Did you want to be an officer?

A. No, I was a sergeant major. That was what I always wanted to be. Just a sergeant major.

Love Me Do

John Saul

I love you Diane. When you tie back your hair then I love you.
It's the same when you just stand there in a room with your
hands deep in your pockets. When you wear white. When your
laughing goes out of control. Only I can't agree with you over Paul
McCartney. Paul McCartney was a great singer, that is undeniable.
If he is still a great singer I don't know. Does saying was imply
isn't? Anyhow I agree that he was, we may treat that as a fact, one of
the true statements of our time. Just don't let's make a lexicon out
of his vocal qualities. Of course I love you Diane. Because I argue
with you doesn't mean I don't love you. I do, and I won't say it
again. Things don't become true by being repeated. Certainly not,
no, I would not jump through a ring of fire for you, are you mad? A
paper hoop perhaps. What John Lennon would have done for
Yoko Ono is hardly relevant. All I'm saying is that John Lennon
was a great singer too. Take A Hard Day's Night. Diane if you say
you would go through fire for me that's all very well, all very
terrific. Not to say a load of baloney. If I said to you now, move that
saucepan to one side and put your hand in the flame you wouldn't. I
hope you wouldn't. Not even in the direst circumstances, no.
Quite what circumstances did you have in mind? Diane I hardly
think a butterfly tattooed on your thigh would make a lasting
statement about us, do you. Tattoo yourself one by all means but it
will always be your butterfly. What was I saying? John Lennon,
where he takes over from Paul McCartney for the last verse. Mm,
he sang Mm. When did you ever hear anything so brilliant?
Trivial? It was not in the least trivial. You listen to it sometime.
Diane sit down, please. Of course I've heard Revolver, don't be
preposterous. Paul McCartney was everything you say on
Revolver. You don't have to get up in the middle of breakfast to
play it. Why Got to Get You into My Life? If you have something to
say then say it, don't play these games. What? Do you really want
to know that? If you must know, at the time Revolver came out I
was with a girl called Janet. I must have mentioned her before. The
one with rich parents, whose mother made ceramic tables. Had a
Pyrenean mountain dog called Rex? I must have mentioned her.
Since you ask we spent half the summer being idle. Lying prostrate
on an enormous green slope in some park nobody else used. Paul
McCartney floated about the sky singing Good Day Sunshine.
Actually Janet sided for John Lennon too. Said he was the sharp
one. Details, what details? She always brought along lemon juice in

231

a tartan thermos flask. With Janet? Absolutely not. Snogging, that's all. Too comatose from the sun. Mini skirts? Why bring up mini skirts? Yes, if you want to know yes. She had black, purple, maybe pink. Funny when you ask me what she looked like, the funny thing is I always see her face as being in the sunlight. Diane don't. It's nothing to be upset about. No, I can't honestly say that whenever I think of you I see your face in the sunlight. Retract? Retract what? All I can do is tell you the truth. How do you mean, that isn't enough? Please stop hovering by the door and sit down. Hold on, let me close my eyes and think. When I think of you I see . . . you directly in the eyes and your eyes are beautiful. No, I fully admit your face was not in the sunlight if I concentrate. Your hair is tied back, your eyes are beautiful and I love you. What do you mean you'll never play Revolver again? Diane I only told you about Janet because you asked. I thought you wanted to face up to this retrospective jealousy thing. I see, all I am doing is adding to your feeling of guilt, is that right. Mind with the kettle. Could you turn the flame out altogether, if you would be so kind. What is there to get all churned up about? That sunlight, as you call it, that sunlight belongs back in nineteen sixty-six and cannot fall again. Einstein. I tell you something else, I've gone right off this boiled egg. Diane don't fly off the handle. You don't eat I don't eat, what kind of talk is that? And this nicely sliced tomato? Diane, come. I eat – you eat, agreed? You know, when you're putting tomato on your bread and you sort of pat it down with your fingers and look at it with your head on one side, when you do that there's something wonderful about you. Diane when you call someone a creep don't you think you might look at them. What rain, when? I never said I pictured you in the rain. When I closed my eyes just now you were definitely indoors, as it happens, sitting at a table rather like now. Well you were sitting a moment ago. You were not grimacing, you were smiling. No you did not have your I'm Waiting to Meet Paul McCartney look, I never said such a thing. I said that last year in Scotland? What has last year in Scotland to do with anything? I am not shouting Diane kindly do not insist that I am shouting when I am not shouting. I am not, I do not want to and even if I wanted to I wouldn't. My throat is dodgy enough in the mornings as it is. I don't know why it is but it is. Love a duck Diane. Can you once and for all leave walking through fire out of this. I will categorically not go through fire, shoot rapids, swim oceans or stand on aeroplane wings for you but I love you. Mm. Yes. Taste what? I taste of fish. That's great. Crab. Is this another of your games? I don't remember what I dreamed, no. Watch it, somebody's toast is burning. Yes of course we'll relax, being Sunday. Shouldn't I say that? I'm talking to you aren't I, not working through some pasty grammar. Do you know we had a teacher who showed us a sentence with five thats. Dead now. Diane said that that that that that man John Lennon sang was not a patch on Paul McCartney's. I can talk like that if you prefer. Start what? You began. A stockbroker in Rye or roundabouts got it into his head to request She's a Woman for his bride-to-be and you began your same old speech on the glories of a certain rock singer's voice. That wonderful gravel or whatever you called it at the bottom of his throat. You spoke up for him so I spoke up for John Lennon. So what if they were, fed up being compared, it was bound to happen. And I tell you something that's generally overlooked which you can't compare to Paul McCartney, and that is that John Lennon played the most astounding rhythm guitar you ever heard. All My Loving. This Boy. Remember This Boy? I suppose it is about jealousy, yes. Though I would hardly say that emerges through the guitar work, would you? Diane I am not out to provoke you. Why should I say precisely what snogging means to me, if I tell you that you'll still be on about it this time next year. I have no reason to believe my snogging was special, no. No, Janet's was not special either. I know because I know. What great experience without parallel, what are you talking about? I just know, the same as I know the money in my pocket is my own, the same way I know no one in your family will polevault to an Olympic medal. What's more I don't enjoy snogging, so there. Diane. If I say I don't enjoy liquorice that does not imply I chewed some last week. Diane a person can be over-sensitive. There was no blazing great unparalleled experience of teenage love. The dizzy climax was reached, the true meaning of passion revealed, I freely divulge, with a face and name I don't remember, on a coach whose purpose, starting point and destination have sunk their deepest in the bogs of past time. Yes it must have lurched sideways at roundabouts, what an unncessary question. It's called centrifugal force. Diane that is entirely speculation on your part. She had a musty smell, there my memory begins and ends, it came as a shock at the time and it's not much of a fact to cling to you'll agree! I know that she sweated because I saw the patches under her arms, how's that. My head aches. Must you play records on a Sunday morning, and so loud. That's better, a little, thank you. Diane I told you, I don't remember any dream. Not since the one with the river and the purple dinner last week. Guess, how can I guess what you dreamed about? Paul McCartney, uh-huh, I might have guessed. You went shopping with Paul McCartney and you bought matching striped shirts. I bet when they recognised him they wouldn't take his money, did they? I see, star shopping after hours. He played you a song with an accordion, standing in a taxi, how very decent of him. Let me guess which song. He composed it there in the corner of the taxi with his face to the window. It was a limousine type of taxi. And? It was called Gold, and it was. You mean in quality. Really. I suppose you didn't ask when the release date was. Exclusively for you Diane, uh-huh. Do you know that or did he tell you that? Diane I didn't say I didn't trust him, it occurred to me as it would to anyone, perhaps he says that to all of them. I know that he's married and lives on an island, that doesn't make him a monk, if he's remote what's he doing with you in a taxi in the first place. He asked if there was a man in your life and you said sort of. Marvellous. I presume you mean sort of in your life, not sort of a man. I wouldn't say I was flattered Paul McCartney asked after me, no. John Lennon? I couldn't imagine him asking after me at all somehow. Then you and Paul were off to the Swiss Alps, like in Help. You stood in the snow and shared a pair of headphones. Did he keep his accordion on all the time? I had a chalet next to yours, well that's something. He had to go to a recording and you and I made a snowman. Diane if he flung off his accordion exclusively for you or went recording it's all the same to me. He was sensitive, I'm glad. Doubtless the artistic temperament. In what way sensitive? You could just tell, I see. It must have been terrifically psychic for you. You noticed he was not clumsy for instance. I get the idea. Don't tell me, I burst into your chalet and fell down in a heap of skis. Diane sometimes I'm not so sure you love me at all. It's nothing to laugh about, Christ. Not when I love you like I do.

3 exceptional **1st** novels from the publishers who launched Peter Ackroyd, William Boyd, Clare Boylan and Jane Gardam . . .

1 ▶ **THE GLASS HOUSE**

MONIQUE CHARLESWORTH

Obsession, blackmail and murder – the other face of the German economic miracle – in an outstanding first novel set in Hamburg.
£9.95   July

2 ▶ **BARS OF AMERICA**

NEIL FERGUSON

Interstate freeways and down-town bars, gas stations and fast food cafes, these provide the background to a vivid series of encounters between assorted fugitives from the American Dream – black and white, cops and cowboys, bartenders and prostitutes.
£9.95   June

3 ▶ **BORROWED TIME**

AMNON JACKONT

A powerful political novel illuminating the conflict of loyalties facing those caught up in the Arab/Israeli confrontation. It has already provoked a furore in Israel.
£9.95   April

hamish hamilton

THE
TIPPERARY
FANALE

Desmond Hogan

Olivieri Di Fazio wrote home in 1954 that there were beacons in the sky over County Mayo like lavish, celestial messages, stars, fat, puffed out stars over a flat landscape which ran with stones and splintered rocks. From that letter on Gisella wanted to join her brother in this country, Ireland, and in particular in the country within a country which the West of Ireland, Olivieri's stamping ground, seemed to comprise. In fact it was not just Gisella who followed her brother to Ireland but two other brothers. Olivieri had laid claim to a few shelled shop premises on the main streets of decrepit towns and was turning them into cafés. Old counters swore with the pain of being renovated, drapery store counters, millinery counters, and being turned into food counters. Run down streets, dowdy town halls baulked at these new spots of energy but there they were, the gleaming Di Fazio facades, usually a sanguine red which retained its freshness long after it was painted and reminded Gisella when she arrived of one of her reasons for leaving Italy, wanting to forget.

Olivieri Di Fazio, then a young man of twenty five, with the curly, pale copper Di Fazio hair, had encountered Breda Finuacane on her pilgrimage to Assisi in the holy year, 1950, on one of those trips she took away from the focus of her pilgrimage. He encountered her in a village square and walked, almost mechanically, up to her, his smile somehow electrified by her strangeness, red, flossed hair, a face with all the dramatic brown twinges of a bog in it.

She would gurglingly relate that incident for years afterwards, becoming, unnoticed to herself, plump and grey, in the telling of it, though still retaining the floss in her hair, a Virgin Mary pale blue coat on her springy bosom in the cafe which she and her husband looked after. Near the café was a bog, a bog coming close to the main street, the bog a sea behind the main street, a reminder with its few, isolated lights of the fatalities of life. It was these lights which inspired Gisella to christen her café 'The Tipperary Fanale' — 'The Tipperary Beacon' — though her café was not situated in County Tipperary. It was as if she, like a dazed traveller, had mistaken her location at first but in fact she just liked the name Tipperary. It was in a song she remembered from childhood and she was surprised to find that Tipperary, a verbal signpost of her childhood, was to be found in Ireland.

Her husband had the cement business and the builders'

providers business behind the cafe. There was also a shed full of wood chippings there, the chippings spilling out into the sun, blond, and giving off an immaculate smell at odds with the smells of the rest of the yard, which was about her only reminder of Italy in those first few years of marriage, the smell of the wood chippings invoking the smell of the covert yet spacious depths of forests near her home in Italy.

The Di Fazio's had set up in Ireland very swiftly, thanks initially to the benign lump of money left to his son-in-law by Breda Finuacane's father who died after the marriage between his daughter and the young Italian, without much delay. Olivieri started a small industry and his brothers came and fostered some of the cafés. Gisella opened her own, on the premises of her husband's house. She'd met Ciarán Ward shortly after arrival in Ireland and allowed herself to be wooed by him, in the spirit of swift Di Fazio nuptuals on Irish soil. He had blond hair that was leaving his head, came from County Galway and held a suppliant hat in his hand on front of the suit he always donned to make the point that he was interested in her.

Gisella became an Irish girl. Her parents came to none of the weddings in Ireland. One by one the Di Fazio's were renouncing their family in Italy, that grandmother with the pigeon silver hair and the bottom that stuck out like that of a pigeon, a worried arch on her nose, the grandfather who forever sat, still in black, on a bench outside the family home, his eyes hopeless, almost unmoving since the war, the parents who'd rarely come out of the house since the war.

After two sons she nearly forgot Italy but ironically the sons had Italian names, Vincenzo and Salvatore and there were those links to Italy, the name over her café, the names of her sons, the café now the meeting place of town bard – a national school teacher in a chocolate coloured suit who spoke Russian and who wrote poems on children's school exercise books – and of town profligate, a big, burdensome man in a heavy coat who exposed himself on the main street after midnight, pulling back that coat to surprise some homeward going, dance-loving virgins.

There was a river in the town and Gisella sat by it and sun bathed in summer; she wrote letters beside it, back home. Italian was breaking down and Italian words careered into English words on the page. She wanted to forgive the family secret but now family was integrated into Ireland, and the idea of forgiveness became distant. Her parents no longer seemed to belong to her. There was the warm air, sensuality on her legs, lightwaves behind duomas of tree tops on the other side of the river. A boy came to her one day beside the river when there were teddyboys, he one of them, about to emigrate to England, recognising her from the café, and brought her under a hawthorne tree recently relieved of its blossom and made love to her, the white chest of his over big, funereal black swimming togs wearing a little floret of ash hair. Later she heard he'd been killed working on a rail line by a juncture of a myriad rail lines in Birmingham.

Before long Vincenzo was as old as that boy. Vincenzo played on the local hurling team, covered his own languid white chest in the blue and white local stripes, emerged as a hero from one or two games which decided mastery, was hoisted on local shoulders where he fitted easily. Vincenzo was a photograph in the local press. Ancestral looks had emerged in him, black hair which split over his face in a furnace, cheekbones that cracked in an orange, painted colour, sculpted, berry lips. 'The Italian' Vincenzo was called. As if he was the only one of them worthy of his race, the 'the' becoming a gruffer 'de' with time on the lips of men who spent most of their summer days fishing for pike. There were forebodings in that. Vincenzo had been assimilated into the preconceptions of Irish machismo. This sense of machismo had been well fostered when, after a short course, he got a job as a television repair man in County Donegal. He chose the job because it brought him far from home and allowed him to veer around roads under drunkenly undulating mountains in a landscape at times harsh, unrelenting, tobacco coloured and at times a piquant green as if he was on the loose in the Wild West. There was a lot of anarchy about County Donegal. Little wayside post offices which also sold sweets; 1950's cigarette signs outside as if they were messages pleading vulnerability, cigarette smoke static over yellowed cigarettes since the nineteen fifties, being constantly robbed by I.R.A. men and little old ladies being gagged and tied up, their pale blue uniforms still on, beside cages which boasted rare breeds of budgie. In the meantime, while Vincenzo was acquainting himself with burly and bearded hordes in pubs in Letterkenny, raucously singing with them into the small hours, Salvatore, a frailer specimen, was attending the local boys' school, attaining academic honours. There'd been little communication between them as they grew up, five years between them, and now communication and liaison of personalities were extinct. Salvatore was the one who talked of Italy, who reminded Gisella when it was early spring near her home in Italy, who quested for Italy with the determination of a catechetics student. He wore his hair in an aggravated thickness as was fashionable in the mid seventies; a nonchalence about his shoulders in their anemic anorak. 'Salve' the local boys called him. He had his great grandmother's nose, a bony and contorted arch to it. The boys' secondary school was built in the nineteen thirties, a bland, pale square of a building. There were cherry blossoms outside, in concentrated abundance where they were permitted, only at the side of the building, and cherry blossom creeping around the Ceylon Road like military marchers in a painting by Uccello, when Salvatore's father died suddenly in his late fifties. The smallness of grief Gisella felt made her realize how little of a marriage there'd been, what a non-event of a relationship there'd been; all these years she'd been forgetting Italy behind the archetypes of another country – only the two sons the marriage produced seemed real, manifest, involving for her. So she withdrew from her husband's grave without grief and set back to work in the café which had now expanded into the adjoining premises and could cater for busloads of soccer players or busloads of pilgrims who'd set down in an interim between travelling on their bus to some site of a miracle or an apparition, the sight of these ladies under their scarves tucking into a meal of chips with pornographic deluges of ketchup on them becoming common. Gisella had walked away from her husband's grave but with a little withered pink chiffon scarf around her neck. It was taken as a nuance of Italy. But in fact it was an excuse to wear the brooch which clasped it, a brooch her youngest brother had given her years before, the one who was killed during the war.

'Madame,' the smelly aged town profligate called her over, 'Madame, I sympathise with you.' He took her hand and manouvred it in his, feeling for her ring with the jade in it. The town poet said: 'Your heart will go down to the grave with him only to fly out. I know what it feels like.' His mother had died the year before. Vincenzo was home, having taken over the cement and builders' providers business, working away in the yard.

He was changed, squatter, masked in a fluffy and aggressive

looking beard. There was even a little touch of a Northern accent in his Southern accent, the Northern accent of County Donegal a twin accent to that of the television world of Northern Ireland troubles, County Donegal she'd forgotten hemming in the Northern Ireland state in fluid little crevices. These crevices were the ones I.R.A. men on the run jumped over. Gisella thought, incongruously: 'He has an I.R.A. accent. There was a little pub in town which had the tricolour always unfurled on the wall and this was the pub Vincenzo went to now. There were dark congregations under this flag. But Vincenzo's demeanour insulated him from questions; he was very much the male presence; the fulcrum. He took over, swinging with his arms and working in the yard. He cut his beard off and cut his hair to marry. That was the first time Gisella's parents came to Ireland.

There was a photograph taken in the fair green, near the hotel, all the Italians and Irish, Gisella's parents and the young nephews and nieces from Italy, the brothers in Ireland, the sons and daughters of Gisella's brothers, but prettiest of all were three Italian nephews who'd come with Gisella's parents, three mascots, all of her part of Italy gathered into their faces, rounded, jovial faces with dumpy chins, dumpy eyes, freckles sieved on their faces, three identical suits on them, black shoes shining, blue, pink and blue again collars respectively open on them like the colours of shop fronts on a more flagrant Irish street.

After that there was collusion with Italy; letters; conviviality. Italy had made a mark in town and it was no coincidence that in Saint John's Church on the hill, a squat Protestant building, during the autumn harvest thanksgiving that the Italian Renaissance was mentioned by the rector as a metaphor of ever renewing hope. His daughters looked out from their pew, three girls with the hair of Botticelli angels. They'd had little affairs with Italian boys over for the wedding. They looked guilty now, their hair a pristine, almost silver blonde.

There was a rush of correspondence between Gisella and her mother; domestic things, ignored in and unfed into their minimal correspondence, were covered and quickly saturated. The rhythm of conversation started up in their correspondence, the frenetic, rising pitches of voices, the convulsed higher notes. The drama of conviviality, of closeness. It had not happened since before the war. Gisella's parents were old traitors, They were both emerging from their shame now for some crumbs of intimacy; old, mangy dogs both of them, lean in the stomach, dun coloured, their disproportionate heads drooping on front of them. Zammìo had died for them, had sacrificed his life for them or at least for Gisella's father when Gisella's father was abruptly going to be done away with, by hanging, by mutilation, by a gun, no one was sure. A liberated, hysterical horde gathered around the house where the black shirts had been burnt inside, one on top of another, the remains of them still in a grate, Zammìo had proferred himself; his chest had been very bold in that white shirt of his, it had stuck out, with adolescent defiance, the replete breasts of his chest. Maybe it was because he'd looked so well fed and defiant that the crowd took up his offer, ritualistically, and one of the men shot him in the head outside town. Afterwards the mob faded into non-existence and people of the village claimed they'd had no part in it; that this mob was comprised of inhabitants of the fields, the mountains, the borders of one distant field and another. Everybody had it mentally annihilated. There was a truce in that. Zammìo was buried and it might have been that he'd never lived. Gisella had taken the white shirt with the blood on it off his body and walked with it as though with a wounded bird whose life could still be saved. She'd walked as though hypnotised, in the direction of the village church. But there she'd found a flock of geese who'd escaped from the war and, suddenly screaming, she left the white shirt in the holy water font parched of water, three saints sculpted at the base of the font, three indifferent medieval male presences.

'Mrs. Ward, I'm sorry to hear about Vincenzo. But it's still a good cause after all. He was doing it for Ireland.'

Two years after his marriage Vincenzo was taken away after a Garda swoop on 'The Tipperary Fanale' and particularly on the yard at the back and convicted of manufacturing cement containers for bombs and arranging their transport up to the Donegal and Tyrone border. Nobody else in the family had known; nobody could have known. The ordinary looking containers could have been anything in the way of industrial implements. Vincenzo and his wife had lived in the adjoining house to Gisella, on the expanded premises of 'The Tipperary Fanale'. A flat had been made for them on the first floor. The wife now, a girl from the outer townlands, left the flat, arranged a legal separation – realizing she'd never really known Vincenzo very well – and the last that was heard of her was that she was a secretary in a modelling agency in Dublin, male modelling it was said, as well as female modelling.

The first time Gisella saw Vincenzo in prison – it was summer – he had a little nugget of black hair in the middle of his chest which despite summer was very white, his shirt off, and she was reminded of Zammìo's chest. Nakedness was the demense, the password of Irish politics. But Vincenzo's beard was shaved, he looked changed, his hair was neater. He was an adolescent among other adolescents and among hairy specimens of Irish heroes. The building was unwisely built. You might have been entering Auschwitz. It took you in a grey, Victorian grasp and seemed not willing to let you out. The summer heat had denuded the yellow irises growing in the town river, right down to their feet. They stood up, vacantly, from the water and little spirals of mud patches. 'Vincenzo.' The young man on the other side of the bars was a stranger, someone whose development she had ignored for years. When the image had become explicit, that of the Irish revolutionary, the politics went. Confronting her was just a pale, adolescent-looking shell.

Observing his neat, fashionable hair cut she informed him that the barber, Gregory De Mare, at home had died, a man of reputed French Huguenot extraction, who'd clipped away in town with a scissors since he'd gone bald at the age of twenty two, only a black bushy tail left around his head since that time.

Vincenzo did not respond. She saw not just a prisoner behind bars but a prisoner of his own self deceptions; only now that he was jailed was Vincenzo changing and a sensitivity, always implicit in him, not just emerging but enveloping him. The shaved, almost wounded looking jaws were evidence of this. He looked at her with another history from that of Ireland, one she'd tried to repress. He looked for the first time as if he was acquainted with his origins, cut off from them for a long time, with only debased superficialities connecting him with them. 'De Italian.' A young man looked at her with a face that wanted to go back to where it rightly belonged but could not, among the pale florets of young men's faces standing around a dancefloor in her adolescence.

The people of town were subdued, charitable in their response to the event; she could take a bus back to the town as though to a bosom whose darkness would take hold of her and let her lose her splintered and throbbing heart in it.

It was not an unusual story in Ireland at the time; in fact it was in many ways unsensational; only 'The Tipperary Fanale' gained from it and sent out new, dangerous signals which allured many more people into it.

To everybody's surprise Salvatore, the frail, literary shouldered one, decided to study engineering at Galway University. He wanted something as an antidote to the works of literature he read all through adolescence. He began to study in a rectangular modern building. He still moved around, in that fawn anorak. He started the year Vincenzo went to prison.

Two boys; Salvatore had always felt repressed by Vincenzo. Now that Vincenzo was in prison Salvatore began playing football in Galway, running around a muddy field near the lake, more for the colour of the soccer jerseys than anything else, bright red. He enjoyed pushing forward his legs as he wore the bright red jersey, exhibiting himself with drama. It was his invocation of Italy.

And as Salvatore was becoming more physical, even going for winter swims in the sea at Blackrock, exposing a guache, white, though oddly full body with embarrassed spider-grey hairs on the legs, Vincenzo was conversely becoming literary in prison, poring over books on religious matters, inspired by an I.R.A. colleague who decided to turn to God but not the God of the religious paintings in the church in Ballymurphy, Belfast, but a more tender, less Irish God.

Near the prison lived a Protestant parson, once parson in the environs of Walsingham in Norfolk, England, and this man in his cottage with its honey coloured thatch was making a study of the Gnostic gospels and their relation to the cult of Isis in Egypt. He had little pamphlets printed by a local press which purported to presage a new age of peace. These pamphlets had got into the prison and to the I.R.A. man, Vincenzo's friend. An I.R.A. warrior became docile, ameliorated by what he read, his face frankly shedding its beard and shining with a kind of dazed gladness.

The parson tried to visit his new converts but this man, all in black, with the wide brimmed black hat of a Victorian priest in Ireland, was considered by the prison authorities as a possible subversive, having no family business with the prisoners and after a period of him dangling, literally – his figure was long and lean – in

244

the waiting room he was turned away. The incident had only added an extra grimace to Vincenzo's face when Salvatore came to see him at the Easter after he'd started at university. Outside in a yard men traipsed around, repeating the same patterns of walking, Irish heroes, now grey motifs against a grey background. Inside Vincenzo asked him, through bars, for certain books. So in the next months Salvatore ferried books into Vincenzo, books about the Egyptian cult of Isis, about the Gnostic gospels, about the symmetry and mathematics of Chartres Cathedral. In a prison cell Vincenzo had started his own renaissance.

Easter 1984 there were prints of Botticelli paintings on the wall of 'The Tipperary Fanale', over the trough of bubbling chips, a rectangular tableau of economically muscular Italian soccer players in demon red. The place had changed; the time had changed; Vincenzo was being let out of jail a year later. Gisella, her hair having turned from copper to grey, was going back to Italy that Easter, for a wedding, her first time to Italy since she'd left. The grey of her hair was not the grey of wisdom, she'd lost two sons, one to jail, the other to England – Salvatore had given up his studies and was being very successful in the insurance business in London, making a lot of money, having already purchased a flat. He'd tired of academic things, ideas. He was gruff and well dressed now. Vincenzo, by contrast, was docile and, Gisella thought sometimes, almost senile. They both seemed somewhat deranged and outside her scope, beyond the limits of her sympathy, not because she didn't want to care but because they had made themselves dream-like, their gestures had wrought an emotional collapse in her towards them; she had no language to translate their gestures for herself. She felt herself virtually impotent towards them. Her two sons gone from her nearest concern her mind was preoccupied elsewhere. It was as if thoughts were rising over the landscape of her life, like marchers approaching over a distant hilltop. There was 'The Tipperary Fanale' always to keep her thoughts from her, to buffet her against them. But they kept approaching, a funeral march from long ago, the bringing of a body from the countryside. She had to reckon not just with Zammìo's death but with all the filaments of adolescence she'd left behind in Italy. 'The Sandpiper' starring Elizabeth Taylor and Richard Burton was playing at the Town Hall cinema for the umpteenth time when she left for Italy, persuading customers away for the umpteenth time the night before she left, to see Elizabeth Taylor in a shaggy painter's tunic going out to encounter the sandpipers of beaches near Monterey. So few people realized that Gisella was packing. Her face had been a kind of cinematic experience for her customers for years, the attraction of momentary, inscrutable images on it.

That Gisella was making a much wider journey was only evident to Marylin, her main assistant, the night before Gisella left, in a gesture which scared Marylin. As the café was closing, emptied, Gisella reached a fingernail to the Italian soccer players on the wall and scratched one of their faces, leaving a visible abrasion in the picture and a surprised look in an adolescent face.

The plane journey was to Pisa; Dublin had looked jubilant in sunshine, inviting her to stay. The drone of the plane went way inside her, a fearful, tense, drilling reverberation, an anticipation of the echoes of war which would inevitably reach her in Italy.

Zammìo had brought a dead rabbit home one day, holding the rabbit by its hindlegs. The rabbit had been tortured. Zammìo had confronted his father with it as though confronting him with an image of his beliefs but Zammìo's father had only seen in the blood and mutilation a kaleidoscopic equivalent to the bolder passages of Italian history.

Gisella and Zammìo had buried the rabbit, holding one another over the clay when it was settled again. Zammìo's chest had been generous and unrecoiling against her body. Zammìo's body had notified her of the male body; she picked out other young men from the dancefloor but their neat chests, their laundered and genteel embraces always sent her back to Zammìo. There had been something burlier about his body which had made her inquisitive. His chest had grown bigger in the course of their affair, the breasts of his chest more rotund. That no one knew of their affair was a mark of their mutual deviousness and of their exhilaration with one another which determined them to keep the secret. That she had been pregnant by her brother when he'd died had been a secret she'd kept all these years. She'd gone to Florence to have the baby but lost it. A mangled embryo had merged into an image she'd kept with her all these years, that of a little boy, as heir to the love between herself and Zammìo and as mental talisman. At Pisa airport there was a little boy in a blue and white striped tee shirt who looked at her as if she was the mother he was expecting from the plane and then he looked away. She had registered the untroubled waves of auburn of his hair though.

After staying the night with relatives a car brought her through the hills; the yellow blobs of mustard seed hills. Towers pivoted on hills, modern water towers and medieval-domicile towers. They refreshed themselves at an open air café in the hills which was packed with tourists but tourists from other parts of Italy. It was Holy Thursday. Light ran amok over the windscreens of jammed, parked cars. Gisella breathed deeply before getting into the car again. In half an hour she would be home. She was a grey haired woman in a demure, grey Irish suit, a snake skin handbag on front of her, acrobatic wriggles of red in the patterns of the bag. She looked almost like one of those pilgrims that alighted in her cafe. All she needed was the little vinegar or perfume bottle of holy water beside her, holy water scooped in the course of the pilgrimage. The sun in her hair made it look white and somewhat mad though. There was a green in her eyes which had not been noticeable for years but the green was part of a middle aged woman's face now and not that of a girl and the green looked fierce and demanding among the pallor of skin and hair. Gisella clutched the handbag awkwardly. She had lost the language of Italian self-confidence with items like handbags.

There was a fiera in the village the first days she stayed in it. Young men came out onto the steps leading to the square in the late afternoons, ties on them, many coloured shirts, spectacular shouldered jackets. Old men mingled with almost unnoticeable movements with the boys. Young and old looked eventually like actors coming on stage for the applause at the end of a drama. The difference between the old men's faces and the young men's faces was that the young men's faces looked more faraway, more enthralled. Maybe it was because it was near Easter but there was something devotional and silent in the stance of young men. The women just went home with bread. The young men had infiltrated the fiera with the gestures of standing too, silent effigies around the bumpers, the sun prodding purple and emerald shirts. In the evening the mystically unchanging village towers and the gaudy turrets of the fiera merged, the big wheel going around and around and making you dizzy to the music of young girls' rhythmic squeals.

She had not found what she had been expecting, the werewolves

of history, public and personal, waiting to grab her. The
werewolves had gone. But instead she'd discovered that she'd been
grabbed by another country's history and inexorably trapped in it.
The arc of Irish history, that perennial, green landscape-haunting
rainbow had touched her life and trapped her much more than
Italian history had ever done. In trying to get away she'd made a
cage for herself of much tougher wires. She was bound now, by her
life, by her children, to Ireland's tragedies and mistakes. Italy was
an escape for her, a revelation, maybe even a renaissance. The
biggest revelation being that ghosts don't stay around. The village
had lost its ghosts. But there was one ghost or remonstrance of the
past that had stayed and flourished, the image of a little boy.

You have children but they are not your real children. There
were children long ago who are more real for you. The image of the
little boy had stayed with Gisella all these years. For some reason he·
wore a blue and white striped tee shirt now. When she bumped into
a boy on the steps of the church on Easter Sunday the child in her
mind suddenly had that boy's bony nose and ethereal cheekbones.
There are things in you that grow and grow, ideas, put together
from the bits of experience that confront you in everyday life. They
are the things that ultimately save you from insanity. They are also
the things that give you a pivot to escape from, to start again.

On Easter Sunday night Gisella managed to free herself of her
female company, company of assorted ages, and saunter off by
herself, cardigan hanging from her shoulders, and grasp something
of the fiera at night by herself. A young man laconically looked at
her against a rouge background, a few sharpshooters lined up
beside him, backs to the fiera, aiming at targets patterned against
the rouge. His arms were folded on front of him and his stance, like
that of so many young men in this country this mesmeric weekend,
distilled silence and seemed to challenge you into similar heights of
silence and stillness. This time Gisella was, guardedly, still and
silent, looking, her body and head poised sideways, towards the
boy. There was a tiny retraction in the arms of the boy but the eyes
became bigger, bolder, more black hued. There was curiosity,
indolence, respect in them. He knew this was someone different.
They became sloe-black, child's eyes, expansive, unbiddable,
direct. There was now contact made between them which she
could not back out of. So she continued to be still and told the boy,
by telepathic messages, the story of her life. There was a furnace in

his black eyes when the big wheel swept into them and an explosion of his white shirt when some wagon lit up in its descent near him or some stall's light went on and off, catching him momentarily in going on. Stalls were lighthouses, signalling. Gisella went on. Stalls tried to ravish her, lighting up with their wares of pink teddybears with prostrate, gangly legs. Gisella had lost the boy. She encountered a man's face between a pile up of porcelain, idiot faced, bonneted dolls. He looked at her accusingly. There were doughy jowls beneath his keenly unshaven face. She was one of them, the fascisti. He had the face of a cabbalist. There was emnity in it, contempt. Gisella had to go away with his spittle on her face. The spittle reflected the wounds of three awkward red bulbs. She was back at a fiera long ago, once when she tried to step out of the house despite her parents' warning. There had been red blotches on her white dress that night and they'd become further encumbered, at the back, her arms folded precipitously on front, by dashes of a purple substance someone had thrown. Gisella had not noticed until she'd got home. But something had been achieved that night, an attempt at freedom, a stubborn attempt to integrate herself into the fiera and dissolve her past in it. She'd come home though from the attempt, like a bird with a sprained leg and inanimate wings. But there had been still movement in those wings, a movement she'd tested more and more and finally became joyous and somewhat potent with. One day she took off.

'The Tipperary Beacon' waited for her in Ireland. There was a loose hair of heather, fallen from a bunch of heather further on on the shelf, under the tableau of the Italian soccer players the night she got home, the cafe closed. It was already actually the small hours of the morning. Her fingers pulled the hair of heather over and off the shelf where dust had been allowed to accumulate. It came as no surprise to anyone when a few months later she sold 'The Tipperary Fanale' and returned to Italy, waiting first to bring a son who had an Irish tricolour inerasibly tatooed on the billow of slightly jaundiced muscle on the uppermost part of a feebler and more impotent arm.

Poems/Hugo Williams

Sonny Jim in Love

They left me alone with the pens
and I have gone over my loved one's face
in ink, for something to do.
I wanted to see how she looked
telling me not to, so I let my hand
trail on her cheek like a hook.
Wasn't I her pet? Her little marmoset?
I traced a well-worn path
back and forth between her eyes
in search of crumbs.
I ran the gauntlet of her tantrums.

When she drew ahead of me
I scribbled for my life. Jagged lines
shot this way and that like looks
blurring her skin. Nervous attention
(glance towards) alternated rapidly
with nervous submission (glance away)
until I felt dizzy. I gave her
horn-rimmed spectacles, blacking them in
where her eyes accused me of
following her round the room. I broke a nib
crossing out her kindness to the dog.

I wasn't satisfied
till I had joined up her eyes and mouth
in a rough-hewn triangle,
a monkey-face. I watched a pen
snag the corner of her mouth, spattering
ink on my cuff. I went through
the paper and the paper beneath
in my efforts to make good.
When they asked me what I was drawing in my book
I told them everyone looked like that
by the time I had scribbled my gaze on them.

Sonny Jim's House

The cistern groans under a new pressure.
Little known taps are being turned on
in obscure regions of the house,
cutting off the water for his tea.
Jim forwards her mail to the garden, laughing
because he has hidden the marmalade.

At nine they both stay home and do nothing,
out of work. The ring in the bath and the
hacked loaf prove he is on the track
of his elusive wife. Her movements displace
the usual volume of elegant soft-porn: face-
creams and cigarettes. Now Jim has razor-burn.

By the end of the afternoon he will have taken
a thousand pairs of sex-oriented shoes
back to her dressing-room. Jim swears
he can still see the funny side of life
in a halfway house where even the shoes
exist in limbo and the hand-rail is loose.

He puts his ear to the door of the study,
rushes in, sees the back of his head.
This is where he sits alone, in coffee-shock,
making lists of women. Photos of his wife
line the walls, reminding him of her.
The cupboard is open. He can't decide what to wear.

When the front door bangs he imagines his wife
has gone out and runs upstairs to look at
her clothes. Blocked by her breakfast tray,
he comes back down again, asking himself
whether the hall is part of the original house
or something to do with the street.

Jim thinks there are two houses here,
each one overlapping the other, like towels,
the spiral stair acting as a kind of hinge
for correct and incorrect behaviour. He stands
for hours on end, rolling his eyes
in soapy water dreams, unable to go up or down.

251

Poems/Steve Ellis

Cornwall I walked the aisle, between the menagerie:
Tudor pew-ends of foxes, dogs and hares
trained on the altar, their shapes sleeked
with years of hands over the black oak.
Outside, rain; rain to drown the village,
while I sat like Noah in his dark hold
silent among beasts, feeling light weaken
through the grey, saintless glass. The lady
— those cruel scars a flaw in the stone
or mad husband?, the vicar had riddled —
kept a look-out for the Last Day
from her corbelled crow's-nest in the choir.
Weather-bound I waited, reading the text
spread on the eagle; and then they entered,
along the nave, men, women and children
shaking the soil from ancient clothes,
from caps, leggings, jerkins, gowns, smocks,
filing into pews, settling for the sermon,
their eyes upon me as I began the verse:
'He that believeth shall be saved'.
I preached this theme to the full church;
to the bullet-snouted hounds, to the hares
with ears like flails along their backs
couched dimly beside the pews, aware
of a low chuckling, that strengthened:

I looked up to see the human faces
melt into muzzles, noses join with chins,
foreheads sink behind spreading ears,
hair streaming, rooting over skin,
and the laughter loud above my voice —
laughter in rows of gloating, goatish eyes,
hooting fur throats in cotton collars,
yelps, and kids' squeals, and foxes' shrieks.
I ran, between the pews and out into air,
outran the rain that coursed the roads
to the cottage; Maggie and John were getting tea
as if nothing had happened, but I knew.

Visiting
Home

He weeds while I watch. I remember
how I always had to help him as a boy
and how bored I was seeding out
the summer's lines of different leaves.
I liked some bits: the bonfires,
the chance of digging up a roman coin,
but hung around mostly, required yet unnecessary,
blasting birds with my fingers
while he jawed green wisdom over council railings
where disciplined oblongs mirrored our own:
crops at right angles to a path running
straight down the middle; gardens combed
then parted like haircuts. I always wished
he'd grow flowers like other kids' dads,
but now I'm glad of his thrift: vegetables
embody the agreement between man and mud.

Later, me just into Lawrence, him just past
his prime, he was black-haired and silent,
deep amongst the greens, escaping
mother's chatter and her awful friends,
absorbing soil's intimate solace . . .

Change now. I'm the age he was,
he nears the pension. In the evening
I wander in the garden when he leaves it:
the circling concrete houses hold a well
of winter air, grey and empty across
the estate's various shares of earth, dug,
deserted. Cats have come like litter,
and young men minus old skills
growing weedaria or prairies, while we keep
on with the old rules, the straight lines,
the trusted packets of seed as wilderness
waits in the wings. Though this doesn't upset;
rather, the corruption of cuttings,
the sure start of old age. Already
some forsythia holds fire in a corner,
some pampas grass looks fay by the Rhubarb —
one day I'll come back to this: him standing
by a lawn rosy with advanced health,
sun silvering specs and dentures, wearing skirts
of cheap vague tarty hardy annuals.

An old plate's farewell to the table
(*after Geoffrey of Vinsauf*)

Once in the springtime of my glaze
I lustily upshouldered, Atlas-like,
whole earths of meat and mash;
young and old in the gravy shallows
carved my face with strange signs as fleeting as
generations; and nights
I remember of a golden eminence,
when company directors stripped me bare
then spanked me with their knives and forks.

But my brothers gradually died away:
one was exiled to feed the cat,
one cracked in the oven, two more
shattered in the terrible kitchen war
of '79. I survived, an oddment.
Now, despite baptism twice a day
I begin to feel the shame of age
and am passed over. My old face fades:
Table, I depart, farewell.

Saint Francis's 'Cantico di Frate Sole'
done into Hollywood gangsterese

Boss, you got it all —
admiration, pull, status, the works —
it's all yours.

It's yours for being top —
there ain't no guy not too green
to mention you.

Thanks, for you and your organisation,
specially this guy Sun
who's always around with some light;

there's class stamped all over him,
a real smart guy —
he could only be one of your boys Boss.

Thanks, Boss, for these dames Moon and Stars,
platinum blondes in the night
you made real sweet.

Thanks, Boss, for this guy Wind
and the Weather boys, Air, Cloud, Sky,
bringing your gang the goods.

Thanks, Boss, for this dame Water —
she's a cute kid
and don't try to come over too big.

Thanks, Boss, for this guy Fire
who keeps his eye open after dark,
don't squeal and can handle himself.

Thanks, Boss, for old Ma Earth —
she looks after us real good,
always flowers and stuff around the joint.

Thanks, Boss, for the guys who take the rap
when you tell 'em,
that get roughed up and see trouble;

the smart guys know to keep their mouths shut
'cause you'll see to it Boss
they're on the payroll.

Thanks, Boss, for this cold dame Death
no guy can escape.
Nuts to the guys that die playing dirty.

Smart guys die in your good books.
There ain't no second show-down.

O.K. you guys, get prayin' —
say thanks to the Boss
and don't get big ideas.

THE CREAMERY
MANAGER

John McGahern

The books and files had been taken out but no one yet had stopped him from entering his office. Tired of sitting alone listening to the rain beat on the iron, he came out on the platform where he could look down on the long queue of tractors towing in the steel tanks, the wipers making furious, relentless arcs across the windscreens as they waited. He knew all the men sitting behind the glass of the cabs by name. That he had made his first business when he came to manage the creamery years before. Often on a wet summer's day, when there could be no rush at hay, many of them would pull in below the platform to sit and talk. The rough, childish faces would look up in a glow of pleasure at the recognition when he shouted out their names. Some would flash their lights.

Today no one looked up, but he could see them observing him in their mirrors after they had passed. They probably already knew more precisely than he what awaited him. Even with that knowledge he would have preferred if they looked up. All his life he had the weakness of wanting to please and give pleasure.

When the angelus bell rang from Cootehall, he began to think that they might have put off coming for him for another day, but soon after the last stroke he heard heavy boots crossing the cement. A low knock came on the door. Guard Casey was in the doorway but there was no sign of the sergeant. Guard Guider was the other guard.

'You know why we're here, Jim,' Guard Casey said.

'I know, Ned.' Quickly the guard read out the statement of arrest.

'You'll come with us, then?'

'Sure I'll come.'

'I'm sorry to have to do this but they're the rules.' He brought out a pair of bright handcuffs with a small green ribbon on the linking bar. Guider quickly handcuffed him to Casey and withdrew the key. The bar with the green ribbon kept the wrists apart but the hands and elbows touched. This caused them to walk stiffly and hesitantly and in step. The cement had been hosed clean but the people who worked for him were out of sight. The electric hum of the separators drowned their footsteps as they crossed to the squad car.

In the barracks the sergeant was waiting for him with a peace commissioner, a teacher from the other end of the parish, and they began committal proceedings at once. The sergeant was grim-faced and inscrutable.

'I'm sorry for that Sunday in Clones,' the creamery manager blurted out in nervousness. 'I only meant it as a day out together.'

The grimness on the sergeant's face did not relent: it was as if he had never spoken. He was asked if he had a solicitor. He had none. Did he want to be represented? Did he need to be? he responded. It was not necessary at this stage, he was told. In that case, they could begin. Anything he said, he was warned, could be used against him. He would say nothing. Though it directly concerned him, it seemed to be hardly about him at all, and it did not take long. Tonight he'd spend in the barracks. The cell was already prepared for him. Tomorrow he'd be transferred to Mountjoy to await his trial. The proceedings for the present were at an end. There was a mild air of relief. He felt like a railway carriage that had been pushed by hand down rails into some siding. It suited him well enough. He had never been assertive and he had no hope of being acquitted.

Less than a month before he had bought stand tickets for the Ulster Final and had taken the sergeant and Guard Casey to Clones. He already knew then that the end couldn't be far off. It must have been cowardice and an old need to ingratiate. Now it was the only part of the whole business that made him really cringe.

They set off in the Sergeant's small Ford. Guard Casey sat with the sergeant in the front. They were both big men, Casey running to flesh, but the sergeant retained some of an athlete's spareness of feature. He had played three or four times for Cavan and had been on the fringe of the team for a few seasons several years before.

'You were a terrible man to go and buy those stand tickets, Jim,' Casey had said for the fifth time as the car travelled over the dusty white roads.

'What's terrible about it? Aren't we all Ulster men even if we are stranded in the west? It's a day out, a day out of all our lives. And the sergeant here even played for Cavan.'

'Once or twice. Once or twice. Trial runs. You could hardly call it *played*. I just wasn't good enough.'

'You were more than good enough by all accounts. There was a clique.'

'You're blaming the selectors now. The selectors had a job to do. They couldn't pick everybody.'

'More than me has said they were a clique. They had their favourites. You weren't called "the boiler" for nothing.'

A car parked round a corner forced the sergeant to swerve out into the road. Nothing was coming.

'You'd think the car was specially parked there to deliver an accident.'

'They're all driving round in cars,' Casey said, 'but the mentality is still of the jennet and cart.'

It had been a sort of suffering to keep the talk going, but silence was even worse. There were many small flowers in the grass margins of the roadside.

They took their seats in the stand halfway through the minor game. There was one grace: though he came from close to Clones, there wasn't a single person he knew sitting in any of the nearby seats. The minor game ended. Once the seniors came on the field he started at the sudden power and speed with which the ball was driven about. The game was never close. Cavan drew gradually ahead to win easily. Such was the air of unreality he felt, of three men watching themselves watch a game, that he was glad to buy oranges from a seller moving between the seats, to hand the fruit around, to peel the skin away, to taste the bitter juice. Only once did he start and stir uncomfortably, when Guard Casey remarked about the powerful Cavan fullback who was roughing up the Tyrone forwards: "The Gunner is taking no prisoners today."

He was not to be so lucky on leaving the game. In the packed streets of the town a voice called out, 'Is it not Jimmy McCarron?' And at once the whole street seemed to know him. They stood in his path, put arms around him, drew him to the bars. 'An Ulster Final, look at the evening we'll have, and it's only starting.'

'Another time, Mick. Another time, Joe. Great to see you but we have to get back.' He had pushed desperately on, not introducing his two companions.

'You seem to be the most popular man in town,' the sergeant said sarcastically once they were clear.

'I'm from round here.'

'It's better to be popular anyhow than buried away out of sight,' Casey came to his defence.

'Up to a point. Up to a point,' the sergeant said. 'Everything has its point.'

They stopped for tea at the Lawn Hotel in Belterbet. By slipping out to the reception desk while they were eating he managed to pay for the meal. Except for the sergeant's petrol he had paid for the entire day. This was brought up as they parted outside the barracks in the early evening.

'It was a great day. We'll have to make an annual day of the Ulster Final. But next year will be our day. Next year you'll not be allowed to spend a penny,' the sergeant said, but still he could see their satisfaction that the whole outing had cost them nothing.

Now that the committal proceedings were at an end an air of uncertainty crept into the dayroom. Did they feel compromised by the day? He did not look at their faces. The door on the river had to be unlocked in order to allow the peace commissioner to leave and was again locked after he left. He caught the sergeant and Guard Casey looking at one another.

'You better show him his place,' the sergeant said.

To the right of the door on the river was a big, heavy red door. It was not locked. Casey opened it slowly to show him his cell for the night.

'It's not great, Jimmy, but it's as good as we could get it.'

The cement floor was still damp from being washed. Above the cement was a mattress on a low platform of boards. There was a pillow and several heavy grey blankets on the mattress. High in the wall a narrow window was cut, a single steel bar in its centre.

'It's fine. It couldn't be better.'

'If you want anything at all, just bang or shout, Jim,' and the heavy door was closed and locked. He heard bolts being drawn.

Casually he felt the pillow, the coarse blankets, moved the mattress, and with his palm tested the solidity of the wooden platform; its boards were of white deal and they too had been freshly scrubbed. There was an old oil can beside a steel bucket in the corner. Carefully he moved it under the window, and by climbing on the can and gripping the iron bar he could see out on either side: a sort of lawn, a circular flowerbed, netting-wire, a bole of the sycamore tree, sallies, a strip of river. He tried to get down as silently as possible, but as soon as he took his weight off the oil can it rattled.

'Are you all right there, Jimmy?' Casey was at once asking anxiously from the other side of the door.

'I'm fine. I was just surveying the surroundings. Soon I'll lie down for a while.'

He heard Casey hesitate for a moment, but then his feet sounded on the hollow boards of the dayroom, going towards the table and chairs. As much as to reassure Casey as from any need, he covered the mattress with one of the grey blankets and lay down, loosening his collar and tie. The bed was hard but not uncomfortable. He lay there, sometimes thinking, more of the time with his mind as blank as the white ceiling, and occasionally he drifted in and out of sleep.

There were things he was grateful for . . . that his parents were dead . . . that he did not have to face his mother's uncomprehending distress. He felt little guilt. The shareholders would write him off as a loss against other profits. The old creamery would not cry out with the hurt. People he had always been afraid of hurting, and even when he disliked them he felt that he partly understood them, could put himself in their place, and that was almost the end of dislike. Sure, he had seen evil and around it a stupid, heartless laughing that echoed darkness; and yet, and yet he had wanted to love. He felt that more than ever now, even seeing where he was, to what he had come.

That other darkness, all that surrounded life, used to trouble him once, but he had long given up making anything out of it, like a poor talent, and he no longer cared. Coming into the world, he was sure now, was not unlike getting into this poor cell. There was constant daylight above his head, split by the single bar, and beyond the sycamore leaves a radio aerial disappeared into a high branch. He could make jokes about it, but to make jokes alone was madness. He'd need a crowd for that, a blazing fire, rounds of drinks, and the whole long night awaiting.

There was another fact that struck him now like coldness. In the long juggling act he'd engaged in for years that eventually got him to this cell – four years before only the sudden windfall of a legacy had lifted him clear — whenever he was known to be flush all loans he'd out would flow back as soon as he called; but when he was seen to be in desperate need, nothing worthwhile was given back. It was not a pretty picture, but in this cell he was too far out to care much about it now.

He'd had escapes too, enough of them to want no more. The first had been the roman collar, to hand the pain and the joy of his own life into the keeping of an idea, and to will the idea true. It had been a near thing, especially because his mother had the vocation for him as well; but the pull of sex had been too strong, a dream of one girl in a silken dress among gardens disguising healthy animality. All his life he had moved among disguises, was moving among them still. He had even escaped marraige. The girl he'd loved, with the black head of hair thrown back and the sideways laugh, had been too wise to marry him: no framework could have withstood that second passion for immolation. There was the woman he didn't love that he was resigned to marry when she told him she was pregnant. The weekend she discovered she wasn't they'd gone to the Metropole and danced and drank the whole night away, he celebrating his escape out to where there were lungfuls of air, she celebrating that they were now free to choose to marry and have many children: 'It will be no Protestant family.' 'It will be no family at all.' Among so many disguises there was no lack of ironies.

The monies he had given out, the sums that were given back, the larger sums that would never be returned, the rounds of drinks he'd paid for, the names he'd called out, the glow of recognition, his own name shouted to the sky, the day Moon Dancer had won at the Phoenix Park, other days and horses that had lost – all dwindling down to the small, ingratiating act of taking the sergeant and Guard Casey to the Ulster Final.

The bolts were being drawn. Casey was standing in the doorway. 'There's something for you to eat, Jimmy.' He hadn't realized how dark the cell had been until he came out into the dayroom, and he had to shade his eyes against the light. He thought he'd be eating at the dayroom table, but he was brought up a long hallway to the sergeant's living quarters. At the end of the hallway was a huge kitchen, and one place was set on a big table in its centre. The sergeant wasn't there but his wife was and several children. No one spoke. In the big sideboard mirror he could see most of the room and Casey standing directly behind him with his arms folded. A lovely, strong girl of fourteen or fifteen placed a plate of sausages, black pudding, bacon and a small piece of liver between his knife and fork and poured him a steaming mug of tea. There was brown bread on the table, sugar, milk, salt, pepper. At first no one spoke and his knife and fork were loud on the plate as the children watched him covertly but with intense curiosity. Then Casey began to tease the children about their day in school.

'Thanks,' he said after he'd signed a docket at the end of the meal which stated that he had been provided with food.

'For nothing at all,' the sergeant's wife answered quietly, but it was little above a whisper, and he had to fight back a wave of gratitude. With Casey he went back down the long hallway to the dayroom. He was moving across the hollow boards to the cell door when Casey stopped him.

'There's no need to go in there yet, Jimmy. You can sit here for a while in front of the fire.'

They sat on the yellow chairs in front of the fire. Casey spent a long time arranging turf around the blazing centre of the fire with tongs. There were heavy ledgers on the table at their back. A row of baton cases and the gleaming handcuffs with the green ribbons hung from hooks on the wall. A stripped, narrow bed stood along the wall of the cell, its head beneath the phone of the wall. Only the cell wall stood between Casey's bed and his own plain boards.

'When do you think they'll come?' he asked when the Guard seemed to have arranged the sods of turf to his satisfaction.

'They'll come sometime in the morning. Do you know I feel badly about all this? It's a pity it had to happen at all,' Casey said out of a long silence.

'It's done now anyhow.'

'Do you know what I think? There were too many spongers around. They took advantage. It's them that should by rights be in your place.'

'I don't know . . . I don't think so . . . It was me that allowed it . . . even abetted it.'

'You don't mind me asking this? How did it start? Don't answer if you don't want.'

'As far as I know it began in small things. "He that contemneth small things . . ." '

'Shall fall little by little into grevious error,' Casey finished the quotation in a low, meditative voice as he started to arrange the fire again. 'No. I wouldn't go as far as that. That's too hard. You'd think it was God Almighty we were offending. What's an old creamery anyhow? It'll still go on taking in milk, turning out butter. No. Only in law is it anything at all.'

'There were a few times I thought I might get out of it,' he said slowly. 'But the fact is that I didn't. I don't think people can change. They like to imagine they can, that is all.'

'Maybe they can if they try hard enough – or they have to,' Casey said without much confidence.

'Then it's nearly always too late,' he said. 'The one thing I feel really badly about is taking the sergeant and yourself to the Ulster Final those few Sundays back. That was dragging the pair of you into the business. That wasn't right.'

'The sergeant takes that personally. In my opinion he's wrong. What was personal about it? You gave us a great day out, a day out of all our lives,' Casey said. 'And everything was normal then.'

That was the trouble, everything was not normal then, he was about to say, but decided not to speak. Everything was normal now. He had been afraid of his own fear and was spreading the taint everywhere. Now that what he had feared most had happened he was no longer afraid. His own life seemed to be happening as satisfactorily as if he were free again among people.

Do you think people can change, Ned? he felt like asking Casey. Do you think people can change or are they given a set star at birth that they have to follow. What part does luck play in the whole shamozzle?

Casey had taken to arranging the fire again and would plainly welcome any conversation, but he found that he did not want to continue. He felt that he knew already as much as he'd ever come to know about these matters. Discussing them further could only be a form of idleness or Clones in some other light. He liked the guard, but he did not want to draw any closer.

Soon he'd have to ask him for leave to go back to his cell.

Empire Building

Deborah Moggach

It didn't look much when he took it over, the Empire Stores, but a man with business instinct could see the potential. The previous owners had been fined by the Health Authority and finally gone bust. Hamid, however, had standards. His wife told people this too, with a small shake of her head as if she were being philosophical about it.

The neighbourhood was a transient, shabby one, with terraces of bedsits and Irish lodging houses. The parade of shops, Hamid calculated, was far enough from the Holloway Road for people to rely upon it for their local needs, which he had all intention of supplying. The shops were as follows: a wholesale dressmaking business, with a curtained window behind which the sewing machines hummed, those Greek ladies knew the meaning of hard work; a dentist's surgery, with frosted glass; a greengrocer's that had ageing fruit and early closing on Thursdays, now how can anyone prosper with early closing; then the Empire Stores, and next door to it a newsagents run by an indolent Hindu and his wife. Hamid put a notice 'Under New Management' in the window of the Empire Stores and re-stocked the merchandise – liquor behind the cash desk, where he sat in control, and groceries along the aisles. His aims were not modest, but his beginnings were.

His own wife and children were installed in a flat in Wood Green, three miles away, where the air was fresher and the neighbourhood more salubrious. The streets around the Empire Stores were not respectable; you need only have taken a look at the cards fixed to the newsagent's window, even a family man like Hamid knew the meaning of those kind of French Lessons. Business is business, however, and it is a wise shopkeeper who is prepared to adapt. Or, as his father was fond of saying: to those who are flexible comes strength.

The local blacks were big West Indians who drove up in loudly-tuned cars and who suddenly filled the shop. They bought party packs of beers in the evenings and left a musky male scent behind them. One of the first things Hamid did was to extend his opening hours until 9 p.m. Then there were the single young ladies who bought Whiskas and yoghurt and disappeared into the sodium-lit streets. How solitary was the life of these young English women, with no family to care for them, no wonder they fell into evil ways. Hamid installed a second cold shelf and stocked it with pizzas, two ranges of yoghurts and individual fruit juice cartons for these bedsit dwellers and their twilit lives. Such items moved fast.

Sitting at the till, its numbers bleeping, Hamid thought of the dinner being prepared for him at home, the hiss of the spices as they hit the pan, the buttery taste of the paratha he would soon be eating. He thought of his son Arif, his neat, shiny head bent over his homework, the TV turned right down. He thought of his own tartan slippers beside the radiator. Passing them a carrier bag, he gazed with perplexity at these lost, pasty-faced English girls.

His main income, however, came from the drunks. It was for them that within the first three months he had doubled the bottle shelf space and increased his range of cans. Business was brisk in Triple Strength Export Lager. These men, their complexions inflamed by alcohol, shambled in at all hours, muttering at the floor, murmuring at the tins of peas. They raised their ruined faces. Hamid avoided their eye; he took their soiled bank notes or the coins they counted out, shakily, and fixed his gaze above their heads. Flesh upon flesh, sometimes their fingers touched his, but he was too well-mannered to flinch. Sometimes they tried to engage him in conversation.

It was bemusing. Not only did they poison themselves with drink, rotting their souls and their bodies, but they had no shame. They leaned against the dentist's frosted glass, lifting the bottle to their lips in full public view. They stood huddled together in the exit of the snooker hall, further up the road, where warm air breathed from the grills. Sometimes he could hear the smash of glass. Lone men stood in the middle of the road, shouting oaths into the air.

Business is business. Sometimes he raised his eyebrows at Khalid, his nephew, who helped him in the shop, but he never offended his wife by describing to her this flotsam and jetsom. One night she said: 'You never talk to me.'

It was the next week that a man stumbled in and steadied himself against the counter. He asked for a bottle of cider and then he said:

'You'll put it on the slate?'

'I beg your pardon?' Hamid raised his eyes from his newspaper.

'I'll pay tomorrow.'

'I'm sorry,' Hamid said. 'It is not shop policy.'

The man started shouting. 'You fucking wog!' he shouted, his voice rising.

Hamid lowered his gaze, back to the dancing Urdu script. He turned the page.

'Get back to the fucking jungle, fucking wog land!' The voice slurred 'Where you belong!'

Khalid appeared from the stock room and stood there. Hamid kept his eye on the page. He read that there was a riot in Lahore, where an opposition leader had been arrested, and that ghee was up Rs 2 per seer.

'Fucking monkeys!'

Khalid put down the crate of Schweppes and escorted the man to the door. The next day Hamid wrote a notice and sellotaped it to the counter.

He sat there, as grave as always, in his herringbone tweed jacket. He held himself straight as the men shambled in, those long lost rulers of a long lost Empire, eyeing the bottles behind him. He had written the notice in large red letters, using Arif's school Pentel. PLEASE DO NOT ASK FOR CREDIT AS A REFUSAL OFTEN OFFENDS.

That was in the late seventies. War was being waged in the Middle East; a man had walked on the moon; Prince Charles had still not found a wife. Meanwhile Hamid filled out his VAT receipts, and in view of increased turnover negotiated further discount terms with McEwans, manufacturers of lager.

In 1980 the old couple who ran the greengrocer's retired and Hamid bought the shop, freehold, and extended his own premises, knocking through the dividing wall and removing the sign H LAWSON. FRUITERER AND GREENGROCER.

Apart from 'good morning', the first and last conversation he ever held with the old man was on completion day, when they finalized the transaction in the lawyer's office down the road.

'Times change' said the old man, Mr. Lawson. The clock whirred, clicked and chimed. He sighed. 'Been here thirty years.'

They signed the document and shook hands.

'Harold' said Hamid, reading the signature. 'So that's your name.'

'You know, I was in your part of the world.'

'My part?' asked Hamid.

'India.'

'Ah.'

'In the army. Stationed near Mysore. Know it?'

Hamid shook his head. 'My family comes from Pakistan.'

They stood up. 'Funny old world, isn't it' said the old man. Hamid agreed, politely. The lawyer opened the door for them.

'How about a quickie' said the old man.

'I beg your pardon?'

'Little celebration.'

Hamid paused. 'I don't drink.'

They reached the head of the stairs. 'No' said the old man. 'No, I suppose you don't. Against your religion, eh?'

Hamid nodded. 'You first, please' he said, indicating the stairs.

'No, you.'

Hamid went first. They emerged into the sunlight. It was a beautiful day in April. Petals lay strewn in the gutter.

'If I'd been blessed with a son, maybe this wouldn't be happening' said the old man. 'But that's life.'

Hamid nodded.

'You've got a son?'

'Yes' said Hamid. 'A fine chap.'

'Expect he'll be coming in with you, in due course.'

Hamid murmured something politely; he didn't want to offend the old man. Arif, running a shop? He had greater things in mind for his son. Hamid had a new, larger sign fitted to cover the new, double shop front and this time had it constructed in neon illuminated script: THE EMPIRE STORES. He extended both his liquor and grocery range to cover the extra volume of retail space, adding a chicken rotisserie for take-outs, a microwave for samosas and a large range of fruit and vegetables, all of a greatly improved quality to those of H Lawson. The old man had left the place like a junk heap; it took seven skips to clear the rubbish out of the upper floor and the backyard. One morning Hamid was out in the street, inspecting a heaped skip, when one of his customers stopped. She was an old woman; she pointed at the skip with her umbrella.

'See that?' she said. 'The wheels? Used to have a pony and cart, Harry did. For the deliveries.'

'Did he really?' Hamid glanced up the street. He was waiting for the builders, who were late again. Unreliable.

'Knew us all by name.' She sighed, and wiped her nose. 'No . . .' She shook her head. 'Service is not what it was.'

'No' agreed Hamid, looking at his watch and thinking of his

builders. 'It certainly isn't.'

Hamid, who always bought British, traded in his old Cortina and bought a brand-new Rover, with beige upholstery and stereo player. He transferred Arif to a private school, its sign painted in Gothic script, where they sang hymns and wore blazers. On Parents' Day the panelled halls smelt of polish; Hamid gazed at the cabinets of silver cups. His wife wore her best silk sari; her bangles tinkled as she smoothed Arif's hair.

The conversion of the upper floors, above the old fruit shop, was completed at last and Hamid stood on the other side of the street with Khalid and his two new assistants. He looked at the sunlight glinting in the windows; he looked at the dazzling white paint and the sign glowing below it: THE EMPIRE STORES. His heart swelled. The others chattered, but he could not speak.

That night Arif stood, his eyes closed and his face pinched with concentration, and recited:

'Earth has not anything to show more fair,
Dull would he be of soul who could pass by
A sight so touching in its majesty.
The city now doth like a garment wear
The beauty of the morning, silent, bare.
Ships, towers, domes, theatres and temples lie
Open unto the fields, and to the sky . . .'

His eyes opened. 'Know who it's by?
Hamid shook his head. 'You tell me, son.'
'William Wordsworth. We're learning it at school.'

For the second time that day, Hamid's heart swelled. He put his arms around his son, the boy for whom everything was possible. He pressed his face against his son's cheek.

1981. Ronald Reagan became President of the USA. In May the Pope was shot and wounded. In Brixton there were riots; Toxteth too. In July Prince Charles married his Lady Di.

Khalid, too, was married by now and installed in the first floor flat, above the shop. National holidays were always good, business-wise; by now the Empire Stores was open seven days a week and during that summer's day, as people queued at the till, Hamid kept half an eye on his portable TV set. A pale blur, as Lady Di passed in her dress; a peal of bells. As Hamid reached for the bottles of whiskey, the commentator's voice quickened with pride and awe, and Hamid's heart beat faster. 'Isn't she a picture' said his customers, pausing at the screen. Hamid agreed that, yes, she was the most radiant of brides. Flags waved, flicking to and fro, and the crowd roared. Our Princess, his and theirs . . . Hamid smiled and gave a small boy a Toblerone.

That night his wife said: 'You should have seen it in colour.'

Hamid pulled off his shoes. 'You've put it on the videotape?'

She nodded and turned away, picking up the scattered jigsaw in front of the TV, where his daughters had been sitting.

'We can watch it later' he said.

'When?' Her voice was sharp. He looked up, in surprise. 'It's not the same' she said, closing the box.

That night a bottle was thrown up through the window of Khalid's flat. It shattered the glass; Khalid's bride cowered in the corner.

The next day, while the Royal couple, oh how happy they looked, departed on their honeymoon, Hamid inspected the damage. He gazed down into the street, through the wicked edges of glass. They were intruders, those people entering the Empire Stores. Yesterday's glory had vanished. Hamid sat down, heavily, on the settee.

'How could they do this to us?' he asked. 'What have we done to deserve it?'

Khalid, who was an easy-going chap, said: 'Forget it. They were just celebrating.' He lowered his voice, so his bride couldn't hear. 'They were one over the eight.'

'What?'

'Drunk.'

Drunk on the drink he had sold to them. Yesterday they had had record takings.

He closed up the shop that night and walked to his car. On the pavement lay a man, asleep, his face bleeding.

That autumn Hamid installed closed-circuit surveillance in the shop. He now had three assistants and an expanded range of take-away food. Children from neglectful homes came in with shopping bags; they had keys around their necks, and runny noses. They bought bars of Kit Kat and crisps and hot pasties. These mothers did not look after their youngsters; they sent them into the streets to consume junk food.

The dressmaker's was taken over by a Massage and Sauna establishment, which installed black glass and a Georgian door. All about lay the ruined and the dispossessed. This was their country but these people had no homes. New, loitering men replaced the old. Strange faces appeared for a week, a month, and then after a while he would realize they had vanished. To where? His neon sign shone out over the drab street. Inside the shop lay the solace of food, and order.

That year his turnover doubled. He fitted out an office in the store room and managed his growing empire from there, drinking tea from his Charles and Di commemoration mug. He had now converted four flats above the shop, and the lease of the newsagent's shop next door was coming up shortly; he had his eye on that.

In an attempt to brighten the neighbourhood, the council had planted young trees along the pavement. Their leaves were turning red, and falling to the ground. Opposite, the sunset flamed above the chimney pots. As he said his evening prayers on the mat behind his desk, he felt both humbled and grateful.

That evening he looked into his girls' bedroom. They were two sleeping heads. Arif was in the lounge, bent over his computer game. Hamid ruffled his hair; Arif smoothed it down again.

'And have you a hello for your father?'

Arif pressed a button. '570,' he said. '680.'

Later, when Arif was asleep and Hamid had eaten, he said to his wife:

'They teach them no manners at that expensive school?'

She turned. 'You think you can buy manners with money?'

He looked sharply at her. She was putting the crockery away in the cabinet.

'What are you trying to say?' he asked.

'Manners are taught by example. At home.'

'And don't I set a good example?'

'When you're here.' She sighed, and shut the cabinet. 'I think he is suffering from neglect.'

'You say that about my son?'

Neglect? Hamid thought of the boys with faces like old men's, and keys around their necks. Pale boys buying junk food.

'It's his age' said Hamid loudly, surprising himself. 'He's fourteen now. A difficult age.'

'If you say so.'

She sighed again and reached up for something on the top of the cabinet. It was a box of Milk Tray. How plump she was becoming; her kurta was strained tight over her belly.

'Come to the shop' he said 'and there I'll show you the meaning of neglect.'

She sat down, shaking her head in that philosophical way. More and more she irked him by doing this. She examined a chocolate and popped it into her mouth. He looked at her and the word rose up: junk food.

He ignored this. Instead he asked:

'Doesn't Arif understand? I'm working for him. For all the family.' He ran his fingers through his hair. 'For the future.' His voice rose higher. She glanced warningly towards the bedrooms. 'I'm working so that he need never work in a shop! You undersand me, woman? Can't you understand?'

Hindus are lazy. History has proved that point. Their religion is a dissipated one; their life style one of self-indulgence, of the inaction that comes from fatalism. Take Mr Gupta's attitude, for example, to the expiry of his lease. He smiled and raised his hands: the new price was too high, he had this trouble with his stomach, he had been robbed three times in the past year. What will be, will be . . .

Hamid would have suggested that Mr Gupta invest in vandal-proof shuttering, as he himself had done. But he could always have that fitted when he took over the lease, which he did just as the trees outside frothed into blossom, in celebration.

Islam is a progressive faith. He progressed, removing Mr Gupta's sign and installing EMPIRE NEWSAGENTS over the door. He now had one double shop and one single; his properties dominated the parade of shops. Indeed, that week several of his customers joked that he'd soon be taking over the street. Hamid smiled modestly.

The state of that shop! The squalor and the unexploited sales area! The possibilities. It was a dusty little con-tob newsagents when Hamid took it over, but after a complete refitment he had doubled the shelf space and the stock and introduced fast-profit items including a rental Slush-Puppy dispenser in six flavours, a favourite with the local latch-key children.

Dirty magazines, he was not surprised to discover, had a brisk sale in his neighbourhood and he increased the stock from seven titles to fourteen. *Knave* and *Mayfair*, bulging flesh . . . he kept his eyes from this nude shamelessness. He placed such journals on the top shelf. Boys little older than Arif came in to giggle and point; they stood in a row on his display bases. These boys, he thought, they are somebody's son; does nobody cherish and protect them?

It was during the first month of business that Hamid opened the local newspaper and read:

'We are sad to announce the death of Mr Harold Lawson, universally known as Harry to his customers and many friends. For thirty years he was a well-loved sight on the local scene, with the fondly-remembered Betty, his pony . . .'

Hamid read on. It concluded:

'A modest man, he seldom mentioned his distinguished army record, serving with the King's Rifles in India and being awarded a DSO for his bravery during the Independence Riots. He leaves a widow, Ivy, and will be sorely missed. It can truly be said that "they broke the mould when they made Harry".'

Outside the petals had blown into the gutter, just as they had lain the day Hamid had accompanied the old man into the street two years earlier. It was the slack mid-morning period and Hamid stood in the sunshine, watching the clouds move beyond the TV aerials. For a moment he thought of the earth rolling, and history turning. He himself was fond of poetry, despite his lack of education. What was it Arif used to recite?

'Deign on the passing world to turn thine eyes,
And pause awhile from letters to be wise.'

That evening he asked Arif who was the English poet who had written those words. William Shakespeare?

'Dunno.'

Hamid placed his hand on his son's shoulder. 'No, that's "All the world's a stage" ' he said. Arif's bones were surprisingly frail. He sat with his eyes on the TV screen where first a house, then a car, burst into flames.

Hamid kept his son's exercise books on a special shelf. He searched through and found the quotation, written in the round, careful writing Arif still had a year or so ago.

'Ah. Samuel Johnson.'

Hamid raised his voice; on the TV a siren wailed.

'Remember?'

He looked at the title: *The Vanity of Human Wishes*.

Arif said: 'You're blocking my view.'

1983. Renewed fighting in the Lebanon, and the film *Gandhi* won eight Oscars. There were fires and floods in Australia and peace people made a human chain around Greenham Common. The future King of England was toddling now; so was Khalid's first born son, in the flat above the Empire Stores. Property was moving again, as the worst of the recession was said to be over, and Hamid converted the upper floors above the newsagent's shop and sold the flats on long leases.

With the profits, and another bank loan, that summer he bought a large detached house for his family, a real family home in that sought-after suburb Potters Bar.

'I have worked twenty years for this moment' he said, standing in the lounge. There were fitted carpets throughout. There was even a bar in panelled walnut, built by the previous owners who had amassed large debts both by drinking and gambling, hence the sale of this house. He pictured his children sitting around the bar, drinking blameless Pepsi.

'This is the proudest moment of my life' he repeated, his words loud in the empty room. Through its french windows there was a view of the garden, a series of low terraces separated by balustrades. Two small figures in orange anoraks stood on the lawn: his daughters.

Arif, however, was nowhere to be seen. Hamid would have liked him to share this moment but his son had been keeping himself to himself recently, growing more sulky. He had even objected to the move.

'Where will we get the furniture?' said his wife, standing in the middle of the room.

'We'll buy it. Look.' He took out his wallet. It was so fat, it couldn't close.

He found Arif sitting in the car, the radio loud. Hamid turned it down.

'Well, old chap' he said. 'What do you think?'

'Great' Arif muttered.

'Earth has not anything to show more fair. . .'

Hamid stood in the garden. The long, blonde grass blew in the wind. It was dusk and he looked up at his home, the fortress where he kept his family safe. A light shone from Arif's attic bedroom – he had insisted on this tiny room, no more than a cupboard up in the roof. Down below were the bedrooms; then, below them, the curtained french windows, glowing bluish from the TV. How solid, his house; solid and secure.

Today he wore his tweed suit from Austin Reed. He stood like a squire amidst the swaying weeds. Summer was ending, now, and grass choked the flowerbeds. Neither he nor his wife were proficient in gardening, but that did not stop the pride.

It grew darker. To one side of him rose the block of his house. To the other side, beyond the trees, the sky glowed orange. This side lay London. He thought of his shops casting their own glow over the pavement; he thought of the blood-red neon of THE EMPIRE STORES, shining in the night. How ashy those faces seemed, looking up at the window to gaze at the comforts within! Ruined, pasty faces; the losers, the lost, the dispossessed. The walking wounded who once ruled the Empire, pressing their noses against his Empire Stores . . .

He thought of their squalid comforts: those rows of bottles and those magazines showing bald portions of women's bodies. Here at home, on the other hand, he had a mahogany bookcase filled with English classics, all of them bound in leather: Dickens, Shakespeare, and the poet he had taken to his own heart, William Wordsworth.

The trees, bulkier now in the night, loomed against the suffused sky.

'Dull would he be of soul who could pass by
A sight so touching in its majest . . .'

A chill wind rattled the weeds and blew against his legs . . . He heard the faint thump of music, if you could call it music, from Arif's window. The long, dry grass blew to and fro in the darkness. He realized that he was shivering.

His wife said she was lonely. She sat in the lounge, its new chairs arranged for conversations, and all day she had the TV on. She talked about Lahore; she said she was homesick. She talked about her sisters, and how they had sat all morning laughing and brushing each other's hair. More and more she talked like this.

'Nobody talks to me here' she said. 'They get into their cars and drive to their tea parties.'

'You must take driving lessons.'

'The car is so big. It frightens me.'

'Then you must have a tea party here.'

She thought about this for some time. Then she said: 'Who should I invite?'

'The neighbours, of course. And then there are the parents of Arif's schoolfriends.'

'But we don't know the parents of Arif's schoolfriends.'

'What about that boy, what's his name, Thompson? His father is an executive with Procter and Gamble.'

'But what shall I cook for them?'

'And that very pleasant couple next door? We've said good morning often enough.'

So it was arranged. A small party for Sunday tea, so that he himself could be present.

For the next week she was restless; she moved about the house, frowning at the furniture and standing back from it, her head on one side. During one evening she moved the settee three times. She took Arif down to Marks and Spencers to buy him a new pair of trousers.

'Christ' said Arif. 'It's only a bloody tea party.'

'Don't you dare insult your mother!' Hamid's voice was shrill. He, too, moved the settee one more time.

The question of food was vexing. His wife thought sandwiches and cake most suitable. He himself thought she should produce those titbits in which she excelled: pakoras, brinjal fritters and the daintiest of samosas. Nobody cooked samosas like his Sharine.

In the end they compromised. They would have both.

'East meets West' he joked; his nerves made him high-spirited. He joggled the plaits of Aisha, his youngest daughter, one plait and then the other, and she squealed with pleasure. 'East, West, home's best' he chanted to her, before she scuttled into the kitchen.

He wanted to tell his family how much he loved them, and how proud he would be to show them off at the tea party. He wanted to tell them how he had stood in the garden, his heart swelling for them. But his daughters would just giggle; his wife would look flustered . . . And Arif? He no longer knew what Arif would do. He only knew that he himself would feel foolish.

On the Saturday he went into the stock room of the Empire Stores and fetched some choice items: chocolate fancies, iced Kunzle cakes. There was little demand from his customers for these high-class items. Only the best would do, however, for those who lived in Potters Bar.

It was a cool, blustery evening. There must be a storm blowing up. Kentucky boxes bowled along the pavement. Further up the street a man stood in a doorway, bellowing. It was an eerie sound, scarcely human. Hamid buttoned up his jacket as he left the shop, carrying his parcels. Far down the street he heard the smash of glass: he clutched the parcels to his chest.

Then it happened. He was just getting into the car. As he did so, he chanced to glance back across the street, towards the parade of shops. It was at that moment that the door of the Sauna and Massage opened and Arif stepped out.

Within him, Hamid's heart shifted like a rock. He could not move. The face was in shadow; all he could see was the glow of a cigarette. Arif smoking? For some reason this only faintly surprised Hamid.

There the boy stood, a slight figure in that familiar blue and white anorak. He turned to look back at the door; he turned round and made his way across the road, towards Hamid.

Hamid opened his mouth to cry out, but nothing happened. Then, as Arif neared him, the street light fell upon his face.

It was a thinner face; thin, and knowing, and much older than Arif. An unknown, shifty, Englishman's face.

Hamid climbed into his car and fumbled with the key. His hands felt damp and boneless. He told himself to stop being ridiculous; he felt a curious sinking, yet swelling sensation, as if he had aged ten years in the last moments.

Driving home, he tried to shake off his unease. After all, it had been a stranger. Nothing to do with his own cherished son. Why then could he not concentrate on the road ahead? He was a level-headed fellow: he always had been.

Sharine was in a state. 'Where have you been?' she cried.

'It's only ten o'clock' he said, and asked, alarmed: 'What's happened?'

'What's happened? I've spilt the dahi and dropped the sugar and, oh my nerves.'

She was standing in the kitchen. The air was aromatic with cooking.

'The children have been helping?'

'The girls, yes, until I sent them to bed.'

'Arif?'

She shrugged. 'Him, help me?'

'Where is he?'

'Where he always is.'

Hamid walked up the stairs, up past the first landing, then up the narrow flight of stairs to the attic. For some reason he needed to see his son. He knew he would be there, but he needed to see him.

His heart thumped; it must be those stairs, he was no longer as young as he was. Thud, thud, went Arif's music. Hamid knocked on the door.

'What is it?' Arif's voice was sharp, yet muffled.

'It's your father.'

'Wait.'

A few sounds, then Arif opened the door.

'What do you do in there all evening?' asked Hamid. 'Why don't you help your mother? We have a tea party tomorrow.'

Arif shrugged.

'Why don't you answer my questions?' asked Hamid. 'Why?'

A pause. Arif stood behind the half-open door. Outside, the wind rattled against the slates. Finally he said: 'Why are you so interested?'

Hamid stared. 'And what sort of answer is that?'

'Ask yourself.' Arif slowly scratched the spot on his chin. 'If you have the inclination.'

And he slowly closed the door.

That night there was a storm. The window panes clattered and shook; the very house, his fortress, seemed to shudder. In the morning Hamid found that out in the garden some of the balustrade had fallen down. It was made of the most crumbly concrete.

'Charming' said Mrs Yates. 'Love the wallpaper, awfully daring. And what sweet little girls.'

Tea cups clinked. Sharine, in her silk sari, moved from one guest to another. Her daughters followed her with plates of cakes. Everything was going like clockwork. Looking at the pleasant faces, Hamid felt a flush of satisfaction. It had all been worth it. The years . . . The work . . .

'And where's the lad?' Mr Thompson asked, jovially.

'He'll be down' said Hamid, looking at the door and then at his watch. 'Any minute.' Silently, he urged Arif to hurry up.

Mr Thompson's wife, whose name Hamid unfortunately had not caught, finished her cup of tea and said:

'Would it be frightfully rude if I asked to see the house?'

Mr Thompson laughed. 'Rosemary, you're incorrigible.'

Other guests stood up, too: Mr and Mrs Yates from next door, old Colonel Tindall from down the road, the teenage girls belonging to the widowed lady opposite.

'A guided tour' joked Hamid, gathering his scattered wits. 'Tickets please.'

Sharine stood in the middle of the lounge, holding the tea pot. She looked alarmed but he gave her a small, reassuring nod. After all, the house was spick and span.

He led the way. Upstairs he pointed out the view from the master bedroom; the two bathrooms en suite.

'Carpets everywhere!' said Mrs Yates 'And what an original colour!'

'Must have cost you' said Mr Thompson, man to man. Hamid nodded modestly, his face hot with pleasure.

'What's up there?' asked Mrs Yates.

'Just the attic' said Hamid.

But before he could continue, she had mounted the stairs and Mrs Thompson was following her.

'Rosemary!' called Mr Thompson, and turned to Hamid. 'Women!'

Hamid hurried up the stairs. Thud, thud . . . the narrow treads shook, he could hear above him the thump of Arif's music, and then he had arrived at the landing and one of the women was pushing open Arif's door.

'May I?' she turned and asked Hamid.

But by then she had opened it.

There are some sights that a person never forgets. Sometimes they rise up again in dreams; in his sleep Hamid saw mottled faces, their skin bleeding, pressed up against the glass of his shop. He saw stumps raised, waving in his face, in those long-forgotten alleys in Lahore. All the wreckage of this world, from which he had tried, so very hard, to protect those he loved.

Throughout his life, which was a long and prosperous one, he never forgot the sight that met his eyes that Sunday afternoon. Arif, sprawled on the bed, his eyes closed. Arif, his own son, snoring as the men snored who lay on the pavements. On the floor lay empty cans of lager, and two scattered magazines, their pages open: *Mayfair* and *Penthouse*.

Explosions, riots and wreckage all around the turning world. The small hiss of indrawn breath, from the two women who stood beside him.

Vietnam Encore

BRIAN ALDISS

The little lieutenant from the Mid West wore a Vietnamese bauble stitched to his hat. It had probably been bought in a Kansas Bazaar. With his general air of confidence, he tried to impress the troops under him. As he told them more than once, this was his second tour of duty overseas.

'Just remember, you guys,' he called above the noise of engines, 'the folk in the South are on our side. We're fighting for them. You can exploit the hell out of them but you mustn't shoot a one of them.'

Huddled together, the troops laughed.

Lieutenants had been saying such things for years. Troops had been laughing like that for years. At thirty-five thousand feet, when you are heading for action in an alien land way across the wide ocean, you laugh. It helps with the nerves.

People get hurt defending Democracy.

From outside the craft, the scene must have appeared beautiful. The big troop carriers look so good, with their heavy bellies and stub wings. As the planes came down through the blue evening air towards a landing, cloud layers floated up to meet and enfold them, burnished with gold. No sign, no whisper, of the catastrophe being played out on the Earth below.

Nor was there in the planes a sign of that vision, that sense of mission, which had involved the American people in this distant struggle.

As the aircraft penetrated the cloud layer, the troops inside fell silent. A lid was closing over them. The thick moisture beyond the ports made the distance to the U.S. almost tangible.

Then we broke through the cloud.

Little could be seen. The sun was obscured. All below us was shadow.

We altered course, sinking. Suddenly the ground was close, dark, without detail. It promised nothing, said nothing, was silent under an ancient sense of outrage.

As we came in to land, a brief glimpse of ocean, with sun split wide like a spilt egg between cloud curtain and horizon. Tension, no speech. Smooth landing.

Amazing silence as the jets cut. Muzak: *Everything's Coming Up Roses* for reassurance. By the look on some of the guys' faces, they were expecting to be fired on straight away. The approach and touchdown lights died. The glow around the perimeter indicated we were on a large base.

An officer in a jeep was waiting for me. The troops moved off under shouted orders. They became anonymous, war statistics. I remembered that eleven per cent of all our casualties were killed without actual combat, killed in enemy booby-traps: just part of the price of involvement in someone else's civil war. At least I was not Infantry.

The jeep drove me around to the far side of the air base. A helicopter gunship was waiting, big and clumsy, floodlights trained on its camouflaged flank. The lights turned the evening to total darkness. I inhaled before stepping aboard, trying to orient myself after several hours of dislocating flight. All I could smell was ozone and gasoline.

Two men searched me without interest or hope. I was then free to greet a tall hollow-chested man with greying hair cut short. He had a leathery countenance, thick eyebrows, and a belligerent jaw. Half-moon spectacles gave him a curiously mild look, despite contra-indications.

'My name is Gratinelli. I'm in Intelligence. You are James Lambard?'

When I said I was, he wanted to see my identification. Then he relaxed.

'Okay, Jim, take a seat right here. We'll be airborne soonest. Welcome to the war zone. We know you're special and we're glad you came over. You were born here, I understand?'

He must have known. He had seen my papers. He must have heard by my accent. He just wanted to hear it for himself.

'Okay, Jim. That's great. We're going to see to it that your mission is made as safe as can be.'

He intended reassurance. I found him creepy. When he smiled, he showed a gold-capped tooth. My feelings were still ruffled from the journey. I felt it as a snub that an ally – that's what I was – should have been made to travel with infantry in a troop carrier when on a special mission. The gold tooth might have been planted just to annoy me.

The gunship lifted almost at once. Gratinelli told me to relax. We were flying ten miles along the coast to an R & R base where I would be properly briefed.

'You won't come cross any VCs in this area.'

Since I had no small talk, Gratinelli, speaking above the roar of the engines, gave me a lecture on how the war was necessary to defend the Free World. An expenditure of fire-power was the only effective argument the enemy understood. And in fact the war would have been won at least a year ago had it not been for the support coming in to the North from outside. He let the word 'outside' linger like a threat between us.

When I said nothing, he eyed me, I thought, with hostility, and began on another tack.

'Also, we would have less difficulty if the goddamned slimeys – I mean, sorry, I mean the South – was not so corrupt. Corruption is everywhere. You probably heard the President's speech. We are pledged to win not only a military victory over here, but a moral victory against hunger, disease, and despair. Vast quantities of material have been airlifted into your country, Mr Lambard. We have increased food relief for the countryside as well as the towns. Vehicles, machinery to build highways.' He ticked the items off on his thumb. 'Pharmaceutical factories, steel plants, garbage trucks. A massive aid programme. What happens? They all disappear. Just vanish. Might as well pour the money down the sink.'

'Too bad,' I said.

'*Too bad* . . .' he echoed, scornfully. 'Widespread corruption. We're after the hearts and minds of these people. What do we get? This shit.'

I sat with my hands on my knees, avoiding his gaze.

The helicopter sank on to its landing pad. Brilliant lights showed round us. A reluctance to leave the machine overwhelmed me, so sure was I that I was on the fringe of some humiliating experience; although his condemnation was couched in familiar terms, it remained oppressive. Gratinelli gestured impatiently. I climbed out with him close behind me.

As we got into a waiting jeep, he said, 'You're assigned to the Metro. Quite a comfortable hotel, if old-fashioned. Get a night's rest, and the men who will escort you on your mission will be round at eight in the morning. Be ready for them.' He gave me an Army pass.

'Where are we, exactly?'

'The troops call this Sugar City. It's where they come for R & R.' He gave a dry laugh, showing the gold-capped tooth again.

The Metro proved to be a large hotel almost on the waterfront.

Its grand crumbling facade stretched upward into the night, seemingly without termination, since a garish neon sign with kicking dancing girls over the main foyer dazzled the eyes, making the darkness darker.

I slung my pack over one shoulder and jumped on to the pavement. The jeep bore Gratinelli away into the night.

A crowd of GIs, garishly dressed local girls, and kids swarmed about the steps of the Metro. Youths roared about on Hondas, miraculously avoiding running into anyone. Beggars and vendors were everywhere. A boy tried to sell me a watch. All along the front by the Metro were hotel signs, dance signs, bar signs, massage signs. American music blared, pop competing with blue grass, country, jazz. I stood there in a mood of dull amazement before pushing through the crowd and entering the hotel.

The foyer was as disorderly as the front.

Military police were on duty, too busy with girls to take any notice of new arrivals. Couples were coming and going everywhere. Raucous laughter sounded from a lounge bar, where a sailor could be glimpsed, dancing on a table. Going up in the elevator after I had checked in, I pushed among men kissing and feeling girls who could scarcely have been more than thirteen.

My room was at the back, small, uninviting. I sat on the bed. The whole hotel pulsed with its transitory life like a coral reef. A painful anguish seized me. Anything was better than solitude, trapped in one cell of this labyrinth. I had to get a girl myself.

She was young and said her name was Velvet. I picked her up in the foyer. Rather, she chose me. She generally worked with a friend, but the friend was ill tonight. She opened her legs and invited me in.

Afterwards, as she washed herself, she did not wish to talk. She knew very little, but she said a general had told her that Sugar Town's population of a half-million had swollen to three million since the Americans had arrived. Surrounding the central area was a city of refugees and derelicts from the war further north. Velvet grew spiteful when I questioned her further. I let her go.

After a restless night, I rose and showered. I watched the TV intermittently while I dressed and drank a cup of coffee. There were only American stations, run by local US Armed Forces Networks. The news concerned the capture of a VC General, Tom Scargill, apparently the most brilliant general fighting for the

North. There was also a one-minute burst of hate for the IRA, fighting against the South, and responsible for blowing up a US naval frigate in Plymouth harbour, with the loss of nine lives. The Irish government was being denounced by Washington for supporting the IRA.

These news items were perfunctorily done. An incest case in San Antonio got more coverage. There were old cartoons and the customary pap, shovelled out in the usual half-joking American way, all interspersed by items from home: how rain persisted in the Detroit area and a high pressure ridge was stable over Seattle and the Pacific Northwest.

In came my two American escorts. One went straight over and switched off the television without invitation.

'Sure thing, American wealth and technology allows us our own little enclaves over here,' one of them said, in answer to a comment I made. 'You don't expect us to exist on their standard of living, for god's sake. The local culture has nothing to offer.'

'A thousand years of history?'

'Forget history. This dump is falling apart at the seams. If you want my personal opinion, we should hand it over to the VCs. But the US always honours its treaties. Worse luck.'

At that they both laughed. The men were in their early twenties. Solid energetic young men with pale heavy faces. Hair short, uniform casual. One wore a big cowboy hat. Both were army officers and carried revolvers. One of them had the Stars and Stripes tattooed on his biceps. They told me their names were Pedro and Len. Pedro was the one with the cowboy hat and the tattoo. Their manner towards me was a mixture of friendliness and insult; I was familiar with it from my years in Florida.

We ate a quick breakfast in the hotel dining room. The windows looked out across the sea. The sun shone as if disaster never happened. With the tide out, the beach glittered in the sunlight.

Already there were guys about, soldiers on R & R, stumbling along, clutching girls. Pedro and Len made a hearty breakfast of pancakes with sausages and hash browns. They complained about the quality of the food as they devoured it. It was better back home. I drank coffee, listening to their contempt.

'You despise this place,' I said to the one who had last spoken. He was Len.

'No offence, Jim, but what else? Look, we have to be over here putting things to rights. We don't have to like it. See, I'm well-informed on the general picture. The country was divided, North and South. It's poor up North, real poor, so they turned to Communism. Those sons of bitches will not stay put in the North. They keep infiltrating across the frontier. It's like a contagion, and the slimeys in the South just don't have the motivation to kill the VCs in any whole-hearted way.'

'We try to slam a little spirit into them,' Pedro said. He smiled a lot more than his partner. 'Like you know why they are called VCs? Because their leader is a Southerner. He got started in a town called Ventnor on an island out in that ocean there.' He pointed through the window with his fork. 'VC stands for Ventnor Commies. Maybe you know. Somehow the name stuck – nostalgia, maybe. But when the US weighed in, one of the first things we did was take out Ventnor and the island, so that at least the South was safe in our hands. I suppose you saw that on TV back in Florida, but I was here on my first tour of duty and I saw it happen. It's history. You feel proud to be part of history.'

He gave a drum-roll with two heavy fingers on the edge of the table.

'History,' Len said thoughtfully. 'Give me Atlanta, Georgia, every time. Stuff history. History is for heroes.'

'What do I have to do?' I asked, when they finally got to the coffee and cigarette stage. They sized me up and Pedro gave a secret smile.

'You went to school at a place called Christ Church College. That right?'

'Not a school. Univeristy. A college at a University. What about it?'

'Okay.' He exaggerated his patience. 'You went to University at a place called Christ Church College?'

'Just called Christ Church. It is a college but it is just called Christ Church. That's the tradition.'

Smiling even more heavily, Pedro slammed his fist to the table. 'Don't give me that slimey shit. From now on it's Christ Church College, okay? Let's be clear, okay?'

'The foundation dates back to the time of Henry VIII. You can't simply change things overnight that –'

He interrupted with another bang on the table. 'Listen, we don't have to take crap, Lambard. Just so you know this dump we're talking about, that's enough. Screw history. How long were you there?'

'Three years. The statutory period.'

'Three years. So you would remember your way around?'

'Of course. If the college is still intact.'

'Jesus. Henry VIII,' Len said, belatedly. 'You slimeys really are a caution. Didn't he have seven or eight wives?'

Ignoring him, Pedro said, 'The VCs have got a VIP locked up in Christ Church College. We want that guy. He is valuable to both sides and we need him. You are going to help us. Understand?'

'Who is this guy? A secret agent?'

'There won't be much danger. The less you know, the better,' Pedro said. He stubbed out his cigarette forcefully, as if illustrating his point.

'Who is he?'

'Code name Hawk,' Len said. 'We need him, okay? Let's move. We're going to get you into local clothing and then we'll hit the ·trail. It isn't going to be dangerous.'

They had both told me that. It did not make me feel happier. Nor did the underlying assumption that because of my nationality I must be a coward. I followed them from the dining room.

We took a route north from Sugar City. I could see for the first time what had become of the land in which I had been born.

The disaster which had overtaken it had been twofold.

Firstly, during the eighties, high rates of unemployment, an indifferent government, and inner city decay, coupled with inevitable problems of racism, had led to demonstrations and ferocious rioting in the North, that part of the country worst hit by the poverty trap. The rioting was met by increasingly repressive measures from a police force once renowned throughout the world for its restraint. Several pitched battles were fought, notably in Leeds, Liverpool and Sheffield. Liverpool had become the HQ of a rebel army supplied with war material coming from the country's traditional enemies in the Marxist camp. As the news bulletin I had seen admitted, the IRA was also active. There are always many who wish to see society destroyed.

In the nineties, decline was rapid. Police were defeated at the Battle of Warrington, with three hundred of them mowed down by machine-gun fire. The government in the affluent South decided to

BRIAN ALDISS

divide the country, leaving the North to its own increasingly anti-establishment devices. Despite trails of refugees wending north and south, a wall – the infamous Cotswold Wall – for many miles little more than a few strands of barbed wire – marked a physical division between the two halves of the country.

Secondly, the USA had moved to the aid of its ancient democratic ally, the land from which so many of its own traditions, legal and cultural, had come. Many voices urged the President not to take such a step. The parallels with the Vietnam War, still a scar in many minds, were stressed. But the military argued that all that was needed was an increased presence. American bases had to be defended. There were treaty obligations through NATO. And there was, as there had been in World War II, strategic value to an island lying off the coast of a Europe also undergoing a series of violent disruptions in many major cities. So a presence was maintained, and increased. Pressure induces counter-pressure. Islam insurgency was added to Marxist strength in the North. Infiltration into the South continued. Month by month, the American presence in the South was increased. There was no pulling back.

'We're after the hearts and minds of these people,' Gratinelli had said, echoing his President's words. But those in the South, in the old capital of London, had seen the corruption that American wealth brought in its wake. They watched hungrily as sky-cranes flew in meat and beer for the daily barbecues behind defended U.S. enclaves. They became sucked into the dirty trades that black-marketeering brings. About the U.S. bases grew tatty tinsel towns constructed from waste, the non-bio-degradables of plastic packing cases and wrappings from which brothels, cafes, bars, dope-shops and the rest could be constructed. Goods and equipment from the base made their way through the wire in a steady stream, paying for services which a ruined country readily supplies. And every weekend, the casualties – the men with AIDS and the new quick-syph and chancres and hepatitis cases with dirty needles and the poisoned and the maimed who had driven drunkenly off the winding local roads – every weekend, these casualties were shipped back to the States on special hospital flights, or flown to secret recovery bases in the Mediterranean, away from the investigative eye of reporters. The States itself was torn apart by this new overseas war.

The route from the south coast northwards ran over downland. Apart from a few encampments, the country looked much as ever. There were few people about. Those who walked by the road froze as we went by. The sight of a US uniform was enough to stop them in their tracks. They knew GIs fired at moving targets, in a war where they could not tell one side from the other.

Over the downs, towards the outskirts of London, change was more apparent. Sprawling shanty towns had gone up. By Purley, these makeshift quarters were visible on either side. The road became fenced and roofed with electrified fencing, so that civilians could not interfere with troop movements. Beyond the fencing people stood, looking into the road, sullen, unmoving. They were in the main the people who had fled from the North and found no shelter, no trust, in the homes of relations.

'Slimeys! Lost the gift of movement,' Pedro said. I thought I disliked him more than Len. It was something to do with his sunny smile.

Our vehicle and the two vehicles escorting us were halted at a barrier. Our credentials were checked. Someone had blown up a lorry a mile ahead and the road was blocked. We were sent on a detour.

So we drove through the heart of London.

Everywhere was stamped the insignia of decay. No building had been maintained. Paint had come near no dwelling in the last fifteen years. Gutters and roofs had not been repaired. Many of the streets we drove through were boarded up, perhaps by the military to facilitate their movements. As we drove along Millbank, burnt out buildings confronted us on either side of the Thames. Military traffic could be seen patrolling on the river.

Some of the famous landmarks had gone.

The House of Commons, that individual gothic building, had disappeared, and Big Ben along with it. The entire structure had been bought by a consortium of billionaires, and shipped to Arizona stone by stone where, with the aid of computers, it had been assembled just as before, to stand on the lip of the Grand Canyon, an object of reverence and curiosity for the tourist trade. It housed an unrivalled collection of old pin-table machines.

'We got to many of the old art treasures before the VCs ruined them,' Len said. 'The entire contents of the National Gallery are now safe in an annexe of the Smithsonian, as maybe you heard.

Worth millions. Millions.' He repeated the word with satisfaction.

The Stars and Stripes flew over Buckingham Palace, dominating the Union Jack. An immense battery of tanks and weaponry was drawn up in front of the palace. There were no tourists, no guards in scarlet uniforms and bearskins.

'That's where we have your royal family, Jim,' Len said. 'They're safe as long as they are there, and we take good care of them.'

Pedro laughed. 'Imagine – the Canadians wanted to take them over. Some chance . . .'

We drove on, to stop for a break in a new barracks area in Hyde Park. Then through Paddington to the Oxford road.

Paddington was in ruins. The whole area had been reduced to rubble. The IRA had been at work. Later, a wide road had been bulldozed through the rubble. Again the local population was kept off the road by electrified fencing. Behind the fencing, clusters of stalls had been set up. I saw men and women climbing over piles of bricks to see what trade was to be had. All were thin and crudely dressed. As our cars went by they froze.

I noted that Len and Pedro kept carbines ready in case of trouble, but there was none.

Vegetation had sprung up among the ruins. Beds of a pink flower, rose-baywillow-herb, created a little beauty among the blackened debris.

Driving up the Thames Valley was no longer the pleasant experience it had been when I had first gone to the University of Oxford. Here were more indicators of the disaster which had overtaken my country. Whole towns evacuated, prison camps set up, immense fortifications, airfields, mobile guns on the move, convoys, once a wood on fire. The only moving figures we saw were Americans. They were everywhere: marching, directing the traffic, swarming over vehicles, drinking. Old Glory hung everywhere, limp in the mild afternoon sun. I was in an occupied country.

Before Henley, we had to detour to avoid a pitched battle. The US forces, perhaps out of contempt for the opposition, were careless. They commanded heavy armour but not vigilance. The average GI had no stomach for defending Europe. So the guerillas from the North, with a few well-placed mines, were often able to raid camps for supplies or capture whole convoys.

Three Tomcats screamed overhead, cannons blazing. The noise went straight through to the very fibres of being.

'Give it to the bastards!' Len shouted after them. He went into a story about how he had been on a patrol outside Norwich when one of the men triggered an IRA mine of the kind known as a Jumping Jenny. When a boot touched a concealed prong, the mine jumped a metre in the air before exploding. Len's friends were reduced to an area of raw shredded meat around the spot, with red tissue and white bone splinters sprayed everywhere. Len was lucky. He had just skipped behind a big tree to urinate. He was the only one to survive. Len seemed more friendly after he had told me this.

'I'm sorry about your friends.'

'Forget it.'

I remembered when I had first gone up to Oxford, to Christ Church, that most beautiful of colleges. The start of my first academic year. Oxford seemed to me a peaceful and civilised place. True, there was much talk of the country's economy declining, with manufacturing industry closing down; and there were strikes and the occasional riot. Troop movements increased, along with demonstrations. But none of it touched Oxford. Oxford had been there since the thirteenth century. It was impossible to imagine its green lawns besmirched, its welcoming libraries looted. Wrapped up in our own little lives, we had not taken alarm.

But my father had. My father ran a successful chain of trendy clothes stores, some in high streets, some within department stores. He often visited his shops in the North.

At the Glasgow store, he received a threatening letter. Someone did not approve of the way the profits of the branch went south. My father ignored the letter. On his next visit, he was attacked by three men in a side street when returning to his hotel. He carried an illegally purchased British Army revolver. As the men came up, he drew the gun and fired. One man fell. Panic seized my father. As the other two froze, he shot them too. I remember his return home in a state of shock.

The incident changed our lives. My father became a haunted man. He saw the civil war coming, sold up the clothes chain and our house, and took us over to live in the States, in Florida, where many other English were settling. I managed to get a porter's job on the local air base.

In Florida we are the poor whites. Why are we so unpopular?

Because the war is unpopular. American viewers are tired of seeing their boys being blown up outside Leicester and Stow-on-the-Wold. Escalating costs, escalating deaths: for these we are in some way responsible.

I believe it. We are responsible. We didn't care enough in the good years. We didn't care when millions of people went on the scrap pile of unemployment. We thought all the American talk about Democracy and Eternal Vigilance was crap. So it may be. But we tried to live without Democracy and Eternal Vigilance and it finished us. Throughout the eighties our divided society had ceased to believe in the idea of equal rights for the individual.

Oxford was only a few miles south of the Cotswold Wall. Big US air bases lay nearby, together with a store of missiles and nuclear weapons – so far unused but kept perpetually on the ready for the next stage of the war, which many saw as inevitable. Infiltration from the North was constant. Both sides saw that when London was blotted out, Oxford would make a suitable second capital for government. Hitler had had the same idea long ago, refraining from bombing the ancient city in consequence.

Now it was less privileged. Evidence of damage was clear, as we studied the city through binoculars from an adjacent hill. I wondered as I viewed it, Did you teach us aright?

Pedro and Len gave me a casual briefing. By now I had the two of them separate and distinct. Their manner was basically sullen, perhaps of a cultivated sullenness in order to keep me in my place but more likely an attitude fostered by their resentment at being here at all. But Len, I now perceived, was the stronger of the two. He was a stolid individual, even likeable in a way. His cold, deliberate manner was part of his approach to life – a life which, from various hints he let fall, seemed to have been spent surviving in the tougher districts of Atlanta, Georgia. He did not like England, but to Len it was merely an extension of back-street existence.

In some curious way, Len – neither he nor Pedro would reveal their surnames – wanted to secure my liking. He explained to me with care that the US was in my country legally, in response to treaty obligations and the obligations of a long-standing relationship between our two nations.

Pedro laughed when he heard this. I did not laugh.

Pedro was from Detroit. His real name was Peter, but his wife was Mexican. Watching him as we travelled – for my life might depend on understanding the two officers – I saw his nervousness. His sullen manner hid fear. He took his cues from Len and tried to imitate his manners. He was a minor academic in civilian life, now trying to be one of the bunch. Perhaps his tattoo was another of his bids to be thought something other than he was; he had acquired it in Sugar City. As he saw that Len and I were reaching a kind of tacit understanding, Pedro became more personally edgy.

Our vehicles were drawn up in what had been the garden of a private house. The house had been hastily fortified at one time, since it commanded a good view of Oxford. It was now deserted, with that woebegone look of a building for whom maintenance is a forgotten word. Sycamore seedlings sprouted in its gutters. Its roof sagged and there were damp stains on its stuccoed walls.

With friendly insults, the soldiers dispersed themselves about the garden, negligently keeping watch. Lighting cigarettes, they adopted casual poses. The radio operator took messages back and forth between the officers and his set. Why was it all like a play? I asked myself. Had Americans so far embraced unreality that they did not believe in death?

The three vehicles were drawn up on what had once been lawn.

We looked over shaggy hedges of lonicera and laurel towards the old city.

'There's Christ Church,' I said. 'You can see Tom Tower.' The famous tower gleamed in the afternoon sun. Something seemed to flutter in my throat as I stared at it. I was looking back at the peaceful past we had lost, which could never return.

The Cumnor Hills to the west of Oxford were yellow, not with autumn but with Agent Orange defoliant. Near at hand, the trees were blighted and woebegone. It was as if we stood on the edge of a bowl of rotting salad.

As we stared, tracer bullets came spanging through the hedge just to the left of us. They hit the side of the house behind us and went ricochetting off into space. We dropped immediately, faces in early summer buttercups.

My first experience of being under fire was immensely exciting. I was not frightened. Rather, it occurred to me that the experience was right and just. Everything that had gone before had prepared me for being shot at in my own native land.

Pedro retrieved his cowboy hat. He jumped up and was peering through cover. There was nothing to be seen. He thrust his fists into his pockets.

'Some bastard's got the approaches covered,' he muttered.

'All those towers down there make great snipers' posts,' Len said. He was very calm. He looked at me almost with approval, one eyebrow raised, as if to say, See what we're up against?

Shivering fits began inside me, although I remained unfrightened. I hid them as best I could, wishing I were back in bed with Velvet, her arms about me.

The two officers lit a joint and shared it between them.

Sheltered by hedge, our backs against the wall of the house, they gave me the rest of my orders, one sitting one side of me, one the other.

Half of Oxford was in enemy hands – that is, held by the North. The South, after initial resistance, had accepted the situation. Separated only by no-go areas, the two sides lived in truce together, thus proving the American hypothesis that both were rotten with Communism. It was left to the States to stir things up in the old city and awaken British fighting spirit now and again.

'We go get Hawk as soon as we get the signal over the air,' Pedro said, leaning his head against the wall behind and inhaling deeply.

'When do we get the signal?'

He shrugged. Neither he nor Len answered me. Pedro's smile had become a grimace. I could not look at him. The soldiers were reappearing from various hiding places, sheepishly lighting up fresh cigarettes.

No more shots sounded. Perhaps the firing had been random. We sat mute.

After a while, Len rose and went across to the radio operator. Pedro followed. Opening his hand, Len took over the operator's headphones.

He stood tethered to the vehicle by the headphones.

'No decision,' he said finally to Pedro. They lit another joint. When it grew dark, Len kicked in the door of the house. We established occupancy, taking the radio with us. Screens were put up against the window of a downstairs room. There was no electricity, but a battery light was lit.

After a while, we ate sausage and beans from self-heating cans, followed by ice-cream and coffee.

Consultations with the men were intermittent. Although they

were there to protect us, the arrangements appeared casual. A machine gun was mounted in the grounds of the house, and a sentry posted. Pedro and Len brought out collapsible beds. I slept beside them, rolled in a khaki army blanket.

Towards dawn, I was woken by their boots on the bare floor and their subdued voices. The other men were in the room, and all were in a state of suppressed excitement. I propped myself on one elbow.

'Get up, Jim,' Len said. 'We're on the move.'

'What is it?'

'Signal came through, that's all. Get up.'

They were looking at each other from under eyebrows, with pleased, eager expressions. I was excluded from their circle of quiet triumph.

'Operation Hawk,' Pedro said, with relish. He shaved with a cordless razor.

Dawn was seeping from behind the blackout. I peered round the screen. The garden was grey, with a discarded look, as if it were an old indoor film set. Nothing moved there. Everything had gone away.

One of the drivers hustled in with a cannister of coffee and mugs. We drank standing up. Still the Americans talked in low voices full of expectation, their occasional glances in my direction excluding me from their secrets.

We pissed in the garden before climbing into the vehicles. As we rolled forward, Pedro opened up a bag and passed me over a revolver. He grinned at me without showing his teeth.

'Stick this in your pocket. Listen to orders. We're aiming to halt before we hit this college of yours, okay? You're to go on on foot. You're an ordinary civilian. Remember, the college is in the hands of the VC, so you say you are from the North. Get inside, ask for a job. Hawk is kept in an upstairs room, so Intelligence says. Get him out of there. We'll be outside to give you support.'

'How do I do that? How do I get him out?'

'We'll be outside with the cars. The quick getaway. First, you bring him out. He's in the Bursary, according to our Intelligence.'

I found myself waving my hands at him.

'Who is this Hawk? What's his real name? This is crazy!'

Len leaned forward and said, reassuringly, 'He's no one. We

need him, Lambard, and we trust you.' Here he gripped my knee to steady my resolve. 'We'd join you, happen we didn't look so American.'

That being undeniable, I sat tight as we bumped down the neglected road, trying to rehearse what I might do. After all, I was going to be among my own people, in my own College. Although I had been out of touch with events, except as reflected through the distorting lens of American TV, I could rely on my native wits to see me through.

The revolver helped my courage. The memory of my father's bravery in killing three attacking Northerners put spirit into me.

As we rolled into the town, past a check-point set up by the forces of the South, a dull roar like that of an earthquake filled the air. Like the roar of an earthquake, it seemed to come from all sides at once.

Overhead in the pale blue sky planes were flying. Pedro pointed upwards with the muzzle of a carbine and let out a cheer. The planes moved steadily, lines of them, high, heading westwards.

At the bridge over the Isis called Folly Bridge stood another check-point. Here our small convoy stopped; the vehicles were backed into a concealing side lane. Christ Church loomed on the rise a short way ahead, its pallid towers seemingly untouched by time. The venerable foundation made an ornamental kind of fortress. The flag of the North, the Red Rose, flew from its towers.

People I passed in the street nursed a skulking look to themselves, a tendency to hide their chins behind their shoulders. Only the old and the very young were represented. Several carried boxes or bore bundles of sticks. Most of the women walked with dogs. Their clothes were neutral in colour, their eyes downcast but mobile in their set faces. I thought, they scarcely look English.

A stone building which had once been a church now harboured down-and-outs, some of whom stared from its windows. A young woman, wrapped in coarse cloth, stood half-supporting herself against the crumbling wall. Since she thrust out a posy to me, I paused. The woman held a small child on her crooked right arm. With her left hand, she grasped a basket full of simple flowers. They were yellow. Once in childhood I had been able to call them by their name, but it had gone from me now.

'Buy my flowers,' she said, half between demand and supplication.

I was attracted to her face. It was a handsome one, with elegant features, though probably hunger had refined it. Over it reigned a sullen, cast-down expression. She stared fixedly at me, the posy still thrust some way towards me, her head lowered in a characteristic pose perhaps, at once suspicious and defiant.

'Do you need money?'

She looked me up and down in calculation, a cool look, before saying, 'How much you pay me for a short time, Mac?'

'I'm English, not American. I don't want that.'

A flash of sardonic humour momentarily softened her face.

'Everyone wants *that*. How much you pay me? Just a quick one?'

Shaking my head, I passed on. Although I was shamed by the encounter, I could not prevent myself thinking, Maybe I'll come back after I've got Hawk . . . Underdogs are always exploited. Why has no one ever devised a better way for society to function?

If she were washed all over . . . Then I thrust that side of life from my mind, to concentrate on the serious business at hand.

A woman with an old tartan rug over her shoulders hobbled to the great gate of Christ Church, under the shadow of Tom Tower. She carried a basket of goods, possibly laundry, her manner anxious, her gaze darting here and there. Someone opened the door set in the gate and she went in. The door clanged as it closed.

Momentarily uncertain, I paused, glancing round. Len was following, some way back down the street. He made no gesture when he saw me looking at him. I went ahead under the shadow of the portal and knocked on the worn door.

It was cold there, waiting in the shadows. Away down the street stood the posy-seller with her child, in sunlight.

When the door opened, I explained to the eye presenting itself that I was looking for work. A porter dragged the door wider and admitted me. I was immediately seized. Two men in camouflage jackets pinned me to the inside of the great gate. They searched me roughly. My revolver was removed from my pocket.

I stood with my face pressed to the rough timber, listening as one of the men examined the weapon. 'No firing pin,' he said, contemptuously. I heard my revolver thrown into a nearby bin. They both laughed and stood back.

They let me go without question, motioning me away.

What had been a spacious quadrangle – Mercury – was now

filled with sheds containing the vehicles of mobile units, battered lorries and Land Rovers. Under the cloisters surrounding Mercury, stalls had been established – to sell what I could not see. People were coming and going, mainly young men in a kind of uniform and young women scantily dressed. A sense of unreality possessed me as I witnessed this degradation of a revered seat of learning. It might all have been a strange charade enacted for my benefit, a parable of folly.

To add to the feeling of unreality, planes were still droning overhead on their westward path. The sky was now full of them. Nobody in the quad was paying them any attention.

A few people were casting glances in my direction. The influence of American propaganda caused me in part to regard the VC as enemies; yet, since I had not been personally involved in the civil war, I felt in part that they were merely fellow-countrymen. All the same, I began to walk as if with innocent purpose towards where the Bursar's office had been situated in my day.

Discreet windows which had once been closed were now thrown wantonly open. Glass was missing in many cases. Trousers, skirts, long-johns, hung over the sills to dry. I reached a stone staircase and ascended to the upper level. Looking back, I saw that one of the soldiers who had frisked me was following me.

This decided me to act fast. I would enter the bursar's office and ask for work. Perhaps I should demand to join the VC. Perhaps I should reveal that I was an old student of Christ Church. Perhaps there would be some clue as to who or where Hawk was.

The door still bore a small brass plate saying Bursar.

I knocked and went in.

An elderly man, very square, sat with arms folded against the window. Nearer at hand was a tough black sergeant in a red beret and green uniform, pointing a sub-machine-gun at me. In that frozen moment, I heard the planes still passing overhead, wave after wave. The Red Rose hung over the stone fireplace.

I turned too late. The soldier who had been following me ran up and stuck a gun into my spine. I did as I was told, moving reluctantly into the room. The door was slammed behind us. The three men regarded me with satisfaction.

The man in the window came over to inspect me. He had an immense expanse of face, most of it whiskered or wrinkled, with a great nose and a mouth that remained slightly open, as if he were about to bite. He scrutinised me unblinkingly, almost as if I were a piece of furniture.

'Papers,' he said, holding out a hand.

'Are you Hawk?'

'Papers.'

I handed them over.

'James Malcolm Lambard. Good. Sit in that chair.'

I did as I was told and the tension in the room eased.

'Your father, Arthur Lambard, is a war criminal.'

'My father is dead. And he was certainly no criminal.'

'His name remains registered as a war criminal with the Government of the North. Three deaths to answer. His anti-communist activities are well-known.'

Terrible confusion ran through me. Among the old college photographs and engravings on the wall was a portrait of Lenin. It disoriented me.

'There's been a misunderstanding,' I said. 'I have come just to meet a man called Hawk.'

'We'll be sending you to a prisoner-of-war camp near Bootle, Lambard. A tribunal will try you and adjudge your classification. There is no Hawk. It's a code name. Once you step into Christ Church with a revolver with no firing pin and ask for Hawk, you are delivered. Like a parcel.'

He was turning away as he spoke, throwing my papers on his desk and motioning to the armed men to march me off. I jumped up. Before I could take a step towards him, I was seized roughly and held.

'This is all crazy. I've done nothing wrong. Let me go at once.' I shouted madly until the sergeant punched me in the ribs.

'You're co-operating with the American enemy.' The man at the window spoke without looking round at me.

'But if I understand you, you are co-operating with them too.'

'Not co-operation. It's an arrangement on a war footing.' He turned round to me as if suddenly pleased and said, 'We collect little men like you, Lambard. The Yanks are happy to hand you over. When we get enough of you we exchange you for a Big Name the Yanks are holding. There's another war going on – a diplomatic war – and it looks good for both sides if we exchange a few bodies we don't need. The United Nations approves of that sort of thing. Keeps the Third World quiet. You may be part of a deal for our

General Scargill, held by the Yanks. Just behave yourself, you'll be okay.'

As the guards led me from the room, I shouted, 'I thought you people hated the Yanks. You're in league with them.'

He had returned to the window, to stand looking out at the planes overhead, and did not reply. The door slammed.

As they led me away, the black sergeant said, 'You want to keep your mouth shut, mate, or you'll be in trouble. Course we hate the bloody Yanks, but the real enemy's the South. The Yanks'll have to go away in the end, same as they did in Vietnam. Pack up and go.'

'They'll never go. The believe they have a duty to this country. They still have a vision of saving the world.'

We came out into Mercury. Armed vehicles were revving up. I could see other prisoners, a dejected bunch, standing handcuffed behind a lorry.

The sergeant gave me a push from behind. 'Saving the world from what? That persistence of vision will ruin them – and us. You know nothing, Lambard. You bloody chose to clear off – into their camp. The Yanks will over-reach themselves, like they did before. Then the US public'll get pissed off of the whole shooting match. They won't want to know about Europe, will they? – won't want to stump up the taxes necessary to save the world.'

A fit of trembling made me weak. I staggered, and the stone buildings seemed to whirl about me. I fought not only to keep my balance but to fend off the extent of my betrayal.

'They saved the world before . . . Europe . . . World War II . . .'

His hand was tight round my arm, steadying me and shaking me at the same time. His big face came close to mine.

'They're too stinking rich to go through that stuff again. Too stinking rich. Now stop blowing your mouth and move it.'

'Listen – when I get back – if I'm exchanged . . . I'm going to tell this whole rotten Hawk story to the world. Then you'll –'

He hit me with his fist in the stomach, so that I doubled up, gasping for breath. So much fury at the injustice of things rose in me that it burst out as hot tears, springing from my eyes to the stones below my feet.

The sergeant straightened me up, saying, quite gently, 'Who's going to believe what you say? No one will listen – on our side, or on their side. You're discredited, Lambard. Now, come on, move it, man.'

His words were lazily delivered, without malice, and he stood there a moment while I got my breath back, thinking there was rough justice in what the sergeant said. Much had been discredited by war – not I alone. The planes still roared overhead.

'Saving the world for Democracy, shit!' he said, and laughed.

I said nothing. He was producing a chit and signing me over. As a corporal took me into custody, the sergeant said, almost pityingly, 'You're dumb, Lambard. What price their latest move? Didn't the Yanks tell you before they sold you down the river? They're re-enacting Cambodia now.'

Seeing that I didn't immediately take his meaning, he said, 'Washington has just decided to attack the IRA direct. The loonies have begun the strategic bombing of Ireland. A neutral country . . .'

Raising my eyes, I saw the long-range bombers crossing a sky that was now a clear hard blue.

As we prisoners were herded into the waiting trucks, loudspeakers round the quadrangle blared forth the martial noise of the national anthem, 'There'll Always Be North England'.

Notes on the Authors

Brian Aldiss was born in Norfolk in 1925, served in the Royal Signals in the Far East and worked as a bookseller and journalist before devoting himself entirely to writing and editing. His fictional autobiography *The Hand-Reared Boy*, *A Soldier Erect* and *A Rude Awakening* was published in the 1970's, by which time he was well established as one of the major SF writers in the country. *The Malacia Tapestry*, *Frankenstein Unbound* and his collections of short stories *Space, Time and Nathanial* and *The Canopy of Time* are among his best known works and *The Helliconia Trilogy* (1982, 1983, 1985) has crowned his achievement in this field.

Tim Aspinall was born in Hampstead in 1935 and lives in London with his family. He is a freelance director, producer and playwright.

Dirk Bogarde was born and brought up in Sussex, and now lives in a seventeenth-century farmhouse in Provence. He is well known as one of Britain's most distinguished film actors, having appeared in such films as *Darling*, *Death in Venice*, *The Servant*, *The Night Porter* and *Providence*. He is also a distinguished writer, having published two volumes of his autobiography — *A Postillion Struck by Lightning* and *Snakes and Ladders* — and three highly regarded novels. His third, and final, volume of autobiography will be published in autumn 1986.

Maggie Brooks was born in 1951 and studied at the National Film School. Her work includes scripts for feature films and a television play. She has also written two novels, both published by Chatto & Windus: *Loose Connections* (1984) and *Heavenly Deception* (1985).

Charles Bukowski was born in 1920 in California, where he still lives today. He is a controversial figure who rose to prominence in the 1960s via the underground literary culture of Los Angeles and San Francisco. His first work, *Flower Fist and Bestial Wail*, was published in 1960, but it was not until the late 1960s, when he was taken on by the publisher Black Sparrow, that he began writing full time. Since his first novel, *Post Office,* he has written over forty books of poetry and prose, most of which are in print in America. Airlift Books distribute 10 of his publications in the UK, the latest of which are the novel *Ham on Rye* (1983) and the screenplay *Bar Fly* (1984).

Elizabeth Burster was born in 1956 and studied English at King's College, University of London. She completed an MA in American Studies and went on to do research in modern American fiction.

Simon Burt was born in Wiltshire in 1947 and educated at Trinity College, Dublin. He started writing seriously in 1981 and was first published in *The Fiction Magazine. Floral Street,* published by Faber & Faber in 1986, was his first collection of stories, although his work has been included in several anthologies and his stories in *Mae West is Dead,* edited by Adam Mars-Jones, were singled out for acclaim.

Duncan Bush was born in Cardiff in 1946 and studied at the universities of Warwick and Oxford. He is lecturing at Gwent College of Higher Education, working on media studies and film, and has had his short fiction published in several magazines including the *London Magazine, Stand* and *Granta.*

A. S. Byatt was born in Yorkshire in 1936. She was educated at Newnham College, Cambridge, and lived for a year in Pennsylvania, USA. She is a distinguished essayist and critic and until 1984 was a lecturer in English at University College, London. She has written a critical study of Iris Murdoch, *Degrees of Freedom,* and a number of novels all published by Chatto & Windus. *A Shadow of a Sun* was published in 1964, *The Game* in 1968 and there are two volumes of a quartet called *The Power House,* the first being *The Virgin in the Garden* (1979) and the second, *Still Life* (1985).

Raymond Carver was born in 1939 in Oregon and now lives in Washington. He has taught at the universities of Iowa, Texas and California and written several collections of stories and poems published in America. Picador published in one volume *The Raymond Carver Stories* (1985), which included his three earlier collections, *What We Talk About When We Talk About Love* (1981),

Cathedrals (1983) and *Will You Please Be Quiet Please* (1976). His collection of poems, *Fires*, was published by Collins in 1985 and will soon be out in Picador.

Judy Cooke was born in Wiltshire in 1938 and educated at King's College, University of London. She lectured in the Department of Extra-Mural Studies, University of London and became Head of the English Department at Richmond College, Surrey. Before editing *The Fiction Magazine* she was a freelance journalist, reviewing fiction regularly for the *New Statesman*. She has published short stories, critical essays and a novel *New Road* (Gollancz, 1975).

Janice Elliott was born in Derbyshire in 1931. She read English at St Anns, Oxford and then worked as a journalist on *House & Garden, Harpers Bazaar,* where she was beauty editor, and later on the *Sunday Times* Women's page. She left in 1962, the year her first novel, *Caves and Echoes*, was published and since then she has written a distinguished list of novels, the most recent being *Secret Places* (1981), *The Italian Lesson* (1985) and *Doctor Gruber's Daughter* (1986), all published by Hodder & Stoughton.

Steve Ellis was born in York in 1952. He studied English at University College, London University, where he completed his doctorate on Dante and Modern Poetry; this was published by Cambridge University Press in 1983. He won an Eric Gregory Award for his poetry in 1982, and a collection of his work is soon to be published ·by Bloodaxe. He is currently teaching in the Department of English at the University of Birmingham.

Georgina Hammick was born in Hampshire in 1939. After studying at Salisbury Art School and the Academie Julian in Paris, she taught in primary and secondary schools. Her poems have appeared in many magazines and anthologies and she was one of the contributors to *A Poetry Quintet* (Gollancz, 1976). She now lives in Wiltshire and is working on a collection of short stories.

Helen Harris has lived in London for the last eight years, writing short stories and working first as a translator and a tourist information officer, and then as a freelance magazine researcher.

She has travelled very widely, including India and the Middle East, and has spent a year living in Paris. Her first novel, *Playing Fields in Winter*, was short-listed for the first Betty Trask Award and published by Century Hutchinson in 1986. Her short stories have appeared in numerous magazines including *Punch* and *The London Magazine*.

Aidan Higgins was born in Co. Kildare in 1927. He is the author of four novels, the most recent of which, *Bornholm Night Ferry*, was published by Allison & Busby in 1983, and a collection of short stories, *Asylum and Other Stories*, published by Calder. He has also written several works for radio and his novel, *Langrishe Go Down* was dramatised for television by Harold Pinter. Aidan Higgins is now writing the screen play of *Asylum*.

Russell Hoban was born in Lansdale, Pennsylvania in 1925 and now lives with his wife and their family in London. He is well-known as an illustrator of children's books and has published over 40 titles. His first adult novel, *Lion of Boaz-Joachin and Joachin-Boaz* was published by Jonathan Cape in 1973, followed by *Kleinzeit* (1974); *Turtle Diary* (1975), made into a film starring Glenda Jackson and Ben Kingsley, and *Riddley Walker* (1980), recently adapted for the theatre and performed at the Royal Manchester Exchange, and *Pilgermann* (1983).

Desmond Hogan was born 35 years ago in Ballinasloe, Co. Galway, and now lives in London. He has published two novels, *The Ikon Maker* and *The Leaves on Grey*, and two books of short stories, *The Diamonds at the Bottom of the Sea*, which won the John Llewellyn Rhys Memorial Prize in 1980, and *Children of Lir*. Last year he won an *Irish Post* award. His novel *A Curious Street*, published by Hamish Hamilton in 1983, was brought out by Picador in 1984. His new novel *A New Shirt* is to be published by Hamish Hamilton this autumn.

James Lasdun was born in London in 1958. His stories and poems have appeared in various publications and he received an Eric Gregory Award for his poetry in 1982. His first collection of stories, *The Silver Age*, was published last year by Cape and he is now working on a novel.

George Macbeth lives and works in Norfolk with his wife, the novelist Lisa St Aubin de Terán and their family. One of the leading poets of his generation, he was for many years poetry producer for the BBC. His most recent collections of poems published by Secker & Warburg were *The Long Darkness* (1983) and *The Cleaver Garden* (1986). He has written three novels, all published by Cape; *Anna's Book* (1983), *The Lion of Pescara* (1985) and *Dizzy's Woman* (1986).

Allan Massie was born in Singapore in 1938. He was educated at Glenalmond and Trinity College, Cambridge. He has taught in Ireland and Italy and lived in Rome from 1972-75: he now lives with his wife and three children in the Scottish borders. He reviews fiction regularly and has edited the *New Edinburgh Review*. His four novels published by Bodley Head are *Change and Decay in All Around I See* (1978), *The Last Peacock* (1980), *The Death of Men* (1981), and *Death in Winter* (1984). His most recent novel, *The Hanging Tree*, will be published by Heinemann later this year.

John McGahern was born in Dublin in 1934 and brought up in various places in the West of Ireland. He has written a number of novels and short story collections, the most recent of which are *The Leavetaking* (1975) and *The Pornographer* (1979); his collections of short stories, also published by Faber & Faber, are *Nightlines* (1970), *Getting Through* (1978) and *High Ground* (1985). He is now working on a new novel.

Deborah Moggach was born in 1948, one of four sisters both of whose parents are writers. She spent a year living in Pakistan, where she worked on a local newspaper and there started her first novel, *You Must Be Sisters*. Since then she has written regular reviews and articles for various magazines and papers, as well as five more novels, the most recent of which are *Hot Water Man* (Cape 1982), *Porky* (Cape 1983) and *To Have and To Hold* (Viking 1986).

Amos Oz was born in Jerusalem in 1939. He joined a kibbutz when he was fifteen and now teaches literature and philosophy at the kibbutz high school. A distinguished Israeli writer he has written several novels, the most recent of which, *A Perfect Peace*, was published by Chatto & Windus in 1985.

Lucy Pinney lives on a Devon Farm near Honiton with her family. She has written a country diary for the *Observer* and articles for *Cosmopolitan*.

V. S. Pritchett, born in Suffolk in 1900, is one of the most talented writers of his generation. He has written numerous collections of short stories, a form in which he excels, five novels and countless essays and reviews. His most recent publication, *A Man of Letters*, collected essays on English, European and American writing, was published by Chatto & Windus in 1985. He is President of the Society of Authors, foreign honorary member of the American Academy of Arts and Letters and of the Academy of Arts and Sciences, and an ex-president of International PEN. He received a CBE in 1968 and a knighthood in 1975 in recognition of his services to literature.

Richard Rayner was born in 1955 and lives in London. He is Assistant Editor of *Time Out* and has recently sold his first filmscript. He is currently working on a novel.

Frederic Raphael was born in 1931 and educated at St John's College, Cambridge. A distinguished novelist and screenwriter, he first made his name with a number of screenplays, including *Nothing But the Best, Two for the Road* and *Darling*, for which he won an Oscar. Cape have published several of his novels, the most recent being *Heaven and Earth* (1985), and his collections of short stories *Sleeps Six and Other Stories* (1979) and *Oxbridge Blues* (1980). His best known series for television, *The Glittering Prizes*, was also published in short story form. *Think of England*, a new collection of stories, will be published by Cape in July 1986.

Lisa St Aubin de Terán was born in 1953 and lives in Norfolk with her husband, the writer George Macbeth, and their two children. She has written four novels, all published by Cape: *Keepers of the House* (1982) for which she won the Somerset Maugham Award, *The Slow Train to Milan* (1983), which won the John Llewellyn Rhys Memorial Prize, *The Tiger* (1985) and *The Bay of Silence* (1986).

John Saul lives and works in Germany. He had his first story published in *The Fiction Magazine* in 1985 and is now working on a collection of stories.

Gillian Tindall is a well-known novelist, broadcaster, journalist and historian. She has published a number of non-fiction works, including a highly praised study of urban history, *The Fields Beneath;* a critical biography of George Gissing, *The Born Exile;* and a study of Bombay, *City of Gold.* Her most recent works are the novel *Looking Forward* (1983) and the critical study *Rosamund Lehmann: An Appreciation*, published by Chatto & Windus in 1985. She is currently engaged in writing the screenplay of her novella, set in Bombay, *The China Egg.*

Marina Warner was born in 1946, and went to school in Egypt, Belgium and Berkshire. She read French and Italian at Lady Margaret Hall, Oxford, where she edited *Isis*, the university magazine. She has worked as a feature writer and critic for magazines and newspapers, and until recently regularly reviewed for *The Sunday Times.* Her books incude two historical studies in female symbolism: *Alone of all her Sex, the Myth and the Cult of the Virgin Mary* (1976), *Joan of Arc, the Image of Female Heroism* (Penguin, 1983) and her latest, *Monuments and Maidens, The Allegory of the Female form* (1985). She has also published two novels, *In a Dark Wood* and *The Skating Party*, published by Weidenfeld and Nicholson in 1977 and 1982.

Hugo Williams was born in 1942 and lives in London with his wife and daughter. He is the author of several volumes of poetry including *Symptoms of Loss* (1965), *Love-Life* (1979), and *Writing Home*, published by OUP in 1985. He has also written travel books, the latest of which was *No Particular Place to Go* (1980), and is the TV critic and Poetry Editor of the *New Statesman*.